DIRECTORY OF GRADUATE PROGRAMS IN APPLIED SPORT PSYCHOLOGY

SIXTH EDITION

Editors

Michael L. Sachs, PhD
Temple University

Kevin L. Burke, PhD
Georgia Southern University

Diana C. Schrader, MCAT
Temple University

Fitness Information Technology, Inc.
P.O. Box 4425
Morgantown, WV 26504-4425

Library of Congress Card Catalog Number: 00-134937

ISBN: 1-885693-26-5

Copyeditor: Candace Jordan
Cover Design: Bellerophon Productions
Developmental Editor: Geoffrey C. Fuller
Production Editor: Craig Hines
Cover Illustration: Michael Komarck
Printed by: Data Reproductions, Inc.
Printed in the United States of America

10   9   8   7   6   5   4   3   2

Fitness Information Technology, Inc.
P.O. Box 4425, University Avenue
Morgantown, WV 26504 USA
800.477.4348
304.599.3483 phone
304.599.3482 fax
Email: fit@fitinfotech.com
Website: www.fitinfotech.com

Contents

Introduction vii

New Features viii

Psychologist, Psychology, and Psychological ix

Internships/Practica xi

Background Reading in Sport Psychology xii

Careers in Sport Psychology xiii

Certification/Licensure xiv
   AAASP Certification Criteria xiv

Comments, Questions, Feedback xvi

Taking the Next Step: What to Ask as You Review the Directory
Patricia Latham Bach xvii

How to Use the Directory xxix

Graduate Programs in Applied Sport Psychology

University of Alberta 1

Arizona School of Professional Psychology 3

Arizona State University 6

University of Arizona 9

Ball State University 11

Boise State University 13

Boston University 15

Bowling Green State University 17

California State University, Fresno 19

California State University, Fullerton 21

California State University, Long Beach 23

California State University, Sacramento 25

University of California, Los Angeles 27

University of Canberra 29

✮Chichester Institute of Higher Education 31

Cleveland State University 33

Deakin University, Rusden Campus 35

✮DeMontfort University Bedford 37

✮University of Edinburgh 39

✮University of Exeter 41

Florida State University 43

University of Florida 45

Furman University 47
Georgia Southern University 49
University of Georgia 53
University of Houston 56
Humboldt State University 58
University of Idaho 60
Illinois State University 63
University of Illinois 65
Indiana University 67
Iowa State University 69
University of Iowa 71
Ithaca College 73
John F. Kennedy University 75
Kansas State University 78
University of Kansas 80
Lakehead University 82
Leeds Metropolitan University 84
Manchester Metropolitan University 86
University of Manitoba 88
Mankato State University 90
University of Maryland, College Park 92
McGill University 94
University of Memphis *(Human Movement Sciences and Education)* 96
University of Memphis *(Psychology)* 98
Miami University 100
Michigan State University 102
University of Minnesota 104
University of Missouri, Columbia 106
University of Missouri, Kansas City 108
The University of Montana 110
Université de Montréal 112
Nanyang Technological University 114
University of New Hampshire 116
The University of New Mexico 118
University of North Carolina, Greensboro 121
University of North Dakota 124
University of North Texas 126
University of Northern Colorado 128
Northern Illinois University 130
Oregon State University 132
University of Ottawa 135

The Pennsylvania State University 137
Purdue University 140
Université du Québec à Trois-Rivières 142
Queen's University 144
The University of Queensland 146
San Diego State University 148
San Diego University for Integrative Studies 150
San Jose State University 153
Universitè de Sherbrooke 155
Southeastern Louisiana University 157
University of Southern California 159
Southern Connecticut State University 161
Southern Illinois University, Carbondale 163
Southern Illinois University, Edwardsville 165
University of Southern Queensland 167
Spalding University 169
Springfield College (Graduate Studies) 171
Springfield College (Psychology) 173
Staffordshire University 175
University of Stellenbosch 177
Temple University 179
University of Tennessee, Knoxville 182
University of Texas, Austin 185
Texas Christian University (Kinesiology) 187
Texas Tech University 189
Utah State University 191
University of Utah 193
Victoria University 195
University of Virginia 198
Virginia Commonwealth University 201
University of Waterloo 203
Wayne State University 206
West Virginia University 208
University of Western Australia 210
Western Illinois University 213
University of Western Ontario 216
University of Western Sydney 218
Western Washington University 220
University of Wisconsin, Milwaukee 222
York University 224

Appendices

Guide to Appendices 227

Appendix A: Additions, Deletions, and Changes to Directory Entries 229

Appendix B: Other Programs 231

Appendix C: A Word About Internships 232
Michael L. Sachs, Lois A. Butcher, and Shelley A. Wiechman

Appendix D: Doctoral Programs in Clinical/Counseling Psychology 237

Appendix E: Graduate Training and Career Possibilities 239

Appendix F: Ethical Principles and Standards of the Association
for the Advancement of Applied Sport Psychology 247

Appendix G: Texts in Applied Sport Psychology 257

Appendix H: References in Applied Sport Psychology:
Professional and Ethical Issues 259

Appendix I: Reading List in Applied Sport Psychology:
Psychological Skills Training 264
Michael L. Sachs and Alan S. Kornspan

Appendix J: A Reference List of Mental Training/Sport Psychology Videos . . . 276
Alan S. Kornspan, Christopher Lantz, Bart S. Lerner, and Scott R. Johnson

Appendix K: Geographical List of Graduate Programs 281

Appendix L: Contact Persons 284

Appendix M: Telephone Number List of Contact Persons 288

Appendix N: Email Addresses for Contact Persons 292

Appendix O: Surfing the Net: Using the Internet for Success 302
Kevin L. Burke, David Dillard, Vincent J. Granito, Lindsey Blom, and Michael L. Sachs

Appendix P: Websites for Programs 319

Appendix Q: Locations of Graduate Programs: Physical Education
and Psychology, Master's and Doctoral Level 324

Appendix R: Quick Chart of Program Information: Degrees Offered,
Program Emphasis-Rating, and Internship Possibility 327

About the Editors 332

Introduction

This publication is a directory of graduate programs in applied sport psychology. It has been developed by the Association for the Advancement of Applied Sport Psychology (AAASP) to assist students, faculty, and other interested persons who seek basic information regarding such programs.

The directory contains information about each program, including the following: program address; contact person; telephone and fax numbers; email address; faculty substantively involved in the program and their research/applied areas of interest; degrees offered; student information (number of students in the program, acceptance rates, admissions requirements, financial assistance available); internship information; and special comments concerning the program. The directory is intended to provide a starting point for students who are searching for a graduate program, as well as serve as a reference work for others in the field.

A number of disclaimers/caveats must be offered. First, aspects of programs change over time. It is important to contact programs in which you (in the directory, the word *you* refers to the prospective student) might have interest and confirm the current status of the program (i.e., faculty present, degrees offered, financial assistance available, etc.). Second, no attempt has been made to define what constitutes a "program." A program may be a separate area of specialization within a department, or it may simply be a track within an existing program. The numbers, the types, and the quality of courses and internship offerings differ across programs. Varying levels of preparation for work in applied sport psychology are available. It is *critical* that you check with the contact person for programs that interest you and determine whether your goals can be met adequately within the context of the program.

This directory is composed of self-reported information from the colleges and universities represented. AAASP does not endorse any of the programs per se and has not undertaken an evaluation of any of the programs. It is assumed that students interested in particular programs will evaluate them carefully. The section called "Taking the Next Step: What to Ask as You Review the Directory," written by Patricia Latham Bach, may be helpful to you as you check out the programs that interest you.

New Features

This is the sixth edition of the directory. The first edition was published in November 1986, the second in September 1989, the third in September 1992, the fourth in September 1995, and the fifth in September 1998. All information has been updated as of May 1, 2000, to make it as current as possible.

A listing of a number of doctoral programs in clinical/counseling psychology that have indicated they offer opportunities to do work in sport psychology by taking courses in the exercise/sport sciences and enroll in practica has been provided (see Appendix D). This listing derives from the fact that in recent years many students interested in applied sport psychology have expressed a desire to obtain a doctoral degree in psychology with an emphasis in applied sport psychology. The relatively small number of psychology programs that offer emphases in applied sport psychology necessitates consideration of programs that do not have concentrations in exercise/sport but do allow students the opportunity to do some study in this area.

This is the fifth time such a listing has appeared in the directory. In the attempt to identify programs appropriate for the listing, some may have been overlooked. If you're interested in the exercise/sport area and are planning to pursue a doctoral degree in clinical/counseling psychology, you should check with the programs that interest you to ensure that the program is amenable to providing opportunities in applied sport psychology. Keep in mind that not all clinical/counseling programs consider applied sport psychology (or even exercise and sport) a "worthwhile" area of study or practice; broach the subject carefully to avoid diminishing your chances of acceptance to the program (assuming you would still want to enroll in a program that devalues applied sport psychology).

Programs listed in the fifth (1998) edition of the directory that have been deleted from this sixth edition and new programs that have been added to it can be found in Appendix A.

Psychologist, Psychology, and Psychological

The primary use of the term *applied sport psychology* in this directory focuses on training in educational sport psychology. Educational sport psychology emphasizes the teaching of psychological skills (i.e., PST—psychological skills training) such as goal setting, arousal control, concentration, imagery, and positive self-talk.

Some programs offer training in clinical sport psychology as well, but programs in which expertise can be developed in this area are considerably fewer. Clinical sport psychology encompasses psychological problems that demand expertise in clinical/counseling psychology. These problems, which affect both sport participants and non-sport participants, include depression, anxiety, eating disorders, substance abuse, etc.

There is a continuing debate within the field about the nature of *applied* sport psychology, and work with exercise and sport participants often includes both educational and clinical components. The use of the term *applied* herein has been left sufficiently flexible to encompass programs with a variety of emphases, to provide this flexibility of opportunities for potential students in the field.

A smaller number of programs included in the directory have a primarily academic or research focus in the field. These programs may appeal to those interested in minimizing exposure to applications in the field and maximumizing exposure to the academic or research side of sport psychology.

We have attempted to address questions about the emphases of various programs by including a scale that has been used successfully by Mayne, Norcross, and Sayette in their excellent book, *Insider's Guide to Graduate Programs in Clinical and Counseling Psychology* (New York: The Guilford Press, 2000/2001 edition). (For a fuller discussion of this book, see Appendix D.) We asked program respondants to select one of the seven numbers on the following Likert Scale. Mayne et al. used this scale (with established validity) to allow programs to rate themselves along a clinically oriented to research-oriented continuum. We thought that this might be an effective way (as modified) to address this for our field as well. Program respondants were asked to circle the number that best reflects the emphasis/orientation of their program:

Program Rating

1	2	3	4	5	6	7

Applied Orientation   Equal Emphasis   Research Orientation

____ Please check here if your program offers opportunities to pursue an applied orientation OR a research orientation (as opposed to an equal emphasis on both)

The following note was provided: "At the risk of starting a controversy over definitions, please note that research can be basic and/or applied, but simply indicates a focus upon research during one's program. An applied orientation means that the focus is upon applied/consulting work (which could emphasize education/performance enhancement AND/OR clinical/counseling), with a requirement/encouragement to do such work in one or more settings. Some programs will have an equal emphasis on both, and are encouraged to note this, but many programs are clearly oriented towards one side or the other, and it will be helpful for students to know this."

Most programs provided the information requested. Your feedback on whether this information is helpful (and accurate!) would be appreciated.

The programs contained in this directory offer graduate degrees primarily in physical education/kinesiology/exercise and sport sciences or psychology. You should note that use of the terms *psychologist*, *psychology*, and *psychological* is restricted by laws in each state and province. For more information concerning this issue, contact your state's (or province's) psychology licensing board or talk with faculty members in the programs that interest you.

There is an extensive set of literature on professional and ethical issues in applied sport psychology. Appendix H provides a reference list of books and articles that you may find useful in beginning your investigation of this area.

Internships/Practica

The directory provides information on internships available in various programs. It should be emphasized that there are internships and there are "internships." More clearly, the term *internship* has different connotations for different programs. When used with an APA-approved clinical/counseling program, the term refers to a program requirement and is likely to mean a full year's work that may entail 2,000 hours of supervised work in an applied clinical/counseling setting. This setting may or may not (it usually does not) involve any sport psychology work. It should be noted that internships are not affiliated with clinical/counseling programs per se. However, internships must be approved by the programs and usually, but not always, by the APA. Internship sites are often separate from the university and are generally quite competitive.

The term internship, when used with many of the physical education/kinesiology programs listed, is likely to refer to a supervised, applied experience ranging from 90 hours or so to several hundred hours of work. This type of experience is often called a practicum, rather than an internship. In any case, we use the term *internship* quite liberally in this directory, and it encompasses both traditional internships and practica, with a focus on applied experiences in exercise and sport. You should be sure to investigate specifically what internship/practicum opportunities are available in the programs that interest you. A few thoughts on internships are offered in Appendix C.

Background Reading in Sport Psychology

Questions are often posed about general background reading in sport psychology that examines theory, research, and practice (application). Appendix G provides a listing of basic texts in sport psychology and exercise psychology, as well as several general references. The following list contains journals specific to sport psychology, in addition to several related journals in the sport sciences with frequent articles relevant to the field:

Specific: *International Journal of Sport Psychology*

Journal of Applied Sport Psychology

Journal of Sport and Exercise Psychology

The Sport Psychologist

Related: *Journal of Applied Psychology*

Journal of Interdisciplinary Research in Physical Education

Journal of Sport Behavior

Perceptual and Motor Skills

Research Quarterly for Exercise and Sport

Individuals particularly interested in applied sport psychology often search for useful books, both professional and trade publications. To help students locate some of these volumes, we have included in Appendix I an updated version of an article by Michael Sachs (with assistance from Alan Kornspan, a faculty member at the University of Akron) entitled "Reading List in Applied Sport Psychology: Psychological Skills Training," which appeared in *The Sport Psychologist* (vol. 5, pp. 88–91) in 1991.

Fitness Information Technology, Inc. (FIT) is the publisher of this sixth edition of the directory. FIT's address is 1137 Van Voorhis Avenue, Morgantown, WV 26504-4425 (phone: 1.800.477.4348 or 304.599.3483; fax: 304.599.3482; email: fit@fitinfo tech.com; website: www.fitinfotech.com). FIT offers a number of other publications in exercise and sport psychology; be sure to get on their mailing list. Another publisher of note is Human Kinetics. Human Kinetics is a major sport sciences publisher, and you can obtain a catalogue of their publications by calling 1.800.747.4457 or by writing them at Box 5076, Champaign, IL 61820. Their email address is orders@hkusa.com and their website is www.humankinetics.com. There are other publishers in this area, but these two are the most specialized in exercise and sport psychology, as well as other areas within the sport sciences.

Careers in Sport Psychology

One of the most frequently asked questions about sport psychology concerns what one can do with a degree in the field. Division 47 (Exercise and Sport Psychology) of the American Psychological Association (APA), in joint sponsorship with AAASP and NASPSPA (North American Society for the Psychology of Sport and Physical Activity), has published a helpful brochure, *Graduate Training & Career Possibilities in Exercise & Sport Psychology*. We have reproduced the brochure in Appendix E.

The Division 47 Education Committee is also the author of an excellent brochure entitled *How Can a Psychologist Become a Sport Psychologist?* This brochure can be found on Division 47's website (www.psyc.unt.edu/apadiv47/).

Certification/Licensure

As noted earlier, licensure as a psychologist is governed by state or provincial law (for the United States and Canada). Use of the terms *psychologist*, *psychology*, and *psychological* is restricted by these laws. For more information concerning this issue, you should contact your state's (or province's) psychology licensing board or talk with faculty members at the programs that interest you.

Certification, however, differs from licensure in that requirements are not based upon laws per se but are generally established by academic or professional organizations. These organizations attempt to identify the academic/practical background and sets of competencies that an "experienced professional" in the field should have. Certification programs are available in various areas of specialization within psychology, including sport psychology. Specifically, AAASP has a program that provides for certification as a "Certified Consultant, Association for the Advancement of Applied Sport Psychology." The criteria for certification are the following:

AAASP Certification Criteria

Necessary levels of preparation in the substantive content areas generally require successful completion of at least three graduate semester hours or their equivalent (e.g., passing suitable exams offered by an accredited doctoral program). However, up to four upper-level undergraduate courses may be substituted for this requirement (unless specifically designated as requiring graduate credit only). It is not always necessary to take one course to satisfy each requirement. However, one course or experience cannot be used to satisfy more than one criterion, except for number 2.

1. Completion of a doctoral degree.

2. Knowledge of scientific and professional ethics and standards (can meet requirement by taking one course on these topics or by taking several courses in which these topics comprise parts of the courses or by completing other comparable experiences).

3. Knowledge of the sport psychology subdisciplines of intervention/performance enhancement, health/exercise psychology, and social psychology as evidenced by three courses or two courses and one independent study in sport psychology (two of these courses must be taken at the graduate level).

4. Knowledge of the biomechanical and/or physiological bases of sport (e.g., kinesiology, biomechanics, exercise physiology).

5. Knowledge of the historical, philosophical, social, or motor behavior bases of sport (e.g., motor learning/control, motor development, issues in sport/physical education, sociology of sport, history and philosophy of sport/physical education).

6. Knowledge of psychopathology and its assessment (e.g., abnormal psychology, psychopathology).

7. Training designed to foster basic skills in counseling (e.g., course work on basic intervention techniques in counseling, supervised practica in counseling, clinical, or industrial/organizational psychology) (graduate level only).

8. Supervised experience, with a qualified person (i.e., one who has an appropriate background in applied sport psychology), during which the individual receives

training in the use of sport psychology principles and techniques (e.g., supervised practica in applied sport psychology in which the focus of the assessments and interventions are participants in physical activity, exercise, or sport)(graduate level only).

9. Knowledge of skills and techniques within sport or exercise (e.g., skills and techniques classes, clinics, formal coaching experiences, organized participation in sport or exercise).

10. Knowledge and skills in research design, statistics, and psychological assessment (graduate level only).

At least two of the following four criteria must be met through educational experiences that focus on general psychological principles (rather than sport-specific ones).

1. Knowledge of the biological bases of behavior (e.g., biomechanics/kinesiology, comparative psychology, exercise physiology, neuropsychology, physiological psychology, psychopharmacology, sensation).

2. Knowledge of the cognitive-affective bases of behavior (e.g., cognition, emotion, learning, memory, motivation, motor development, motor learning/control, perception, thinking).

3. Knowledge of the social bases of behavior (e.g., cultural, ethnic, and group processes; gender roles in sport; organizational and systems theory; social psychology; sociology of sport).

4. Knowledge of individual behavior (e.g., developmental psychology, exercise behavior, health psychology, individual differences, personality theory).

Further information concerning the certification process may be obtained from either Michael Sachs or Kevin Burke (see addresses and telephone numbers in next piece, *Comments, Questions, Feedback*). AAASP is currently the only association providing certification in applied sport psychology.

You may also wish to consult an excellent brochure developed by the AAASP Organization Outreach and Education Committee entitled *Certified Consultant, Association for the Advancement of Applied Sport Psychology: Questions and Answers*. The current Certification Committee chairperson is Dr. Damon Burton (University of Idaho).

While students entering graduate programs will not be eligible for certification unless they hold the doctoral degree and meet the other criteria listed, this information may be of interest in planning a program of study and/or selecting a program in the first place. It should be noted that *programs* are not certified; *individuals* are certified as consultants. Certainly, your course of study should be determined by you and your adviser, and you can prepare for work in applied sport psychology in many ways. However, designing your course of study to meet (at a minimum) AAASP certification criteria, as well as state licensing criteria for training in psychology (at least the course work/areas of study component), may provide additional options for you if you are interested in working in this area. The degree to which a program can prepare you for these goals may be an important consideration in your selection of a graduate program in applied sport psychology.

Comments, Questions, Feedback

We welcome your comments, questions, feedback, etc., on this directory, particularly concerning ways in which we might enhance its usefulness in the future. Your editors are Michael Sachs, in the Department of Kinesiology at Temple University (and a past president of AAASP); Kevin Burke, in the Department of Health and Kinesiology at Georgia Southern University (and a former secretary-treasurer of AAASP); and Diana Schrader, a doctoral student in exercise and sport psychology at Temple University. Please feel free to contact us:

Michael L. Sachs, PhD
Department of Kinesiology—048-00
Temple University
Philadelphia, PA 19122
215.204.8718 (office)
215.204.8705 (fax)
msachs@nimbus.temple.edu

Kevin L.Burke, PhD
Department of Health and Kinesiology
Georgia Southern University
PO Box 8076
Statesboro, GA 30460-8076
912.681.5267 (office)
912.681.0381 (fax)
KevBurke@gsaix2.cc.GASOU.edu

Diana Schrader, MCAT
Department of Kinesiology—048-00
Temple University
Philadelphia, PA 19122
dschrade@thunder.temple.edu

Taking the Next Step: What to Ask as You Review the Directory

Patricia Latham Bach, RN, MS

The process of becoming a sport psychologist is, in many ways, quite similar to that undertaken by an athlete who desires high-level achievement and excellence in a given sport. The attainment of this vision requires commitment, goal setting, attentional focus, positive self-talk, resiliency, and motivation, as well as the support of significant others, friends, and faculty. As you review this directory, realize that you have embarked upon one of the first of many steps that, taken together, constitute the process of becoming a professional.

Your review of the material will help in narrowing the number of schools and types of programs that warrant further investigation and contact. Your decision is generally based upon a variety of factors but should be most strongly influenced by the *vision* that you hold for yourself in the future.

Sport psychology, as a discipline, is the offspring of two strong parents: psychology and sport/exercise. As part of the maturation process, it has experienced some of the "growing pains" inherent in the development of a profession and has struggled to develop a precise definition of itself, one that can be uniformly agreed upon.

As an example, to date, no universally accepted operational definition of the designation *sport psychologist* exists. The same holds true for a) the lack of specific and consistent educational requirements (other than those mandated for AAASP certification), b) varying degrees of emphasis placed on research versus practical application in different programs, and c) ultimately, the nature and scope of practice itself. Though there is agreement *in principle*, the discipline exists with a degree of "professional ambiguity" in that the roles and responsibilities of individuals in the field vary based on the chosen educational path and type of degree. Therefore, the term *sport psychologist* should be considered a generic title.

Basically, sport psychologists function in three different roles. Because these roles are not mutually exclusive, a degree of overlap may exist for a given individual and within a given position. Cox (1998) identified the three specialized roles as a) the research sport psychologist, b) the educational sport psychologist, and c) the clinical/counseling sport psychologist.

Cox describes the researcher as an individual who is a "scientist and scholar" (p. 10). This person may conduct theoretical and/or applied research, and may teach both undergraduate and graduate courses in sport psychology and related areas. These individuals are generally found in positions at the university level and generally require a PhD.

An educational sport psychologist is described as one who "use[s] the medium of education to teach correct principles of sport psychology to athletes and coaches . . . develop[s] psychological skills for performance enhancement [and] help[s] athletes . . . to enjoy sport and use it as a vehicle for improving their quality of life" (Cox, 1998, p. 10). This person enjoys a broad spectrum of opportunities in that the use of performance enhancement techniques is not unique to athletes and can be applied to a variety of nonathletic consultation settings (e.g., business and industry, music and other performing arts). This person is also sometimes called a performance enhancement consultant or a sport consultant or something similar. Training for this position is generally at the master's or doctoral level.

Clinical/counseling sport psychologists are "prepared to deal with emotional and personality disorder problems that affect some athletes" (Cox, 1998, p. 10). This role requires completion of a doctoral degree in clinical or counseling psychology and may lead to licensure as a psychologist. Some individuals with preparation as clinical social workers may have some applicable background in this area. Based on training, these individuals may conduct research and work in educational and/or clinical environments, and may be eligible to receive third-party reimbursement.

Superficially, the distinctions among the three roles may seem an issue of semantics. There is a tremendous amount of educational diversity among sport psychologists. However, the differences are critical to you as an interested student in that they may strongly affect both your educational focus and training and, eventually, your ability to function within certain environments. There are a myriad of opportunities that may be found if you are willing to invest time and energy exploring the realm of professional possibilities. As a profession, sport psychology is moving to a point in its development wherein sport psychologists, by virtue of their educational choices, may choose more clearly defined career paths based on interests that may be focused on one or more of the three areas of academics, performance enhancement, and clinical practice.

As a parallel, consider the model of contemporary medical education. Students apply to either allopathic (MD) or osteopathic (DO) medical schools. In general, their standardized medical education consists of 2 years in basic sciences and 2 years in clinical rotations. Following graduation, they may enter research-oriented or clinical specialty programs, which culminate in expertise within a particular area of research, education, or practice. The educational process and requirements are well established and ultimately lead to a well-articulated terminal goal.

Unlike traditional medical education, sport psychology has not yet matured to the point wherein a uniform curriculum provides a standard foundation and subsequent systematized practice opportunities. Furthermore, the precise outcome goals of the educational process are also less clearly distinguished. Choice of a program, especially at the doctoral level, may seriously affect a student's opportunities to work with athletes and to develop expertise in an applied practice setting. Traditionally, the nonclinical PhD has been a research degree; therefore, the emphasis of most educational PhD programs in sport psychology remains one of research, not of practice. Students interested in a more applied focus should bear this in mind when making program choices for graduate education in sport psychology.

The "Process-Product" Equation

As a general strategy for evaluation, Daniel Gould (personal communication, May 1, 1995) uses a very simple, yet effective, "process-product" equation that may help guide you in your decisions relative to graduate school and, later, through your educational program. An easy way to conceptualize this equation is to ask the following question: "Is the process congruent with the product (and vice versa)?"

In virtually any situation, the *product* is the anticipated goal or desired outcome. In this case, the product is an identified role as a sport psychologist in education, research, or practice, or some combination thereof.

The *process* constitutes the *means* by which the outcome is obtained or achieved. In this case, a master's or doctoral program is the educational process by which one is prepared to become a sport psychologist.

The process-product equation is especially helpful in two important ways: (a) it will assist you in clearly *defining* your professional objectives (by asking yourself "What do I hope to achieve as a sport psychology professional?"), and (b) it will assist you in selecting programs that are *congruent* with your goals by helping you determine the type of process necessary for your chosen career path.

For example, a student who hopes to work exclusively in the area of sport psychology research would probably be happiest in a nonclinical PhD program with a strong research focus. Alternatively, a student who desires intensive contact with athletes in developing performance enhancement techniques may be best suited to a master's or doctoral program that provides numerous opportunities for actual practice in a supervised environment. In these examples, the tone and focus of the programs are congruent with, and supportive of, the professional goals established by the student.

Training in sport psychology can be completed at the master's and doctoral levels. Because of this, it is important that prior to embarking on your educational journey, you determine *which* (or both) of the two degrees will best prepare you to meet your projected goals. In some cases, a *terminal* master's degree (i.e., one that prepares you for a career requiring no further formal education) may prove more useful than further education at the doctoral level, based on your personal career choices.

The *Graduate Training and Career Possibilities* booklet (see Appendix E) states that "[m]ost of the professional employment opportunities in sport psychology require doctoral degrees from accredited colleges and universities . . . [Individuals] with master's degrees . . . compete at a distinct disadvantage for the limited number of full-time positions available in exercise and sport psychology." This statement holds true when "professional employment opportunities" incorporate more traditional university-related, academic, or research positions, and/or individual clinical practice opportunities requiring licensure. However, given the true paucity of traditional sport psychology positions, even doctoral preparation provides no guarantee of gainful employment. It merely strengthens the chances for a position in higher education or satisfies licensure requirements for practice as a psychologist. In this profession, more (i.e., doctoral vs. master's preparation) is not necessarily better but merely provides a different focus.

It is also important to note that given national trends, decreased funding is available to support educational programs in general. Given this trend, in addition to changes in the economic environment for mental health care (which may affect clinical sport psychologists), the complexion of those positions for which doctoral level preparation is required may be significantly altered. Furthermore, performance enhancement is seldom, if ever, reimbursed by third-party payers.

Students interested in graduate education in sport psychology should be aware that lucrative *and* exciting positions in research and practice are very difficult to find. Many positions may be exciting, but few, if any, are lucrative. However, the field is dynamic and growing, and there is hope for the future. There is a great need for those whose vision recognizes the importance of current work as a bridge to the almost limitless possibilities for this future. Therefore, master's and doctoral programs that promote high standards of academic achievement coupled with creativity, entrepreneurial skills, and flexibility should be considered to best prepare neophyte professionals for this field.

Sport Psychology Program Focus

One difficulty for aspiring students exists in learning to "read between the lines." Universities do not provide materials that intentionally foster misrepresentations. However, *perceptions* of program orientation may be skewed, or good intentions not made clear, due to a lack of clarity in the use of particular terms. For example, some schools allude to "applied" work. This may be interpreted as "direct contact" with athletes. However, the *intention* of that word may be far different in that it may be meant to imply *research* that has an "applied" focus. This disparity in perceptions represents quite a significant variation in actual work, and students should be clear about program focus to ensure a mutual understanding that is in everyone's best interest. It is always sad to hear about students who go to programs expecting one focus and find that that focus is not really available, making for unhappy students and faculty.

A critical difference among sport psychology programs rests in the specific program focus; that is, some programs provide greater concentration in the area of research (whether theoretical or applied), while others are oriented more towards a practice model (often considered an "applied" emphasis). To represent it graphically, one could envision a model with four quadrants, wherein emphasis on both research and practice can be evaluated. In this case, a modified Likert scale is incorporated to facilitate the process (Low = 1, High = 7):

Research and Practice Sport Psychology Program Focus Model

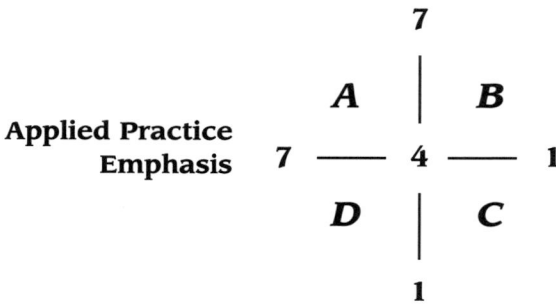

Quadrants:
A — High Research/High Practice
B — High Research/Low Practice
C — Low Research/Low Practice
D — Low Research/High Practice

It is critical to determine exactly *where* your interests lie in this model and to *identify a compatibly matched program and advisor*. For those more interested in academic research (and less so in applied/practice work), a program in Quadrant B would be most appropriate. Students who desire greater emphasis on consultation and first-hand experiences with athletes in performance enhancement, but less emphasis on research, would probably be most comfortable with a program in Quadrant D. Those who wish a mix of the two would find themselves most comfortable with a program in Quadrant A. Those most comfortable with a program in Quadrant C may be in the wrong field.

This model can be used to conduct a threefold evaluation. First, use it to identify your own interests relative to research and practice. This can be accomplished by re-examining your outcome goals or projected professional *product* (refer to the "Process-Product Equation" section). By determining what you would like to do, you will be able to identify where you most appropriately fit in the model. This will help you determine the type of program that will best meet your needs.

Second, the model can be beneficial in evaluating prospective programs. As you read materials and assimilate information, use the research/practice scales to rate your program choices. During your conversations with faculty and students, ask *them* to rate their program. Compare their evaluation with your own, based on your reading and your information gathering. Importantly, determine the degree to which these are congruent; if they are not congruent, why aren't they?

Finally, ask your potential advisor to rate his or her research versus practice focus, because an individual professor may have a somewhat different approach towards these variables than does the program as a whole. If this rating varies from *your* desired rating (i.e., your program preference), consider the difference carefully. A good match between student, program, and advisor is one in which there is a strong degree of congruence relative to both the educational process and the projected product. If your interests are in contrast with the interests of either the program or your advisor, the likelihood exists that no one will be happy. It is best to enter a graduate program that facilitates the possibility of a "win-win" situation, wherein a common purpose and a mutually satisfactory approach have been established. By using the model and thinking through the process-product equation, you will have a much stronger chance of completing your program in an effective and satisfying manner.

Developing Awareness

One of the best ways to prepare for entry into the field is to develop an understanding of and familiarity with the issues that challenge our development as a profession. In this way you will be better prepared to ask the questions that will lead to a clear distinction between the programs that ideally represent your interests and those that do not.

The directory, aside from simply listing programs and institutions, offers valuable information for those willing to invest a few hours in reviewing it carefully. Although this requires some time and energy now, it will save a great deal of effort in the future.

Appendix H provides an excellent overview of references that will prove helpful in developing a perspective relative to the field. These will contribute significantly to your global fund of knowledge about sport psychology. However, a number of articles and books on selected topics will prove particularly helpful to you:

1. Developing an Overview of Sport Psychology (Definitions, roles, history, and current issues.)

    Feltz, D. (1992). The nature of sport psychology. In T. S. Horn (Ed.), *Advances in sport psychology* (pp. 13–22). Champaign, IL: Human Kinetics.

    Williams, J. M., & Straub, W. F. (1998). Sport psychology: Past, present, future. In J. M. Williams (Ed.), *Applied sport psychology: Personal growth to peak performance* (3rd ed., pp. 1–12). Mountain View, CA: Mayfield Publishing Company.

2. Variations in Scope of Practice (Overview of three different roles in which sport psychologists function.)

    Anshel, M. H. (2000). The science of sport psychology. In *Sport psychology: From theory to practice* (4th ed. Scottsdale, AZ: Gorsuch Scarisbruck, Publishers.

3. Career and Future Directions in Applied Sport Psychology

    Taylor, J. (1991). Career direction, development and opportunities in applied sport psychology. *The Sport Psychologist, 5*, 266–280.

    Vealey, R. S. (1988). Future directions in psychological skills training. *The Sport Psychologist, 2*, 318–336.

4. Guidelines for Clinical Psychology Graduate Programs (Helpful hints for developing personal essays, for successful interviewing, and for program analysis and

evaluation. Specific to clinical psychology programs. Provides excellent model for sport psychology program evaluation as well. Highly recommended.)

Mayne, T. J., Norcross, J. C., & Sayette, M. A. (2000). *Insider's guide to graduate programs in clinical and counseling psychology* (2000–2001 edition). New York: The Guilford Press.

When you have completed these readings, the differences in focus, theoretical frameworks, and projected directions of the various programs will have become much more evident. However, to discern the most subtle variations, it is best to spend time in discussion with others, both students and faculty.

Becoming a Wise Consumer

As a prospective student of graduate-level training, you must learn to become a wise consumer. Given your potential investment of time (master's programs—2 years; PhD programs—3–4 years), energy (lots), and financial resources (varies, dependent upon funding, but can be *substantial*), it is critical to learn as much about the program and faculty as possible. Remember, once accepted and with your program initiated, you have established a working relationship that must endure the rigors of the program and the idiosyncrasies of higher education. Though certainly not cast in stone, transfer between graduate programs is much more difficult than transfer at the undergraduate level. In fact, few doctoral programs will consider transfers with advanced standing. (Most PhD students wishing to transfer must initiate the entire process again from scratch. Some credit for courses taken may be applied, but generally relatively little.) Therefore, it is especially important in this situation to thoroughly investigate all aspects of potential programs and to choose wisely.

Given all this, it is vital for students to learn to assimilate information. Primary sources of information include the following:

1. *Written materials* provided by the university (these usually detail particular graduate school requirements) and the specific department (may elaborate on individual program philosophies, options, requirements, electives, etc.). This directory is one place to start, but it is important to get materials from the programs themselves.

2. *On-site visit* to the university enables first-hand observation of faculty-student interactions, facilities, current research projects, and interviews with students and faculty. This can be very helpful and is strongly encouraged for your top choices. Arrangements should be made to meet with several current graduate students or, at least,to be provided with names and telephone numbers for 3–4 current students (and graduates, as appropriate) with whom you can talk about the program.

3. *Telephone interviews* with faculty and current students (when site visits are not possible). This is very helpful in that you can develop a "flavor" for your ability to speak and interact effectively with a professor. Students are also generally very forthcoming and will share perceptions of the program, ideas, and thoughts about faculty-student interactions—a host of information not readily evident in brochures. This is often great for establishing the "bottom line."

It is strongly encouraged to contact a program, at least by telephone, before applying. Some faculty have indicated amazement at students who apply to programs yet have never contacted the faculty or students. Written materials often do not provide enough information on which to base application decisions! Even if on-site visits or meetings at conferences are not possible, you should at least talk with faculty and current students by telephone (the faculty should be happy to give you names of students with whom you can talk) to get a feeling for what the people and the program are like. This is also helpful in the admissions process: making a positive impression over the telephone can be helpful in tilting an admissions decision your way, as opposed to your being "just a name" on an application.

Remember that your decision to enter a graduate program will affect the rest of your professional life. Your ability to work with and learn from faculty and other students is dependent upon mutual educational interests and effective communication skills. First-hand knowledge and assessment of these interests and skills cannot be gleaned solely from the directory. The time and money you spend talking with faculty and other students is a worthwhile investment in your future.

4. *Conference meetings* may be your first exposure to particular faculty or students from identified schools. Take advantage of these opportunities; introductions often anchor positive memories of individuals and may serve you well in the future. These meetings are especially helpful if you have many programs in which you are interested, and you want to get some information and develop impressions before narrowing your list to a more manageable number.

5. *Networking* with other students in the field is a tremendously valuable resource. Most students enrolled in a sport psychology graduate program have spent a great deal of effort investigating the realm of program possibilities and may be able to steer you in the right direction, saving you time, energy, and money. In many cases, department secretaries (if not the faculty) will be happy to pass your telephone number or address (including email address) along to current students, who understand the importance of making a well-informed choice of a graduate program.

6. *Literature searches* conducted through several of the available databases (e.g., SPORTDISCUS, PSYCH-LIT) can help you to determine the types of publications and work completed by prospective faculty. This information may serve as a springboard to further questions about your potential advisor, and demonstrates the type of preparation and motivation that faculty value in prospective students.

Above all, it is important to *ask questions* to clarify specific issues, concerns, and thoughts that may arise relative to a program. The following list provides a sample of the types of questions that may facilitate the process necessary to make your vision a reality and incorporates those that appeared previously in the 1998 Directory. Use these questions to develop a profile for each program. As you rule out certain options and narrow your list, the answers to these questions may become more critical in helping you make your final decision.

An effective method of initiating this process is to develop an understanding of your needs and goals relative to your education and future career aspirations. Self-knowledge and self-awareness are central to our work as sport psychologists. It is especially important, therefore, to take some time for introspection and reflection, to help you establish baseline criteria for your search.

Questions for Introspection/Reflection

1. What aspects of the educational process are most important to me?

2. What do I wish to accomplish through my educational experience?

3. Where do I see myself professionally in 5, 10, 15 years?

4. What are my professional goals for teaching, research, and service to the profession and community?

5. What salary range would be acceptable upon graduation?

6. What type of academic/nonacademic environment would best suit my needs?

7. What resources (other than money) will I need to help me through my education? Are these accessible? If not, how will I develop these?

Note: It would be helpful to identify a faculty member who can walk you through this process. Ideally, this should be someone who has an excellent grasp of the field and who can advise you accordingly.

General Questions

1. What is the size of the institution?

2. Does the institution operate on a semester or a quarter system?

3. What type of grading system is used (e.g., letter grades, pass/fail)?

4. What is the cost per credit hour (for in-state and for out-of-state students)?

5. Where is the institution located (e.g., urban, suburban, or rural setting)?

6. What type of housing is available?

7. Are out-of-state tuition waivers available? If so, are they this available for the duration of the program, or for one year only?

8. What types and amount of financial aid are available?

The Program

1. What are the entrance requirements for the university and for the program?

2. How long has the program been in existence? Do the faculty anticipate any major changes in the program in the foreseeable future?

3. What is the usual length of the program for both master's and doctoral work?

4. Is a thesis optional for completion of master's programs? What other options, if any, are available?

5. How flexible is the program (i.e., are many electives available)? What is the relationship of the program with others on the university campus? Are students welcome to join other departments for course work and/or research or applied practice experiences?

6. Is some form of comprehensive exam required for completion of the degree programs? Are these exams written, oral, or both?

7. What are the strengths and weaknesses of the program? (This question should be asked of *both* faculty and students.)

8. What is the core curriculum? How is it structured? Are the courses taken in sequence available every year so that the sequence can be followed without interruption? Are these outlined on a semester-by-semester basis? Are these courses taught by graduate students or by faculty?

9. What textbooks are used, and in which courses? (This is where your familiarity with books and readings will be quite useful. See Appendix G for a helpful list.) For example, the Jean Williams text, *Applied Sport Psychology: Personal Growth to Peak Performance*, is a very "applied" text. If the school indicates a strong preference for applied work but fails to consider this book (or others like it) in any course, you may need to keep this in the back of your mind; it may serve as a "red

flag." Do the text selections represent a broad spectrum of sport science knowledge that embraces both the research and the practice areas?

10. What is the prevailing "theoretical framework" of the department? How open-minded is the department to more creative, less scientific, and less traditional thinking? Would this be welcomed or discouraged?

11. If the department is in psychology or counseling, is the program APA approved? If it is in these departments, does the program still provide good exposure to sport-related course work and actual practice? The same question can be posed in the opposite direction for those programs housed in departments of physical education, kinesiology, or exercise and sport sciences.

12. Describe the department's operational definition of *applied work* as it is provided for students at both the master's and the doctoral levels. Rate the program on the Research and Practice Sport Psychology Program Focus Model shown previously.

13. What is the ratio of *applied experience* to *research experience* at both the master's and the doctoral levels?

14. What opportunities exist for *structured, consistent, supervised* hands-on applied experiences? What types of relationships has the department developed with the athletic department, the community, and others to facilitate your exposure to real-world situations within the learning environment?

15. Do opportunities exist for multicultural and cross-cultural experiences and training? Is there a process or approach taught to develop sensitivity to and awareness of the cultures inherent in different types of sport and exercise populations?

16. What courses address the following topics, and in how much depth: ethics, clinical and counseling issues (if not a clinical/counseling program), communication, professional development, business practices, use of technology, leadership skills, and creative approaches to entrepreneurship.

17. What time of the day or evening are classes generally scheduled?

Practica/Internships

1. Are internships required to complete the program? If so, what are the requirements, and how are these arranged and supervised? Are these readily available, or must they be developed by students? Are they paid positions? If not required, what opportunities exist for student internships? When does this contact begin in the program sequence? Who arranges these experiences, how are they supervised, and how often is supervision available? What other opportunities have been designed to facilitate professional development activities?

2. Is academic credit available for independently arranged internships?

3. Have collaborative relationships been developed within the community to facilitate a broad spectrum of practicum experiences?

Faculty

1. What research areas are being pursued by faculty and students?

2. How are students involved in the research process? Do all students have the opportunity to engage in research, or only those who have received assistantships?

3. In what journals do the faculty publish? What books have they written? On what topics do the faculty focus?

4. What conferences do the faculty attend, and where is their work presented?

5. Regarding authorship, who is the first author on research projects, papers, book chapters, etc.? Is this a consistent practice, or one that is negotiated up front, prior to the initiation of research or writing? How often do students appear as coauthors on papers presented at conferences and published in journals—either as first author or as second, third, etc., author?

6. What are the faculty's terminal goals for their students? How would they describe the students' marketable skills upon completion of the program?

7. Does the program allow and encourage independent research (other than that done for thesis or dissertation purposes)? Are faculty available on a consistent basis to provide feedback and guidance?

8. What is the faculty's travel schedule? How easily can students make appointments? Do other commitments (committees, etc.) play a major role in the expenditure of faculty time?

9. What types of jobs have the program's recent graduates (at both the master's and doctoral levels) obtained?

Students

1. In general, how do students like the program?

2. What attracted the students to the school and the program?

3. What do the students see as the strengths and the weaknesses of the program?

4. How flexible do the students feel the program to be regarding independent and creative thinking, individual and nonmainstream academic efforts, entrepreneurial pursuits, or membership on a student's thesis or dissertation committee?

5. What types of hands-on learning experiences are available?

6. Are funds available for student research and travel to conferences?

7. How much independent-study work is realistically allowed?

8. What type of relationship exists between students and faculty?

9. What type of relationship exists between students—competitive, cooperative, collaborative?

10. What types of work do student assistants perform?

11. Would the students choose the program again, given their present knowledge and experience?

Some Global Considerations

While no one can prescribe a means to measure the pulse of the profession, there are a few tips, easily applied, that may help create a picture of the field, the players, and the situation as it exists today.

1. Consider that *best* is a relative term: Good educational experiences result when the seeds of excellence are sown within a supportive environment. The best pro-

gram for one student may be another's nightmare, despite the program's reputation. A best fit occurs when there is congruency in philosophy, focus, and direction between the educational team members, consistent for faculty and students. Be guided by well-informed decisions, not popular opinion.

2. Maximize your educational investment: Make program choices that will provide the greatest potential return on your educational investment. The time, energy, and effort committed to graduate programs in sport psychology should prepare you as a professional with marketable skills applicable to a variety of settings, whether your focus is research or practice. Consider programs that aspire to the Biggest Bang for the Buck Theory.

3. Maximize cross-training opportunities: Many current students and recent graduates have emphasized the importance of using elective opportunities to become well rounded, with exposure to a multidiscipline-enriched fund of knowledge. Recommendations, at a minimum, include course work in counseling, psychopathology, eating disorders, and alcohol and chemical substance abuse. These are especially important for students in nonclinical sport psychology programs. Other excellent recommendations include organizational development, entrepreneurship, and computer technology courses. The demands of the workforce are changing much more quickly than the traditional system of education. To be successful, you must be proactive, future focused, and willing to take risks.

4. Learn to create your own opportunities: One of the most important tasks in this emerging profession is gaining access to athletes. There are many ways to *create* opportunities for working with athletes of all ages. Consider programs in the community, with Little League, park and recreation sessions, and amateur athletic events. Skill development necessary for excellence as both a researcher and practitioner can be enhanced in this way, while you increase your visibility and presence in the athletic community.

5. Become a multimedia and multifaceted consumer: Much valuable information for sport psychologists comes from academically nontraditional sources. A tremendous amount of research and information on teamwork and competitive performance comes from business sources. Anecdotal information gleaned from newspapers, TV news and sport broadcasts, popular sport magazines, and a variety of other sources provide both real life examples and validation of our mission as sport psychologists. An increased awareness of our world and of the potential application of our knowledge and experience can only enhance the growth of the profession.

6. Become a sponge and browse the Net: The Internet provides one of the most fertile resources for information gathering. The sport psychology listserv (SPORTPSY), run by Dr. Michael Sachs at Temple University, is a bulletin board that provides a bird's-eye view of the salient issues in the field. This and several other interesting website addresses can be found in Appendix O. They will provide food for thought for prospective students and professionals alike.

Putting It All Together

The list provided above is lengthy but is intended to develop your thinking relative to important issues in sport psychology graduate education. You need not ask each question, of course, nor pose the questions exactly as phrased above. However, to get the big picture, these questions address many concerns that have arisen in the experiences of those who have gone before you.

As a sport psychologist in any of the specialized roles, the use of intuitive skills and tacit knowledge is very important. Developing these skills and learning to trust yourself in using them is a sequential process. This can be accomplished through a firmly established fund of knowledge coupled with a heightened, multisensory awareness of people, places, and dynamic situations.

As you investigate potential programs, begin to practice these intuitive skills and incorporate them into your decision-making process. Learn to assimilate information from several of the sources previously discussed (see the section on "Becoming a Wise Consumer"). Look for *patterns* of consistency in attitudes and responses among faculty and students, and for congruency between verbal responses and printed materials. The important message is often not what is said, but what remains unsaid. Learn to trust your gut-level feeling relative to the program, the students, and the faculty.

Despite all your efforts to know a program, this cannot truly happen until you have become a *part* of it. You must live the reality to know the program in its entirety. Your goal is to make the best possible choice, considering all the information available. Recognize that *every* program has benefits and drawbacks. The important issue is to decide which program will work best for *you!*

In Summary

The purpose of this chapter has been to present issues and to provide questions for students who are considering graduate education in the field of sport psychology. This chapter has attempted to represent the many issues you should consider as you enter this dynamic and exciting field. However, there will always be other, perhaps more personal, issues that may concern you, and your introspection will help you become aware of and sensitive to these needs as you explore the various graduate programs. Remember, like that of an athlete, your journey to success is determined by your energy and effort in preparation. Best wishes in making your vision become your reality!

Reference

Cox, R. H. (1998). *Sport psychology: Concepts and applications* (4th ed.). Dubuque, IA: Wm. C. Brown, Inc.

Endnote

The author would like to express her thanks to the editors, and especially to Michael Sachs, for their assistance and valuable suggestions in preparing this chapter.

How to Use This Directory

This directory, as noted in the introduction, is designed to provide a starting point for students seeking a graduate program in applied sport psychology, or for faculty or other individuals interested in a reference work of graduate programs in the field. The basic information provided can guide the individual toward programs in specific geographic areas, with particular faculty involved, with internships available, and with particular degrees offered.

The information requested from programs was, of necessity, brief and is not intended to provide a basis upon which to make a final selection or rejection of a graduate program. Rather, the directory provides some basic information for a preliminary screening of programs and for contacting the appropriate person for further information. The previous section, "Taking the Next Step: What to Ask as You Review the Directory," will be helpful in directing your search to obtain the additional information necessary to select a graduate program in applied sport psychology.

Please note a number of important points concerning this directory:

1. The information requested for each program in this directory included the following: address, contact person, telephone and fax numbers, electronic mail address, World Wide Website, faculty substantively involved in the graduate program and their research/applied areas of interest, degrees offered, program information (students in the program, acceptance rates, admissions requirements, financial assistance available), internship information, and special comments concerning the program. However, not all programs provided all the information requested (in some cases the information may not have been available). In cases where information was not provided, that category (such as financial assistance available or internship information) has simply been omitted from the program entry rather than left blank.

   Additionally, more specific information about available financial assistance has been included. Programs were asked for information about the percentages of current students in the program receiving the following forms of assistance:

   - Fellowships

   - Research assistantships

   - Teaching assistantships

   - Tuition waivers

   - Other forms of financial aid

   While most programs provided this information, the data should be used with caution. Temple University (home institution for two of your editors) is a perfect example. None of our current students has a fellowship, although fellowships are available for qualified students. The information in the directory entry can, therefore, give you a feeling for what students are currently receiving, but it also helps to know what is available and to find out about all your options.

   Also note that some students receive more than one form of funding at any one point in their programs. Thus, percentages reported may exceed 100.

2. Faculty members substantively involved in each graduate program are listed alphabetically.

3. The degree(s) held by the faculty, such as PhD or other degrees, are *not* indicated. Since this information was not always available, it was thought best to omit it from the listing. However, most of the faculty listed hold a doctoral degree in physical education, psychology, or a related field.

4. Most of the programs listed focus on applied sport psychology. Some, however, are oriented towards research, with little, if any, applied component. In trying to improve our directory, we reviewed some other publications, including the excellent *Insider's Guide to Graduate Programs in Clinical and Counseling Psychology* (2000/2001 edition), by Tracy Mayne, John Norcross, and Michael Sayette (New York: The Guilford Press, 2000). In response to a request from many students for a better way to evaluate programs on their focus on research, applied work, or both, we asked programs to select one of the seven numbers on the following Likert Scale. Mayne et al. used this scale (with established validity) to have programs self-rate themselves along a clinically oriented to a research-oriented continuum. We thought that this might be an effective way to address this for our field as well. We asked program repondants to circle the number that best reflects the emphasis/orientation of their program:

1	2	3	4	5	6	7

Applied Orientation   Equal Emphasis   Research Orientation

___ Please check here if your program offers opportunities to pursue an applied orientation OR a research orientation (as opposed to an equal emphasis on both).

We also included the following Note: At the risk of starting a controversy over definitions, please note that research can be basic and/or applied, but simply indicates a focus upon research during one's program. An applied orientation means that the focus is upon applied/consulting work (which could be focused upon education/performance enhancement AND/OR clinical/counseling), with a requirement/encouragement to do such work in one or more settings. Some programs will have an equal emphasis on both, and are encouraged to note this, but many programs are clearly oriented towards one side or the other, and it will be helpful for students to know this.

Please let your editors know if this information is helpful to you. It can be revised for the next edition to make it as useful to you as possible. Some programs did not respond to this question, and so no self-rating is indicated. In addition, we caution you again to check programs carefully. A program may self-rate as a "1" (very strong applied orientation) when they still do or require a considerable amount of research. The information is useful as a guide, not as a definitive rating.

Please also note that some programs in psychology are not applied sport psychology programs per se, but do have faculty interested in the area. This is indicated where appropriate.

5. In some cases, the number of students in the program may not seem to be consistent with the number of students that appear to be admitted each year. Some programs have provided information on the number of students in the overall department (or number admitted to the overall department) as opposed to the number of students in (or admitted to) the sport psychology area specifically. This is a good example of a program feature you would be wise to check when considering a particular program.

6. The information provided is current as of May, 2000. You should still check all information when considering a given program. New features of a program may be added: new financial resources may become available, faculty may change, etc.

Key to Abbreviations:

APA . . . . American Psychological Association

APS . . . . Australian Psychological Society

GPA . . . . Grade Point Average

GRE . . . . Graduate Record Examination

MAT . . . . Miller Analogies Test

PST . . . . Psychological Skills Training

Degrees Offered:

CAS . . . . Certificate of Advanced Study

EdD . . . . Doctor of Education

MA . . . . Master of Arts

MAP . . . . Master of Applied Psychology

MAS . . . . Master of Applied Science

MEd . . . . Master of Education

MHS . . . . Master's in Human Movement Studies

MPhil . . . . Master of Philosophy

MPsych . . . . Master of Psychology

MPE . . . . Master of Physical Education

MS, MSc . . . . Master of Science

MSEd . . . . Master of Science of Education

DPE . . . . Doctor of Physical Education

PhD . . . . Doctor of Philosophy

PsyD . . . . Doctor of Psychology

GRADUATE PROGRAMS IN
Applied Sport Psychology

UNIVERSITY OF
Alberta

Department of Physical Education and Sport Studies

University of Alberta
Edmonton, Alberta
Canada T6G 2H9

Contact Person:	Anne Jordan (faculty gradute coord.)
....	John Hogg
Phone:	780.492.3198
....	780.492.2830
Fax:	780.492.2364
....	780.492.2364
Email:	Ajordan@PER.UALBERTA.CA
....	jhogg@PER.UALBERTA.CA

Faculty and areas of interest

Kerry Courneya	Behavioral medicine/exercise psychology
John Dunn	Anxiety, aggression, motivation, and perfectionism; secondary interest in scale construction and quantitative statistics
John Hogg	Psychology of performance enhancement: applications for athletes and coaches
Brian Maraj	Perceptual motor behavior
Ron Plotnikoff	Exercise and health behavior change
Wendy Rodgers	Social psychology of exercise, health, and lifestyle behavior
Billy Strean	Sport and exercise psychology: play, games, and fun; sport and physical activity instruction

Degrees offered

- MA (Thesis)
- MSc (Thesis)
- MA (Course based)
- PhD (Dissertation)

Approx. number of students in program

- 12–15

Approx. number of students in each degree program
- 14 Master's/8 PhD

Approx. number of students who apply to/are accepted by program annually
- 12–15 apply/6–8 accepted

Admissions requirements
- 4-year degree in physical education (or equivalent)
- Master's degree in a related field

The program has available for qualified students
- Graduate assistantships
- Scholarships
- Other forms of financial aid

Internship possibility
- Not officially

Internship required for degree completion
- N/A

Number of hours required for internship
- N/A

Core Graduate Course Offerings:

PEDS 540:	The Psychology of Performance in Sport and Physical Activity
PEDS 542:	Social Science Perspectives in Physical Activity, Fitness, and Well-Being
PEDS 543:	Seminar in the Learning and Memory of Movement
PEDS 545	Exercise Oncology
PEDS 582:	Psychosocial Dimensions in Sport and Physical Activity
PEDS 642:	Advanced Seminar in the Psychology of Sport and Physical Activity
PERLS 541:	Social Cognitive Appoaches to Health-Promoting Behavior
PERLS 542:	Social Science Perspectives of Physical Activity, Fitness, and Well-Being

Arizona
School of Professional Psychology

2301 West Dunlap Avenue, Suite 211
Phoenix, AZ 85021

Program Rating

1	**2**	3	4	5	6	7
Applied Orientation			Equal Emphasis		Research Orientation	

Contact Person: . . . . Frank Gardner
Phone: 602.216.2600
Fax: 602.216.2601
Email: . . . . Fgardner@azspp edu
Program web site: . . . . www.azspp.edu

Faculty and areas of interest

Frank Gardner	Sport psychological services in professional sports, performance enhancement and mental skills training in business, psychological assessment in sport and exercise, counseling in sports medicine
Robert Harmison	Performance enhancement, athletes' attitudes toward sport psychology, sport psychology counseling and consulting
Sheryl Harrison	Equestrian studies, arousal regulation
Bart Lerner	Goal setting, imagery, self-confidence, counselor certification, exercise and sport science
Brian Rice	Counseling psychology, addictive behavior, performance enhancement

Program Information

Degrees offered
- PsyD (Clinical psychology with specialty in sport psychology)
- MA (Sport psychology with specialty in counseling)

Approx. number of students in program
- 15–20 (MA)
- 6–10 (PsyD)

3

Approx. number of students in each degree program

- 65% MA/35% PsyD

Admissions requirements

GRE *not* required

GPA 3.0 (MA), 3.25 (PsyD)

The program has available for qualified students

- Work study
- Teaching assistantships
- Other forms of financial aid

Internship possibility

- Yes

Internship required for degree completion

- Yes

Number of hours required for internship

- MA = 500 hours in applied sport psychology
- PsyD = 500 hours in applied sport psychology and 2000 hours of combined clinical and sport psychology

Number of credit hours required for internship

- MA = 9 trimester hours
- PsyD = 27 trimester hours

Description of typical internship experience

- Work with university and junior college athletic teams; work in health and exercise settings; work with professional teams; work with private practice sport psychology services

Comments

Our master's (MA) program is designed to develop strong applied consultants and sport counselors. Students are expected to utilize their degree to work in coaching/education, performance consulting, sport and mental health counseling, exercise/wellness consulting, and as a solid foundation for further graduate (doctoral) training. The program curriculum blends exercise-sport science with counseling and clinical psychology, and applied sport psychology all in one academic department. Students are provided a 500-hour practicum (minimum) with college athletic teams, exercise/wellness facilities, sports medicine facilities, youth sport organizations and professional sport teams. Students have the opportunity to take a minor in professional counseling which meets the requirements for certification as a professional counselor in the state of Arizona.

Our doctoral (PsyD) program in clinical psychology with a formal specialty concentration in sport-exercise psychology, leads to licensure as a professional psychologist and meets the requirements for AAASP certification. The curriculum blends the standard doctoral curriculum in clinical psychology with a 21 to 27 credit sequence in exercise-sport science and applied sport psychology. In addition, students are required to complete, and are provided, a 500 hour (minimum) practicum in applied sport psychology working with collegiate and /or professional teams, exercise and wellness facilities, youth sport organizations and sports medicine/fitness facilities. Doctoral students also complete a doctoral research project under the close guidance of the sport psychology faculty.

These programs are housed within a School of Professional Psychology. Our program is interdisciplinary in nature with faculty from exercise-sport science, counseling psychology and clinical psychology, together comprising an independent department of sport psychology. This unique program structure allows students to be trained in a truly interdisciplinary manner, covering all of the curriculum requirements of AAASP certification, with a clear professional identity of their own.

Arizona State
UNIVERSITY

Department of Exercise Science and Physical Education

PEBE 112
Arizona State University
Tempe, AZ 85287-0404

Program Rating

1	2	3	4	**5**	6	7
Applied Orientation			Equal Emphasis		Research Orientation	

Contact Person:	Darren C. Treasure
Phone:	480.965.8489 (office)
. . . .	480.965.3913 (secretary)
. . . .	480.965.4676 (laboratory)
Fax:	480.965.8108
Email:	DARREN.TREASURE@ASU.EDU
Website:	www.asu.edu/clas/espe/

Faculty and areas of interest

Debra Crews	Psychological benefits of exercise for special populations
Jennifer Etnier	Age, physical activity and mental health
Daniel M. Landers	Arousal/anxiety/attention and performance
Darwyn E. Linder	Social perception of athletes, pain and performance
Darren C. Treasure	Motivational aspects of physical activity
Ellen Williams	Performance enhancement

Degrees offered
- MS
- PhD

Approx. number of students in program
- 15

Approx. number of students in each degree program

- 75% MS/25% PhD

Approx. number of students who apply to/are accepted by program annually

- 40 apply/6–7 accepted

Admissions requirements

- Minimum of 3.00 Jr./Sr. GPA
- Minimum of 50th percentile GRE (verbal + quantitative)
- Sport or exercise psychology courses
- Letter of intent indicating goals that are consistent with program
- Mentor willing to work with student
- Major research experience (undergraduate honor's thesis or master's thesis) required of PhD applicants

The program has available for qualified students

- Research assistantships
- Teaching assistantships
- Other forms of financial aid (including out-of-state tuition waivers)

Assistantships

0%	Fellowships
50%	Graduate assistantships
50%	Teaching assistantships
100%	Tuition waivers (out-of-state)
20%	Other forms of financial aid (in-state fee waivers)

Internship possibility

- Yes

Internship required for degree completion

- No

Number of hours required for internship

- 10 hours per week for 15 weeks or 20 hours per week for 15 weeks

Description of typical internship experience

- Graduate students who are enrolled in programs in exercise science, psychology, or related fields and who are being mentored by one of the listed faculty members, may gain experience in applied sport psychology by assisting in the provision of psychological skills training to intercollegiate athletes or to other subject populations. Most often, these programs are part of a research effort designed to test the efficacy of interventions or to explore psychological processes that mediate the effectiveness of applied sport psychology interventions. The major focus, therefore, is on the research effort rather than on the acquisition by the student of a broad range of intervention skills.

Comments

The program primarily prepares individuals for *research* in the psychology of exercise and sport. Students are expected to immerse themselves in research and to take research credits from their first semester to the conclusion of the program. Two teaching assistants teach several sections of an undergraduate course entitled *Psychological Skills for Optimal Performance*. This experience is open to doctoral students in exercise science who are committed to becoming sport researchers.

UNIVERSITY OF
Arizona

Department of Psychology
University of Arizona
Tucson, AZ 85721

Program Rating

1	2	3	4	**5**	**6**	7

Applied Orientation   Equal Emphasis   Research Orientation

Contact Person: . . . . Jean M. Williams
Sport Psychology Information
. . . . Peggy Collins
Psychology Graduate Secretary
Phone: 520.621.6984
. . . . 520.621.7456
Email: . . . . williams@u.arizona.edu
. . . . lcollins@u.arizona.edu
Website: . . . . www.arizona.edu/~psych/

Faculty and areas of interest

Jean M. Williams   Psychology of injury, relationship of psychological states to performance, performance enhancement, coaching behaviors, group dynamics

Degree offered

- PhD

The program has available for qualified students

- Fellowships
- Teaching assistantships
- Other forms of financial aid

Assistantships

2%   Fellowships
8%   Research assistantships
90%   Teaching assistantships
0%   Tuition waivers
0%   Other forms of financial aid

Note: Percentages are approximate; however, 100% of the students receive fellowships, research assistantships, or teaching assistantships for at least 4 years.

Internship possibility
- Yes, up to 400 hours in sport psychology

Internship required for degree completion
- No, except for the clinical program

Description of typical internship experience
- Internships are available with community athletes and in the Athletic Department's mental training program, primarily for performance enhancement but also for life skills development. Internships are also available at substance abuse centers, corporations, and fitness/wellness centers; primarily for stress management, general health promotion, and personal development.

Comments

In the fall of 1996, the graduate program in sport psychology was transferred from the Department of Exercise and Sport Sciences to the Department of Psychology. The move resulted in the elimination of the MS in sport psychology. The Department of Psychology offers only a PhD program, with majors in the following areas: clinical psychology, cognitive psychology, developmental psychology, psychobiology, policy and law, and social psychology. Students within these major areas, in addition to fulfilling the requirements for the major, can declare a minor in sport psychology and thereby pursue course work, research, and internships specific to their sport psychology interests. At any given time, funding is available for two half-time TAs who have sport psychology interests. Because these positions are filled, we will not accept new applications for admission until fall 2002.

Over the last decade, the Department of Psychology has undergone rapid growth and development. The acquisition of faculty actively continues, with the Department fast becoming one of the premier programs in the country. The graduate program emphasizes research training in order to equip students for both academic and applied careers. It strongly encourages interdisciplinary study for students and reflects the faculty's own interdisciplinary orientation to scholarship.

Ball State
UNIVERSITY

School of Physical Education

Ball State University
Muncie, IN 47306

Program Rating

1	2	3	**4**	5	6	7

Applied Orientation	Equal Emphasis	Research Orientation

Contact Person: . . . . S. Jae Park
Phone: 317.285.1458
Fax: 317.285.8254
Website: . . . . www.bsu.edu/physicaleducation/
. . . . www.bsu.edu/cast/pe/index4.htm

Faculty and areas of interest

M. Buck	Teacher education
D. Kraemer	Exercise physiology and bioenergetics
R. Newton	Biomechanics
J. Reno	Administration and sport management
V. Wayda	Sport psychology

Degrees offered

- MA
- MS
- PhD in Bioenergetics

Approx. number of students in program

- 100

Approx. number of students in each degree program

- 70% MA/30% MS

Approx. number of students who apply to/are accepted by program annually

- Varies

Admissions requirements

- 2.75 GPA (out of 4.00)
- GRE recommended

The program has available for qualified students

- Research assistantships
- Teaching assistantships

Assistantships

0%	Fellowships
30–40%	Research assistantships (get tuition waivers)
0%	Teaching assistantships
10%	Tuition waivers
0%	Other forms of financial aid

Internship possibility

- Yes

Internship required for degree completion

- Not for all of them

Number of hours required for internship

- 3 semester hours

Description of typical internship experience

- Internships provide on-the-job experiences.

Boise State
UNIVERSITY

Department of Health, Physical Education, and Recreation

1910 University Drive
Boise, ID 83725

Program Rating

1	2	3	**4**	5	6	7
Applied Orientation			Equal Emphasis		Research Orientation	

Contact Person: . . . . Linda M. Petlichkoff
Phone: 208.426.1231
Fax: 208.426.1894
Email: . . . . lpetlic@boisestate.edu
Website: . . . . www.kinesiology.boisestate.edu

Faculty and areas of interest

Bill Kozar   Motor learning
Linda Petlichkoff   Competitive anxiety, participation motivation, goal orientation, coach/athlete interaction, coach education

Degree offered
• MS

Approx. number of students in program
• 2–4

Approx. number of students who apply to/are accepted by program annually
• 40 apply / 8–10 are accepted into the total MS program

Admissions requirements
• Minimum 3.0 GPA with an appropriate pattern of classes to provide a foundation in physical education, but 3.00 GPA over the last 2 years
• No GRE requirement

The program has available for qualified students
• Graduate assistantships
• Other forms of financial aid

13

Assistantships

0%	Fellowships
15–18%	Research assistantships
0%	Teaching assistantships
15–18%	Tuition waivers
0%	Other forms of financial aid

Internship possibility

- Several possibilities do exist on campus.

Internship required for degree completion

- No

Description of typical internship experience

- Possible practicum experiences available with several teams on campus

Boston
UNIVERSITY

Department of Developmental Studies and Counseling

605 Commonwealth Avenue
Boston University
Boston, MA 02215

Program Rating

1	2	3	**4**	5	6	7

Applied Orientation   Equal Emphasis   Research Orientation

Contact Person: . . . . Leonard D. Zaichkowsky
Phone: 617.353.3378
Fax: 617.353.2909
Email: . . . . sport@acs.bu.edu
Website: . . . . www.bu.edu/education

Faculty and areas of interest

Amy Baltzell	Coping, development of expertise
John Cheffers	Aggression/violence
Mary Ann Kane	Gender issues, career transition, ethics
Leonard D. Zaichkowsky	Psychophysiology/self-regulation, career transition

Faculty in counseling psychology, human movement, and related areas within Boston University.

Degrees offered

- MEd
- EdD

Approx. number of students in program

- 12 MEd/6 EdD

Approx. number of students in each degree program

- 75% MEd/25% EdD

Approx. number of students who apply to/are accepted by program annually

- 20 MEd apply/12 MEd accepted; 15 EdD apply/2–3 EdD accepted

15

Admissions requirements

- Undergraduate GPA of 3.00
- Strong GRE or MAT scores
- Strong references
- Strong exercise/sport experience

The program has available for qualified students

- Teaching assistantships
- Other forms of financial aid

Assistantships

0%   Fellowships
0%   Research assistantships
20%   Teaching assistantships
0%   Tuition waivers
90%   Other forms of financial aid

Internship possibility

- Yes

Internship required for degree completion

- Yes (both MEd and EdD degrees)

Number of hours required for internship

- 20 hours per week for the master's degree, two semesters

Description of typical internship experience

- Students may intern at university counseling centers, university athletic departments, the Academy for Physical and Social Development, wellness centers, or with Olympic and professional sports teams.

Comments

Students may obtain the EdD in developmental studies or counseling psychology, specializing in sport psychology. The program in counseling psychology with a specialization in sport psychology is based on a scientist-practitioner model. Eligibility for admission to the EdD program requires a complete master's degree in counseling or a related field. The EdD program includes a minimum of 2 years of full-time course work, including a half-time, supervised placement at an approved field site in the second year, and a full-time, 1-year internship. The licensing of psychologists is a state function, and students are urged to contact directly the licensing boards of those states in which they are interested in practicing. With appropriate pre- and post-doctoral training, the graduate may be eligible to sit for the licensing exam in psychology.

Bowling Green State
UNIVERSITY

School of HPER

Eppler Complex
Bowling Green State University
Bowling Green, OH 43403

Program Rating

1	2	3	4	**5**	6	7
Applied Orientation			Equal Emphasis		Research Orientation	

Contact Person:	Vikki Krane
....	Bonnie Berger
Phone:	419.372.7233
....	419.372.2334
Fax:	419.372.0383
....	419.372.2377
Email:	VKRANE@BGNET.BGSU.EDU
....	Bberger@bgnet.bgsu.edu
Website:	bgsu.edu/departments/hmsls/gp.html

Faculty and areas of interest

Bonnie Berger	Exercise psychology, psychological well-being, mood enhancement and physical activity, self-concept in sport and exercise
Vikki Krane	Feminist sport psychology, competitive anxiety
Lisa McClung	Sport and gender
Janet Parks	Gender-biased language, sport administration
Nancy Spencer	Sport sociology, sport and gender

Degree offered
- MEd

Approx. number of students in program
- 4–7 in sport and exercise psychology/25–30 in the School of Human Movement, Sport and Leisure Studies

17

Approx. number of students who apply to/are accepted by program annually

- Developmental kinesiology is a new program; the exact number of applicants/students is not yet known.

Admission requirements

- 3.0 GPA
- GRE scores
- 3 letters of recommendation
- Personal statement
- Résumé

The program has available for qualified students

- Research assistantships
- Teaching assistantships
- Other forms of financial aid

Assistantships

0%   Fellowships
40%   Research assistantships*
40%   Teaching assistantships*
80%   Tuition waivers
40%   Other forms of financial aid

* Graduate assistantships account for approximately 40% of all graduate students. These assistantships often include both teaching and research possibilities.

Internship possibility

- No

Comments

The sport and exercise psychology emphasis in the developmental kinesiology program takes an interdisciplinary approach to exercise science. Sport and exercise psychology is one of several concentrations within the program. Course work in this emphasis includes psychological parameters of sport, applied sport psychology, exercise psychology, and seminars and independent study in sport and exercise psychology. Additionally, many students become involved in ongoing research. Other requirements include 4 of 7 classes in the flexible core. Upon completion of core requirements, the remainder of the academic experience is developed in consultation with the student's mentor/advisor. The sport and exercise psychology emphasis places equal importance on theory, research, and applied sport psychology skills. A thesis or directed project is required for a capstone experience.

California State
UNIVERSITY, FRESNO

Department of Kinesiology
5275 N. Campus Drive
Fresno, CA 93740-8018

Program Rating

1	2	3	4	**5**	6	7

Applied Orientation   Equal Emphasis   Research Orientation

Contact Person: . . . . Rebecca Crampton
Phone: 559.278.7094
Fax: 559.278.7010
Email: . . . . rebeccac@csufresno.edu
Website: . . . . www.csufresno.edu/pehp/programs/

Faculty and areas of interest

Rebecca Crampton   Performance enhancement, athletic injuries
Jenelle Gilbert   Exercise and Sport Psychology
Wade Gilbert   Exercise and Sport Psychology

Degree offered

MA, with an emphasis in sport psychology

Approx. number of students in program

10 (first year of program)

Approx. number of students who apply to/are accepted by program annually

N/A

Admissions requirements

Undergraduate degree from an accredited institution

3.00 GPA in the last 60 semester units attempted

Nonphysical education majors can enter as "conditionally classified"

See www.csufresno.edu/gradstudies/index.html

The program has available for qualified students

Research assistantships

Teaching assistantships

Tuition waivers

Other forms of financial aid

Assistantships

0%   Fellowships

15%   Graduate assistantships

50%   Teaching assistantships/coaching

0%   Tuition waivers

20%   Other forms of financial aid

Internship possibility

Yes

Internship required for degree completion

No

Number of hours required/possible for internship

50 hours (minimum) for a semester

Description of typical internship experience

Supervised work with youth sport or high school athletes

Comments

The sport psychology emphasis at CSUF was created in 1999. This degree is intended for students who are interested in careers as (a) sport psychologists, (b) coaches, (c) teachers, (d) sport administrators, or who are (e) preparing for doctoral study. An additional and unique attraction of this program is its emphasis on courses and research in the field of sports medicine.

California State University, Fresno, is one of 23 campuses in the CSU system. Current enrollment is approximately 18,000 students in a 1400-acre campus in northeast Fresno. The university closely approximates the multi-ethnic population of 600,000 living in the San Joaquin valley. Fresno is within easy driving distance of Sequoia, Kings Canyon, and Yosemite National Parks.

The graduate students are diverse in age, racial/cultural background, and experience (athletic trainers, coaches, and elite performers), providing an enriching experience for students and faculty. Teaching associateships are available to qualified students for full-time and part-time positions, depending on departmental needs.

California State
UNIVERSITY, FULLERTON

Division of Kinesiology and Health Promotion

800 North State College Boulevard
California State University
Fullerton, CA 92634

Program Rating

1	2	**3**	4	5	6	7
Applied Orientation		Equal Emphasis		Research Orientation		

Contact Person: . . . . Bill Beam (KHP Graduate Coordinator)
Phone: 714.278.3432
Fax: 714.278.5317
Website: . . . . www.fullerton.edu

Faculty and areas of interest

Patricia Laguna	Performance enhancement, attention control
Kenneth Ravizza	Performance enhancement, peak performance
Carol A. Weinmann	Performance enhancement in sport and exercise, self-control, self-regulation

Degree offered
- MS

Approx. number of students in program
- 25 sport and exercise psychology students

Approx. number of students who apply to/are accepted by program annually
- 40 apply/25 accepted

Admissions requirements
- GPA of 3.20 in major (2.50 in last 60 units)
- GRE
- Essay

The program has available for qualified students
- Graduate assistantships

- Teaching associateships
- Other forms of financial aid

Assistantships

0%	Fellowships
15%	Graduate assistantships
85%	Teaching associateships
0%	Tuition waivers
0%	Other forms of financial aid

Internship possibility

- Yes

Internship required for degree completion

- No

Number of hours required for internship

- 10 hours per week, plus 1-hour weekly conference

Description of typical internship experience

- Using applied sport psychology techniques/interventions with university athletic teams

Comments

The individual involved in this area of study is grounded in the theoretical, research, and practical aspects of motivation and human behavior in relation to sport and exercise for all ages and ability levels. The program is designed to prepare students for (a) a doctoral program in sport psychology; (b) an effective approach to performance enhancement in a multitude of settings; (c) consultation with athletes, coaches, and group and personal clients; and (d) a more effective approach to coaching and teaching. Three faculty serve the students in this emphasis area.

California State
UNIVERSITY, LONG BEACH

Department of Kinesiology and Physical Education

1250 Bellflower Boulevard
California State University
Long Beach, CA 90840

Program Rating

1	2	3	**4**	5	6	7

Applied Orientation   Equal Emphasis   Research Orientation

Program Rating: Program provides an equal balance of applied and research emphases.

Contact Person: . . . . Michael Lacourse
(Graduate Coordinator)
Phone: 562.985.4558
Fax: 562.985.8067
Email: . . . . mlacours@csulb.edu
Website: . . . . www.csulb.edu/~kpe/

Faculty and areas of interest

Sharon Guthrie	Physical and global self-perception, eating disorders, body image, gender-related topics
Michael Lacourse	Psychophysiology of imagery/brain imaging
Dale Toohey	Education in coaching

Degree offered

- MS

Approx. number of students in program

- 25

Approx. number of students who apply to/are accepted by program annually

- 15 apply/12 accepted

Admissions requirements

- Ask for graduate handbook

The program has available for qualified students

- Research assistantships

Assistantships

0%	Fellowships
10%	Research assistantships
5%	Teaching assistantships
5%	Tuition waivers
0%	Other forms of financial aid

Internship possibility

- Yes

Internship required for degree completion

- Yes

Number of hours required for internship

- Will vary

Description of typical internship experience

- Working with university teams

Comments

The MS program allows the student to complete an individualized program in sport psychology.

California State
UNIVERSITY, SACRAMENTO

Department of Health and Physical Education

6000 J Street
California State University
Sacramento, CA 95819

Program Rating

1	2	3	**4**	5	6	7

Applied Orientation　　　　Equal Emphasis　　　　Research Orientation

Contact Person: . . . . Karen L. Scarborough
Phone: 916.278.7309
Fax: 916.278.7664
Email: . . . . scarboro@csus.edu
Website: . . . . www.hhs.csus.edu/

Faculty and areas of interest

Karen L. Scarborough . . . . .Psychological skills training

Degree offered
- MS

Approx. number of students in program
- 10

Approx. number of students who apply to/are accepted by program annually
- 5 apply/3 accepted

Admissions requirements
- 2.80 GPA overall or 3.00 in last 60 units
- Undergraduate physical education degree (major or minor)

The program has available for qualified students
- Teaching assistantships/graduate assistantships

Assistantships

0%   Fellowships
0%   Research assistantships
60%   Teaching assistantships
0%   Tuition waivers
0%   Other forms of financial aid

Internship possibility

- Yes

Internship required for degree completion

- No

Number of hours required for internship

- 3–10 hours per week

  The master of science in physical education provides a concentration in sport performance for those interested in sport psychology, sport sociology, and teaching/coaching. Flexible use of electives provides specific focus opportunities.

Description of typical internship experience

- Individualized mental training for California State University, Sacramento, athletes
- Administration of psychological skills program for a CSUS team
- Administration of psychological rehabilitation program for injured athletes.

UNIVERSITY OF
California,
LOS ANGELES

Department of Psychology

UCLA PhD Program in Social Psychology
1285 Franz Hall/Box 951563
University of California
Los Angeles, CA 90095-1563

Program Rating

1	2	3	4	5	**6**	7

Applied Orientation	Equal Emphasis	Research Orientation

Contact Person: . . . . Graduate Program Director
Phone: 310.825.2617
Fax: 310.206.5895
Email: . . . . Gradadm@psych ucla.edu

Faculty and areas of interest

Robert Bjork	Cognitive psychology, memory
Tara K. Scanlan	Professor and Director of the International Center for Talent Development. Motivation and emotion regarding youth sport through elite athletes, as well as performers in other talent domains (e.g., art, music, education). Includes developmental and significant other issues, and an integration of quantitative and qualitative research approaches Currently developing a model of sport commitment and examining the role of enjoyment within this framework. The model is to be investigated and applied across talent domains. Also interested in effective parenting, teaching, and coaching for the gifted and talented.
Bernard Weiner	Cognitive approaches to motivations, applications to education, achievement motivation, and emotion.
	Additional course work and faculty expertise are available within the cognitive, developmental, and health psychology areas of psychology, as well as in the School of Education and other cross-campus units.

Degree offered
• PhD only (no MS)

Approx. number of students who apply to/are accepted by program annually

- 100–120 apply/5–10 accepted

Admissions requirements

- Three letters of recommendation (preferably from research psychologists)
- The GRE General Test and Subject Test in Psychology
- All *admitted* students must have taken the following courses:
- Statistics
- Two of the following: learning, physiological, or perception/information processing
- Two of the following: developmental, social, or personality/abnormal
- One course in either biology or zoology
- Two courses in physics or chemistry
- At least one mathematics course, preferably calculus or probability

Note: Although it is possible to gain admission with deficiencies in these requirements, they must be remedied within the first four quarters of graduate study.

The program has available for qualified students

- Post doctoral fellowships
- Fellowships
- Research assistantships
- Teaching assistantships
- Other forms of financial aid

All students are covered by one or more of the above.

Internship possibility

- Outreach: See comments (no traditional sport psychology internships).

Comments

Sport psychology is offered within the Department of Psychology's social psychology area and is central to the newly founded International Center for Talent Development (ICTD). The ICTD is multidisciplinary and includes research, instruction, and outreach components. Post-doctoral fellowships and research assistantships are available.

The ICTD focuses on understanding and facilitating the development of talent across a diverse range of domains (e.g., sport, music, art, education) and skill levels (e.g., youth-sport through world-class athletes). Talent development is viewed broadly to include issues such as the development of expertise; motivation and emotion; development (cognitive, motoric, and social); significant other influences (family, coaches, teachers, peers); and the sociology involved in establishing talent domains. Center functions include research, outreach, and education.

UNIVERSITY OF
Canberra

Centre for Sports Studies

University of Canberra
PO Box 1
Belconnen ACT 2616, Australia

Program Rating

1	**2**	3	4	5	6	7
Applied Orientation			Equal Emphasis		Research Orientation	

Contact Person: . . . . John B. Gross
Phone: . . . . (06) 2012009
Fax: . . . . (06) 2015999
Email: . . . . gross@science.canberra.edu.au
Website: . . . . science.canberra.edu.au/sportstud/

Faculty and areas of interest

John B. Gross   Coaching behaviors—attributions and sports performance

Degree offered

• Graduate diploma in Applied Psychology

Approx. number of students in program

• 3

Approx. number of students in each degree program

• 100% Graduate Diploma

Approx. number of students who apply to/are accepted by program annually

• 10 apply/3 accepted

Admissions requirements

• Graduate Diploma—three years of psychology plus a sports science major

Assistantships

0%   Fellowships

0%	Research assistantships
0%	Teaching assistantships
0%	Tuition waivers
0%	Other forms of financial aid

Internship possibility

- Yes

Internship required for degree completion

- No

Number of hours required for internship

- None

Description of typical internship experience

- Graduate Diploma—two weeks' attendance at an academy or institute of sport

Comments

The Graduate Diploma in Applied Psychology involves 1 year of course work, including a major research project and a 2-week placement at an academy or institute of sport. Fees per year for the Graduate Diploma are approximately $12,000 (Australian).

Chichester
Institute of Higher Education

School of Sports Studies

Chichester Institute of Higher Education
College Lane, Chichester
West Sussex, PO19 4PE, England

Contact Person:	Jan Graydon
Phone:	01243 816320
Fax:	01243 816080
Email:	100443.2067@compuserve com

Faculty and areas of interest

Jan Graydon	Gender issues, motor skills
Ian Maynard	Stress management
Terry McMorris	Cognitive processes and fatigue

Degrees offered

- MPhil
- MS
- PhD

Approx. number of students in program

- 6

Approx. number of students in each degree program

- Different system

Approx. number of students who apply to/are accepted by program annually

- 6 apply/1–2 accepted

Admissions requirements

- Good standing undergraduate degree in sport science or related area or psychology

Internship possibility

- Consultancy experience available

Description of typical internship experience

- Funding is difficult. There is sometimes the possibility of laboratory work or governing body-funded consultancy work.

Comments

At present the master's and doctoral programs are not taught per se. Higher degree qualification is by research.

Cleveland State
UNIVERSITY

Department of Health, Physical Education, and Recreation

Physical Education Building 223
Cleveland State University
Cleveland, OH 44115

Program Rating

1	2	**3**	4	5	6	7

Applied Orientation   Equal Emphasis   Research Orientation

Contact Person: . . . . Susan Ziegler
Phone: 216.687.4876
Fax: 216.687.5410
Website: . . . . www.csuohio.edu

Faculty and areas of interest

Susan Ziegler   Performance enhancement

Degree offered

• MEd

Approx. number of students in program

• 30

Approx. number of students who apply to/are accepted by program annually

• 5–10 apply/7–8 accepted

Admissions requirements

• 2.75 GPA

The program has available for qualified students

• Teaching assistantships

Assistantships

0%	Fellowships
0%	Research assistantships
20%	Teaching assistantships
10%	Tuition waivers
0%	Other forms of financial aid

Internship possibility

- No

Deakin
UNIVERSITY, RUSDEN CAMPUS

Department of Physical Education

662 Blackburn Road
Deakin University, Rusden Campus
Clayton 3168, Victoria, Australia

Contact Person:	Rob Sands
. . . .	Sue South (School Administrator)
Phone:	03 9244 7244
. . . .	03 9244 7244
Fax:	03 9244 7407
Email:	rsands@deakin.edu.au

Faculty and areas of interest
Faculty in health and behavioral sciences (School of Human Movement)

Degrees offered
- Master's in Applied Science (Research) in which students must have a 10-unit undergrad sequence of psychology courses, then proceed to a fourth-year Honours course within the School of Psychology
- PhD
- Graduate Diploma in Sport Science and Graduate Diploma in Psychology as pathways to master by course work
- Master's preliminary program

Approx. number of students in program
- 20

Approx. number of students in each degree program
- 80% Master's/20% PhD (currently small but growing numbers)

Approx. number of students who apply to/are accepted by program annually
- 30 apply

The program has available for qualified students
- Graduate assistantships (limited at this stage)
- Other forms of financial aid (only for Australian students)

Internship possibility

- No, not yet

Comments

Human movement students must fully load their 3 years with psychology units in order to enroll within the School of Psychology Honours year. We are currently negotiating with the School of Psychology to jointly develop a number of undergraduate and graduate units for students of both schools (Human Movement and Psychology). We also have to be mindful that the new Professional Association of Sport Science requires 1000 hours of undergraduate study for an individual to become a qualified sport scientist, while the College of Sport Psychology (within the Australian Psychology Society) requires a master's degree in psychology for registration as a practicing member. It seems we are moving into the position of having to fulfill both sets of professional criteria before an individual can be qualified as a sport psychologist.

DeMontfort
UNIVERSITY, BEDFORD

School of Physical Education, Sport &Leisure

DeMontfort University Bedford
37 Lansdowne Road
Bedford MK 40 2BZ, England

Program Rating

1	2	3	4	5	**6**	7

Applied Orientation   Equal Emphasis   Research Orientation

Contact Person: . . . . Howard K. Hall
Phone: . . . . (01234) 793316
Fax: . . . . (01234) 350833
Email: . . . . HKHall@DMU.AC UK
Website: . . . . www.dmu.ac.uk/dept/schools/pesl/spob/
research_psych.html

Faculty and areas of interest

Steve Boutcher	Psychophysiology
Howard K. Hall	Motivation, stress
Alistair Kerr	Stress
Steve Kozub	Team cohesion and player leadership
Ken Roberts	Movement timing and coincident-anticipation timing in children
Daniel Weigand	Psychosocial development via sport, mental skills training, goal-setting
Adrian Taylor	Exercise psychology

Degrees offered
- MPhil and PhD are attained through research
- MS is attained through a taught course

Approx. number of students in program
- 10

The program has available for qualified students
- Research assistantships
- Teaching assistantships

Assistantships

0%   Fellowships

0%   Research assistantships

0%   Teaching assistantships

0%   Tuition waivers

0%   Other forms of financial aid

Internship possibility

- No

Internship required for degree completion

- No

Comments

MPhil and PhD degrees are by research only. The program currently has 10 students enrolled for MPhil and PhD degrees. We also offer a taught MS in sport studies with a specialization in sport psychology. We offer both teaching and research assistantships to support graduate students studying for MPhil, PhD, or MS degrees.

UNIVERSITY OF
Edinburgh

Department of PE Sport & Leisure Studies

University of Edinburgh
Cramond Road North
Edinburgh, EH4 6JD, Scotland

Contact Person:	Dave Collins
Phone:	44-131-312-6001
Fax:	44-131-312-6375
Email:	d.collins@ed.ac.uk

Faculty and areas of interest

Angela Abbott	Talent identification and development
Dave Collins	Interdisciplinary approaches to research and support in sport and exercise psychology
Richard Cox	Mood state profiling, behavioural aspects of sport psychology
Gavin Loze	Sport psychophysiology
Duncan Mascarenhas	Psychology of officiating
Helen Milne	Imagery and MSM
Patrick Mortimer	Team decision making
Hugh Richards	Coping, social identity

Degrees offered

- MSc
- MPhil
- PhD

Approx. number of students in program

- 25

Approx. number of students in each degree program

- MSc,12; MPhil/PhD, 13

Approx. number of students who apply to/are accepted by program annually

- 25 apply; 8 are accepted

Admissions requirements

- First (and possibly master's) degree in a cogent subject
- CV demonstrate interest in, and commitment to, chosen area
- Telephone/personal interview plus university admission requirements

Assistantships

10%   Fellowships
30%   Research Assistantships
20%   Teaching Assistantships

Internship possibility

- Yes

Internship required for degree completion

- No

Description of typical internship experience

- Extremely varied and personalized. Degree of "hands-on" experience depends on time of year, sport season, etc.

UNIVERSITY OF
Exeter

School of Health Sciences

University of Exeter
Heavitree Road
Exeter EX1 2LU
United Kingdom

Program Rating

1	2	3	**4**	5	6	7

Applied Orientation   Equal Emphasis   Research Orientation

Contact Person: . . . . Ken Fox
Fax: . . . . +44 (0) 1392 264792
Website: . . . . www.exeter.ac.uk/education/

Faculty and areas of interest

Sue Bock	Coaching psychology, children in sport, mental training
Ken Fox	Exercise and public health, self-esteem and exercise, body image, weight management
Geoff Meek	Attitude and motivation, special needs
Andrew Sparkes	Interpretive paradigm, body and self, innovation and change

A range of modules in research methods are taught by psychology faculty.

Degrees offered
- MS and MS (European) in exercise and sport psychology
- MPhil by supervised research
- PhD by supervised research

Approx. number of students in program
- 15 MS, 2 MS (European)/8–10 Research

Approx. number of students who apply to/are accepted by program annually
- 40–50 apply (MS)/30 accepted

Admissions requirements

- Good honors degree (2.1) or B average usually in psychology or exercise and sport sciences

Assistantships:

7%	Fellowships
0%	Research assistantships
0%	Teaching assistantships
0%	Tuition waivers
0%	Other forms of financial aid

Internship possibility

- Yes

Internship required for degree completion

- No

Comments

In the exercise and sport psychology group at Exeter, expertise exists in psychometrics and instrument development, as well as data analysis using structural equation modeling, hierarchical class analysis, and meta-analysis. Qualitative data analysis is relatively new to exercise and sport psychology, and in Dr. Sparkes, Exeter has the foremost authority on the topic in European exercise and sport sciences.

Florida State UNIVERSITY

Department of Educational Research

Program in Educational Psychology, B-197
Florida State University
Tallahassee, FL 32306

Program Rating

1	2	3	**4**	5	6	7
Applied Orientation			Equal Emphasis		Research Orientation	

Contact Person:	David Pargman
. . . .	Gershon Tenenbaum
Phone:	850.644.8793
. . . .	850.644.8780
Fax:	850.644.8776
Email:	Dpargman@edres.fsu.edu
Website:	WWW.FSU.EDU/~EDRES/PSYCHOLOGY/ WELCOME.HTML

Faculty and areas of interest

David Pargman	Health psychology issues (stress, injury), perceptual cognitive factors, motivation, learning
Gershon Tenenbaum	Methodological and measurement perspectives and methods in sport and exercise psychology; cognition and decision making in the development of motor skills and expertise; motivation and exertion in physical tasks: a social-cognitive perspective.

Degrees offered
- MS
- PhD

Approx. number of students in program
- 25–30

Approx. number of students in each degree program

- 50% MS/50% PhD

Approx. number of students who apply to/are accepted by program annually

- 40 apply/10 accepted

Admissions requirements (minimum requirements for consideration)

- Minimum GPA of 3.00
- Minimum GRE score of 1000

The program has available for qualified students

- Teaching assistantships
- Other forms of financial aid

Assistantships

10%	Fellowships
10%	Research assistantships
10%	Teaching assistantships
10%	Tuition waivers
10%	Other forms of financial aid

Internship possibility

- Yes

Internship required for degree completion

- Yes, for the PhD

Number of hours required for internship

- A minimum of 8 semester hours

Description of typical internship experience

- Assignment to one of Florida State University's varsity athletic teams
- Assignment to one of Tallahassee's mental health or wellness clinics

Comments

Psychological processes and conditions associated with athletics and sports situations are studied in the graduate program. Although the academic side (research, theory) of sport psychology is emphasized, students are offered practical (clinical, analytical) experiences in various sport programs. Students can be prepared to teach at the university level, to conduct research, and to serve as consultants to athletes, sport organizations, and those who participate in sport.

UNIVERSITY OF
Florida

Department of Exercise and Sport Sciences

College of Health and Human Performance
305 Florida Gymnasium
University of Florida
Gainesville, FL 32611

Program Rating

1	2	3	4	5	**6**	7

Applied Orientation   Equal Emphasis   Research Orientation

Contact Person: . . . . Christopher M. Janelle
Phone: 352.392.0584 x270
Fax: 352.392.5262
Email: . . . . CJANELLE@HHP.UFL.EDU
Website: . . . . www.hhp.ufl.edu/ess/
. . . . www.hhp.ufl.edu/ess/mblab/
. . . . www.hhp.ufl.edu/ess/sppsylab/index.htm

Faculty and areas of interest

James Cauraugh	Processes, variables, and mechanisms involved in skill acquisition and control
Pete Giacobbi	Arousal/anxiety regulation, coping skills, athlete coachability
Heather Hausenblas	Exercise psychology, eating disorders, exercise dependence, body image
Chris Janelle	Attention, visual search, arousal, and expertise
Milledge Murphey	Psychological factors in high-risk and combative sport
Robert N. Singer	Information processing and cognitive operations involved in self-paced and dynamic settings; factors contributing to motivation and achievement
Keith Tennant	Learning strategies in skill development

Degrees offered

• MS
• PhD (sport and exercise psychology specialization)

Approx. number of students in program

• 30

45

Approx. number of students in each degree program

- 40% MS/60% PhD

Approx. number of students who apply to/are accepted by program annually

- 40 apply/8 accepted

Admissions requirements

- 1000 GRE (the higher the better)
- 3.00 GPA (minimum)

The program has available for qualified students

- Teaching assistantships
- Other forms of financial aid

Assistantships

5%	Fellowships
5%	Research assistantships
50%	Teaching assistantships
50%	Tuition waivers
80%	Other forms of financial aid

Two $7,500 Fellowships available for qualified incoming doctoral students (in addition to assistantships); several $3,000 fellowships available for qualified incoming doctoral students (in addition to assistantships)

Internship possibility

- Yes

Internship required for degree completion

- No

Number of hours required for internship

- To be negotiated

Description of typical internship experience

- Flexible

Comments

Emphasis is on the study of cognitive, psychological, and psychobiological factors contributing to learning and performance excellence, as well as on psychological factors associated with exercise and fitness performance. The orientation is to the scholarly aspects of the specialization, with research conducted in laboratory or in field settings. Students can be involved in applied settings. Students at the master's level are primarily prepared for doctoral work, and doctoral graduates are prepared primarily for university positions and secondarily for applied settings.

Furman
UNIVERSITY

Department of Health and Exercise Science

Furman University
Greenville, SC 29613

Program Rating

1	2	3	**4**	5	6	7
Applied Orientation			Equal Emphasis		Research Orientation	

Contact Person:	Frank M. Powell
Phone:	803.294.3418
Fax:	803.294.2942
Email:	frank.powell@furman.edu
Website:	www.furman.edu/

Faculty and areas of interest

Frank M. Powell	Anxiety, arousal, aging
Paul Rasmussen	Clinical intervention

Degree offered

- MA in exercise science, 30 hours required

Approx. number of students in program

- 45 students in MA program; 2–3 focus on sport psychology

Approx. number of students who apply to/are accepted by program annually

- 2 apply/2 accepted

Admissions requirements

- BA or BS from an accredited school
- Two letters of recommendation
- >1000 GRE
- Exercise science prerequisites may be needed

Assistantships:

0%	Fellowships
0%	Research assistantships

30%   Teaching assistantships
60%   Tuition waivers
10%   Other forms of financial aid

Internship possibility

- Yes

Description of typical internship experience

- Performance enhancement and/or stress management intervention with senior athletes (55 years and over)

Georgia Southern

UNIVERSITY

Department of Health and Kinesiology

PO Box 8076
Georgia Southern University
Statesboro, Georgia 30460-8076

Program Rating

1	**2**	3	4	5	6	7
Applied Orientation			Equal Emphasis		Research Orientation	

Contact Person: . . . . Kevin L. Burke
. . . . (Graduate Program Director)
Phone: 912.681.5267
. . . . 912.681.0200 (Dept. Office)
Fax: 912.681.0381
Email: . . . . KevBurke@gsaix2.cc.gasou.edu
Website: www2.gasou.edu/KIN

Faculty and areas of interest

Kevin L. Burke	Performance enhancement, momentum, optimism, humor
W. Kent Guion	Activity epidemiology
Charles J. Hardy	Social influence processes
Barry Joyner	Performance prediction, data analysis
Jim McMillan	Psychophysiological aspects of performance

Degree offered

- MS with a major in kinesiology, sport psychology emphasis

Approx. number of students in program

- 15

Admissions requirements

- 2.75 (on a 4.0 scale) minimum undergraduate GPA
- A minimum of 1200 using the following formula: undergraduate GPA x 100 + GRE verbal score (400 minimum) + either the GRE quantitative or analytical score
- Students who do not meet these admission requirements may be granted "provisional admission" status if they have a minimum of 1050 using the following formula: undergraduate GPA 2.50 minimum (on a 4.0 scale) x 100 + GRE verbal score (minimum 350) + either the GRE quantitative or analytical score
- A full vitae or résumés that includes the following: a) work history, b) professional experiences, c) membership and participation in professional organizations, and d) other experiences related to the academic program
- Contact information for a minimum of three references

The program has available for qualified students

- Research assistantships
- Teaching assistantships

Assistantships

0%	Fellowships
10%	Research assistantships
70%	Teaching assistantships
80%	Tuition waivers
0%	Other forms of financial aid

Internship possibility

- Yes

Internship required for degree completion

- Yes

Number of hours required for internship

- 3 semester hours

Description of typical internship experience

- Students enroll in a practicum course wherein they receive supervision from an AAASP-certified consultant as they structure and apply intervention/performance-enhancement techniques with teams and/or individual athletes or exercise participants.

Comments

The MS program in kinesiology with an emphasis in sport psychology is based on the integration of science and application in performance enhancement. This foundation gives students the opportunity to be both well grounded in the fundamentals of the scientific process and involved in supervised individual and group/team interventions. The program consists of 36 semester credit hours, including course work in research methods, data analysis, individual and team interventions, team dynamics, the psychological aspects of elite performance, and the psychology of youth sports. All students are required to complete both a sport psychology practicum and a research thesis.

KINESIOLOGY CORE . . . . **9 semester hours**

Course Title	Semester Hours
Research Design in Kinesiology	3
Data Analysis in Kinesiology	3
Seminar in Kinesiology	3

SPORT PSYCHOLOGY EMPHASIS . . . . **27 semester hours**

Course Title	Semester Hours
Psychology of Peak Performance	3
Team Dynamics	3
Psychology of Youth Sports	3
Sport Psychology Interventions	3
Practicum in Sport Psychology	3
Guided Elective	3
Free Elective	3
Thesis	6

. . . . **Total = 36 semester hours**

Typical Course Sequence*

Fall Semester #1
Psychology of Peak Performance
Research Design in Kinesiology
Elective

Spring Semester #1
Team Dynamics
Data Analysis in Kinesiology
Elective

Fall Semester #2
Sport Psychology Interventions
Seminar in Kinesiology
Thesis

Spring Semester #2
Psychology of Youth Sports
Practicum in Sport Psychology
Thesis

* Summer semester course offerings may alter this course sequence.

Sport Psychology Laboratory

The purpose of the Georgia Southern University Sport Psychology Laboratory is to provide facilities and equipment for the teaching, research, and service roles of faculty and students interested in the antecedents and consequences of sport performance. The laboratory supports instruction in motor learning, control and skill, the psychology of performance and coaching, and the psychological dynamics of exercise. The research conducted in the laboratory focuses on, but is not limited to, the following topics: momentum, humor, performance slumps, concentration, team dynamics, and social influences. The service activities of the laboratory focus on individual training sessions, team training workshops, and group training for athletes and coaches.

The laboratory space is partitioned into three areas: the instructional area, the testing/consulting room, and the control/observation room. Equipment is available to measure fine, gross, simple, and complex motor skills, as well as cognitive-affective factors associated with sport performance, and psychological responses to physical and psychological stressors. The lab is also equipped with audiovisual equipment for imagery research and training. An IBM computer station, complete with a web connection, is available for word processing, data acquisition and analysis, and laboratory based instruction.

The email address for the Sport Psychology Laboratory is sppsylab@gsaix2.cc.gasou.edu

UNIVERSITY OF
Georgia

Department of Exercise Science

Exercise Psychology Laboratory
University of Georgia
Athens, GA 30602-3654

Program Rating

1	2	3	4	5	6	**7**
Applied Orientation			Equal Emphasis		Research Orientation	

Contact Person: . . . . Rod K. Dishman
. . . . Patrick J. O'Connor
Phone: 706.542.9840
. . . . 706.542.4382
Fax: 706.542.3148
. . . . 706.542.3148
Email: . . . . rdishman@coe.uga.edu
. . . . poconnor@arches.uga.edu
Website: . . . . www.coe.uga.edu/exs

Faculty and areas of interest

Rod K. Dishman — Psychophysiological and neurobiological/immunological effects of acute and chronic exercise; exercise adherence

Patrick O'Connor — Circadian rhythms and sleep; eating disorders; overtraining; pain; mood responses to exercise

Degrees offered

- MA
- PhD

Approx. number of students in program

- 8–10

Approx. number of students in each degree program

- 20% MA/80% PhD

53

Approx. number of students who apply to/are accepted by program annually

- Approximately 10 apply/approximately 2–3 accepted

Admissions requirements (minimum requirements)

- 1000 GRE
- Undergraduate GPA of 3.00 (2.60 for MA)
- Graduate GPA of 3.50
- A TOEFL score of 600 is required for foreign students.
- A student with a BA or BS can be admitted to the PhD program if the following formula is satisfied: undergraduate GPA x 1000 + GRE verbal + GRE quantitative > 4300.
- Preference is given to students who have strong backgrounds in biopsychology and exercise science, and who have research interests compatible with ongoing research in the program.

The program has available for qualified students

- Research assistantships
- Teaching assistantships

Assistantships

29%	Fellowships
29%	Research assistantships
42%	Teaching assistantships
0%	Tuition waivers
0%	Other forms of financial aid

Internship possibility

- No

Comments

The PhD and MA specializations in exercise psychology are research programs designed for advanced study and research related to an behavioral and biopsychological responses and adaptations to acute and chronic physical activity. The PhD program prepares individuals for careers in universities, government, private industry, or the health sciences. The MA program prepares individuals for additional graduate work at the doctoral level and may lead to careers in allied health occupations, adult fitness/wellness, teaching, or research.

Prerequisites for the MA include a background in the behavioral or biological sciences, including chemistry, biology, physiology, and psychology. Undergraduate course work in exercise science is desirable. Prerequisites for the PhD include a background in the behavioral and biological sciences, including biopsychology, chemistry (through organic), biology, and physiology. Students are expected to have an undergraduate or master's degree in exercise science or an appropriate related field (e.g., psychology).

Programs of study are developed by the student and major professor (three person advisory committee for MA; five person advisory committee for PhD) based on the student's background, interests, and career goals.

The Department of Exercise Science has a well-equipped exercise psychology laboratory for assessing psychophysiological phenomena; the lab includes equipment such as GSR, ECG, EMG, and EEG recorders, as well as equipment to measure beat-to-beat blood pressures under laboratory conditions. Ambulatory measures of blood pressure, heart rate variability, and polysomnography are also made outside the laboratory setting. Collaboration with laboratories in pharmacology, biopsychology, and medical microbiology permit studies of psychopharmacologic, neuroendocrine, and psychoimmunologic responses to exercise and behavioral stressors. The exercise physiology and muscle biology laboratories permit cross-disciplinary research in exercise science. A separate fitness center conducts adult fitness, cardiac rehabilitation, and senior adult programs for university faculty/staff and the Athens community.

UNIVERSITY OF
Houston

Department of Health, Physical Education, and Recreation

123 Melcher Gym
University of Houston
Houston, TX 77204-5331

Program Rating

1	2	3	4	5	**6***	7

Applied Orientation	Equal Emphasis	Research Orientation

Program offers opportunities to pursue an applied orientation OR a research orientation (as opposed to equal emphasis of both).

Contact Person:	Dale G. Pease
Phone:	713.743.9838
Fax:	713.743.9860
Email:	DPEASE@UH.EDU
Website:	www.coe.uh.edu

Faculty and areas of interest

Dale G. Pease	Sport psychology, motor learning, leadership, psychophysiology
Charles Layne	Motor learning, motor control
Jin Yan	Motor control, motor development
James Zhang	Measurement, leadership, spectatorship

Degrees offered

- MEd in physical education
- MS in exercise science (emphasis area within motor behavior track)
- PhD in kinesiology (emphasis area in sport/exercise psychology)

Approx. number of students in program

- 15

Approx. number of students in each degree program

- 66% MEd and MS/34% PhD

56

Approx. number of students who apply to/are accepted by program annually

- 15 apply/10 accepted

Admissions requirements

- MEd: 900 GRE (verbal + quantitative)
- MS: 1000 GRE (verbal + quantitative)
- PhD: 1500 GRE (verbal + quantitative + analytical))

The program has available for qualified students

- Research assistantships
- Teaching assistantships

Assistantships

0%	Fellowships
10%	Research assistantships
70%	Teaching assistantships
50%	Tuition waivers
0%	Other forms of financial aid

Internship possibility

- Available, but very limited

Humboldt State
UNIVERSITY

Department of Health and Physical Education

Forbes Complex—Physical Education Department
Humboldt State University
Arcata, CA 95521

Contact Person: . . . . Al Figone
Phone: 707.826.3557
Fax: 707.826.5446

Faculty and areas of interest

Al Figone   Coaching education

Chris Hopper   Health psychology with families, social psychological aspects of sports for persons with disabilities

Degree offered

- MA

Approx. number of students in program

- 40

Approx. number of students who apply to/are accepted by program annually

- 15 apply/12 accepted

Admissions requirements

- 3.00 GPA

The program has available for qualified students

- Research assistantships
- Teaching assistantships
- Other forms of financial aid

Internship possibility

- Yes

Internship required for degree completion

- No

Number of hours required for internship

- Nine credit hours

Description of typical internship experience

- Work with (1) community sport organizations; (2) involvement with college athletic programs; (3) exercise psychology opportunities in Wellness Institute; (4) school-based/family-based/community-based health psychology.

Comments

The MA program has four areas of emphasis: adapted; athletic training; exercise physiology/wellness; and teaching/coaching. Students can pursue an applied exercise/sport psychology area of specialization within each emphasis area. Students are encouraged to complete their thesis in exercise/sport psychology. The Humboldt campus is located on the northwest coast of California, 250 miles north of San Francisco. The quality of life is exceptional.

UNIVERSITY OF
Idaho

Division of Health, Physical Education, Recreation, and Dance

107 PEB
University of Idaho
Moscow, ID 83844-2401

Program Rating

1	2	3	**4**	5	6	7
Applied Orientation			Equal Emphasis		Research Orientation	

Contact Person: . . . . Damon Burton
Phone: 208.885.2186
Fax: 208.885.5929
Email: . . . . dburton@uidaho.edu

Faculty and areas of interest

Damon Burton   Motivation/goal setting, stress/anxiety, coaching education, PST program evaluation, exercise adherence

Degrees offered

- MS
- PhD

Approx. number of students in program

- MS program: 3–4 full-time/1–2 part-time
- PhD program: 2–3 full-time/1–2 part-time

Approx. number of students in each degree program

- 60% MS
- 40% PhD

Approx. number of students who apply to/are accepted by program annually

- MS program: 18–20 apply/1–2 accepted
- PhD program: 12–15 apply/maximum of 1 accepted

Admissions requirements

- MS program: Minimum of 3.00 GPA, 1000 GRE scores
- PhD program: 3.00 GPA undergraduate, 3.50 GPA master's, 1050 GRE scores

The program has available for qualified students

- Teaching assistantships
- One assistantship through Vandal Sport Psychology Services

Assistantships

Master's (4)

0%	Fellowships
0%	Graduate assistantships
75%	Teaching assistantships
0%	Tuition waivers
25%	Other forms of financial aid

PhD (2)

0%	Fellowships
50%	Graduate assistantships
50%	Teaching assistantships
0%	Tuition waivers
0%	Other forms of financial aid

Internship possibility

- Yes—MS and PhD

Internship required for degree completion

- Yes—MS and PhD

Number of hours required for internship

- 6–9 credit hours

Description of typical internship experience

- Master's internships can be conducted as part of Vandal Sport Psychology Services or, by arrangement, in the Washington State University Athletic Department. Previous students have held internships in such sports as basketball, golf, volleyball, tennis, gymnastics, and track and field—all at the university level, except for gymnastics. Normally, sport-related internships involve developing, implementing, and evaluating PST programs for individual athletes and teams. Additionally, doctoral internships can be set up in counseling as well as in sport psychology with the licensed psychologist employed by the WSU Athletic Department.

Comments

Master's Program: Our 2-year master's program is designed to develop good researchers and skilled consultants, with the program placing relatively equal emphasis on research and application. Students typically use their degrees as steppingstones into such career fields as (a) coaching/teaching; (b) sports medicine, exercise and wellness; and (c) PhD work in educational or clinical sport psychology. The program has good flexibility in both curriculum and internship possibilities, and most recent master's students have completed by graduation all course work and about 150 of the 400 hours of supervised sport psychology internship/practicum work necessary to become a certified AAASP consultant. Master's requirements call for 45 credits of course work, with 33 credits in sport psychology and sport science courses, supplemented by elective course work in psychology and counseling. Washington State University is only eight miles away, in Pullman, and employs a sport psychologist in its Athletic Department. Thus, master's internship possibilities are available in a variety of sports, either at WSU or through Vandal Sport Psychology Services (VSPS) in the Idaho Athletic Department. During their first year, master's students attain consultation experience working as mentors in our mental training courses for varsity athletes; then, during their second year, they normally begin consulting with VSPS before doing their 6-credit internships. Master's students may combine their internships and theses to test applied sport psychology questions or to evaluate the effectiveness of PST programs implemented on teams with whom they are consulting. However, many students also select traditional thesis topics in such areas as motivation, stress/coping, anxiety, goal setting, and exercise adherence.

Doctoral Program: Our 5-year-old doctoral program is designed to employ a focus similar to that of our master's program, but most elective course work is taken at WSU in psychology and counseling psychology. Currently, students take 24–27 credits of course work in WSU's APA-approved counseling psychology program as well as 12 credits of psychology foundation courses. Counseling Psychology at WSU is initiating efforts to make this a "joint sport psychology program." WSU counseling psych students specializing in sport psychology would take sport psychology and sport science at Idaho, and our students would be able to take the supervised internships necessary for licensure in addition to the course work they are already taking at WSU. We hope to have this joint program in place by Fall 2001. Doctoral students currently are doing 80% or more of the 60+ hours of service per week we currently provide to the Vandal Athletic Department through Vandal Sport Psychology Services. The doctoral program also places relatively equal emphasis on research and application skills, and students have opportunities to gain practical experience in ongoing research projects, academic teaching, and VSPS/WSU sport psychology consultation.

Illinois State
UNIVERSITY

Department of Health, Physical Education, and Recreation

Horton Fieldhouse - 5120
Illinois State University
Normal, IL 61790-5120

Program Rating

1	2	3	4	5	**6**	7
Applied Orientation			Equal Emphasis		Research Orientation	

Contact Person:	Anthony J. Amorose
. . . .	Bill Vogler (Graduate Coordinator)
Phone:	309.438.8590
. . . .	309.438.5782
Fax:	309.438.5037
Email:	ajamoro@ilstu.edu
Website:	www.ilstu.edu

Faculty and areas of interest

Anthony J. Amorose — Development of self-evaluations and motivational orientations, coaching behavior

Degree offered

- MS

Approx. number of students in program

- 3–5

Approx. number of students who apply to/are accepted by program annually

- 40 apply/3 accepted

Admissions requirements

- 3.20 GPA
- 1100 GRE

The program has available for qualified students

- Teaching assistantships
- Other forms of financial aid (including tuition waivers)

Assistantships

0%	Fellowships
0%	Research assistantships
100%	Teaching assistantships
varies	Tuition waivers (some available)
0%	Other forms of financial aid

Internship possibility

- Yes

Internship required for degree completion

- No

Number of hours required for internship

- Up to 8 credit hours are possible; no more than 6 may apply toward fulfillment of degree requirements.

Description of typical internship experience

- Open for students to arrange

UNIVERSITY OF
Illinois

Department of Kinesiology

University of Illinois
205 Freer Hall
906 South Goodwin Avenue
Urbana, IL 61801

Program Rating

1	2	3	4	5	6	**7**
Applied Orientation			Equal Emphasis			Research Orientation

Contact Person:	Edward McAuley
	Graduate Program
Phone:	217.333.6487
	Academic Affairs Office
Fax:	217.244.7322
. . . .	217.333.1083
Email:	a-mc3@uiuc.edu
Website:	www.grad.uiuc.edu

Faculty and areas of interest

Les Carlton	Coordination, control, skill
Charles Hillman	Exercise psychology, psychophysiology
Edward McAuley	Exercise and health psychology, aging
Steven Petruzzello	Psychophysiology of exercise
Karl Rosengren	Coordination, control, skill, aging

Degrees offered
- MS
- PhD

Approx. number of students in program
- 15

Approx. number of students in each degree program
- 50% MS/50% PhD

Approx. number of students who apply to/are accepted by program annually

- 20 apply/5–7 accepted

Admissions requirements

- GPA of 3.00 on a 4.00 scale
- GRE total score of 1500 (MS), 1800 (PhD)

The program has available for qualified students

- Fellowships
- Research assistantships
- Teaching assistantships
- Tuition waivers

Assistantships

5%	Fellowships
35%	Research assistantships
60%	Teaching assistantships
90%	Tuition waivers

Internship possibility

- No

Internship required for degree completion

- No

Number of hours required for internship

- N/A

Description of typical internship experience

- N/A

Comments

Students are encouraged to pursue interdisciplinary research interests in this program, as many such opportunities exist on campus. Faculty in the area of exercise and sport psychology engage in collaborative research with faculty from Community Health, Medicine, Psychology, and the Beckman Institute for Advanced Science and Technology, as well as with individuals in other areas of Kinesiology. Our faculty have well-equipped laboratories for conducting their own research and that of their graduate students. We encourage prospective students to contact faculty personally to discuss research, teaching, and educational opportunities in exercise and sport psychology at the University of Illinois. In addition, our departmental homepage is very well developed and contains considerable information about the faculty and the program.

Indiana
UNIVERSITY

Department of Physical Education

Indiana University
HPER 168
Bloomington, IN 47405

Program Rating

1	2	3	4	5	6	**7**
Applied Orientation			Equal Emphasis		Research Orientation	

Contact Person:	John S. Raglin
Phone:	812.855.1844
Fax:	812.855.6778
Email:	raglinj@indiana.edu
Website:	www.indiana.edu/~kines/

Faculty and areas of interest

John S. Raglin	Anxiety and athletic performance, personality, over-training, exercise and mental health, psychobiology of sport, exercise adherence

Degree offered

- MS in applied sport science with a specialization in sport psychology

Approx. number of students in program

- 5

Admissions requirements

- GPA 2.80 or higher on a 4.00 scale
- GRE minimum total of 800 for verbal and quantitative

The program has available for qualified students

- Teaching assistantships

Assistantships

0%	Fellowships
0%	Research assistantships

75%   Teaching assistantships
0%   Tuition waivers
0%   Other forms of financial aid

Internship possibility

• No

Description of typical internship experience

Previous students have conducted research projects with varsity athletic teams or with participants in summer youth sport camps. There are no internships per se available.

Comments

The program is a master of science in human performance, with specialization in sport psychology. The degree emphasizes research in issues related to exercise and mental health as well as sport, rather than application. The program is intended to serve as preparation for the student interested in pursuing a doctorate in sport psychology with a specialization in psychobiological aspects of sport.

Iowa State
UNIVERSITY

Department of Health and Human Performance

Iowa State University
Ames, IA 50010

Program Rating

1	2	3	**4**	5	6	7
Applied Orientation			Equal Emphasis		Research Orientation	

Contact Person: . . . . Rick Sharp
Phone: 515.294.8650
Fax: 515.294.8740
Email: . . . . rlsharp@iastste.edu
Website: . . . . www.iastate.edu

Faculty and areas of interest
New faculty will be hired during 2000.

Degree offered
• MS

Approx. number of students in program
• 5 active/5 part-time

Approx. number of students who apply to/are accepted by program annually
• 5 apply/3 accepted

Admissions requirements
• 3.00 GPA
• GRE general test recommended

The program has available for qualified students
• Teaching assistantships

Assistantships

0%   Fellowships

0%   Graduate assistantships

10%   Teaching assistantships

0%   Tuition waivers

0%   Other forms of financial aid

Internship possibility

- Yes

Internship required for degree completion

- No

Number of hours required for internship

- 3–6 credit hours

Description of typical internship experience

- Several general areas are possible: (a) audit undergraduate sport psychology class, develop and deliver lectures, develop test questions, grade test questions; (b) observe, and assist in where appropriate, psychological skills training with teams and individual athletes; (c) work individually, where appropriate, with individual athletes; (d) do performance analysis employing interpersonal process recall (IPR).

UNIVERSITY OF
Iowa

Department of Sport, Health, Leisure and Physical Studies

E102 Fieldhouse
University of Iowa
Iowa City, IA 52242

Program Rating

1	2	3	4	5	6	**7**
Applied Orientation			Equal Emphasis		Research Orientation	

Contact Person: . . . . Dawn E. Stephens
Phone: 319.335.9348
. . . . 319.335.9335 (main office)
Fax: 319.335.6669
Email: . . . . DAWN-E-STEPHENS@UIOWA.EDU
Website: . . . . www.uiowa.edu/~shlps/grad.htm

Faculty and areas of interest

Dawn E. Stephens   Social psychology of sport, motivational issues, moral atmosphere

Degrees offered

- MA
- PhD

Approx. number of students in program

- 10

Approx. number of students in each degree program

- 60% MA/40% PhD

Approx. number of students who apply to/are accepted by program annually

- 16 apply/4 accepted

Admissions requirements

- GRE: 50th percentile in each category (verbal/quantitative/analytical)
- 3.00 GPA
- Three letters of recommendation
- Transcripts

The program has available for qualified students

- Fellowships
- Research assistantships
- Teaching assistantships

Assistantships

varies	Fellowships
25%	Research assistantships
75%	Teaching assistantships
0%	Tuition waivers
0%	Other forms of financial aid

Internship possibility

- No

Internship required for degree completion

- No

Comments

The program's emphasis is on theoretical research in sport and physical activity contexts, with a particular emphasis on female and youth participants.

Ithaca
COLLEGE

227. 83 miles
4 hrs from 10025
4hrs30 from 06902

Department of Graduate Studies in Exercise and Sport Sciences

Ithaca College
Ithaca, NY 14850

Program Rating

1	**2***	3	4	5	6	7
Applied Orientation			Equal Emphasis		Research Orientation	

Program offers opportunities to pursue an applied orientation OR a research orientation (as opposed to equal emphasis of both).

Contact Person:	Greg A. Shelley
Phone:	607.274.1275
Fax:	607.274.1943
Email:	Gshelley@Ithaca.Edu
Website:	www.ithaca.edu/grad/grad1/

Faculty and areas of interest

Jeff Ives	Psychophysiology
Greg Shelley	Counseling student athletes, applied sport psychology
Gary Sforzo	Psychophysiology
Deb Wuest	Stress management

Degree offered

- MS (concentrations in sport psychology, exercise physiology, and sport pedagogy)

Approx. number of students in program

- 6–10 in each concentration

Approx. number of students in each degree program

- 100% MS

Approx. number of students who apply to/are accepted by program annually

- 75–100 apply/10–15 accepted in each concentration

73

Admissions requirements

- 3.00 GPA from accredited institution
- Successful completion of related core courses
- GRE required

The program has available for qualified students

- Teaching assistantships
- Coaching assistantships
- Research assistantships

Assistantships

10%   Research assistantships

20%   Coaching assistantships

40%   Teaching assistantships

30%   Other forms of financial aid

Internship possibility

Yes, internships are available in all three concentrations.

Description of typical internship experience

* Performance enhancement, counseling (in sport psychology). (See comments.)

Comments

Sport psychology is a concentration, along with exercise physiology and sport pedagogy, in a 30-credit MS program with a thesis and a 36-credit MS program without a thesis. The sport psychology concentration is applied in nature, emphasizing the development and implementation of mentor training programs (MTPs) for individual athletes, coaches, and teams. A sport counseling course is also offered, emphasizing practical, hands-on counseling skills development and experience. Internship experiences exist for selected students who have completed all first-year courses.

John F. Kennedy
UNIVERSITY

2903 miles

Graduate School of Professional Psychology

John F. Kennedy University
12 Altarinda Road
Orinda, CA 94563

Program Rating

1	**2***	3	4	5	6	7
Applied Orientation			Equal Emphasis		Research Orientation	

* Program offers opportunities to pursue an applied orientation OR a research orientation (as opposed to an equal emphasis on both).

Contact Person: . . . . Gail Solt (Director)
Phone: 510.254.0110
Fax: 510.254.4870
Website: . . . . www.jfku.edu

Faculty and areas of interest

Mark Clementi	Optimal performance
Lesleigh Franklin	Women in sport
Keith McConnell	Group process, optimal performance
Gail Solt	Children and sports, optimal performance
Betty Wenz	Ethics in sport psychology, optimal performance

Degrees offered

- The MA is offered in both sport psychology and in counseling psychology with a specialization in sport psychology.
- PsyD

Approx. number of students in program

- 50

Approx. number of students in each degree program

- 80% MA in sport psychology/20% MA in counseling psychology

75

Approx. number of students who apply to/are accepted by program annually
- 40–50 apply/20+ accepted

Admissions requirements
- An interview and/or three letters of recommendation
- Strong interest in the field
- Appropriate prerequisites

The program has available for qualified students
- Other forms of financial aid

Assistantships
0%	Fellowships
0%	Research assistantships
0%	Teaching assistantships
1%	Tuition waivers
45%	Other forms of financial aid

Internship possibility
- Yes

Internship required for degree completion
- Yes

Number of hours required for internship
- 12 units for MA in sport psychology
- 18 units for MA in counseling psychology
- PsyD units to be determined

Description of typical internship experience
- Consists of an 11-week experience at a local college, meeting 11 hours per week with a team or with individuals. The student is supervised by an individual supervisor and by attending a counseling case seminar. Internship may include education, optimal performance consulting, and support.

  Sport psychology students have many options for internships, including working with college teams, youth sport teams, sport organizations, mental health treatment facilities, and private sport clubs. Students serve as counselors in JFK's summer sport camps as part of fulfilling their internship requirement. They help design, create, and conduct the camps, which use sport as a vehicle for enhancing self-esteem, building cooperative groups, and developing skills. The sport psychology program has also established a number of ongoing internships that are staffed each year by students. These programs include support groups for injured athletes, sport psychology programs at local high schools, and various intercollegiate teams and athletes in the San Francisco Bay area.

Comments

Students may choose to pursue an MA in sport psychology, which enables them to work as applied sport consultants or prepares them for doctoral work in clinical or consulting psychology. Students may also choose to pursue an MA in counseling psychology, which may qualify them for the Marriage, Family, and Child Counselor License (MFCC) in California.

JFK also offers a certificate program. It consists of 18 units, typically 4–5 quarters in duration. Individuals already in a related field typically pursue this option.

Kansas State
UNIVERSITY

Department of Kinesiology

Natatorium 8
Kansas State University
Manhattan, KS 66506

Contact Person:	David Dzewaltowski
Phone:	913.532.0708
Fax:	913.532.6486
Email:	DADX@KSU.KSU.EDU

Faculty and areas of interest

David Dzewaltowski   Motivation, exercise adherence

Mary McElroy   Sociocultural, qualitative methods

A faculty search is in progress to fill an exercise psychology position

Degree offered

- MS

Approx. number of students in program

- 5–10

Approx. number of students who apply to/are accepted by program annually

- Variable apply/variable accepted

Admissions requirements (minimum requirements to be considered for admission)

- GRE scores
- 3.00 GPA
- Three letters of reference

The program has available for qualified students

- Research assistantships
- Teaching assistantships

Internship possibility

• Yes

Internship required for degree completion

• No

Number of hours required for internship

• 3–6 credit hours

Description of typical internship experience

• Practicum/internship experiences are available in exercise settings (corporate, cardiac rehabilitation, adult) through the Kinesiology Department's Center for Exercise Research. Practicum/internship experiences with athletic teams are possible.

Comments

The Department of Kinesiology, located in the College of Arts and Sciences, is strongly committed to graduate education and research. Kinesiology faculty study human movement from several perspectives, including biomechanical, physiological, neurological, psychological, and sociocultural. The psychology emphasis draws on faculty's strengths in exercise and health psychology to develop students' understanding of elite and nonelite (youth, older adults, etc.) populations.

UNIVERSITY OF
Kansas

1246 miles from 10025

Department of Health, Sport, and Exercise Sciences

161 Robinson
University of Kansas
Lawrence, KS 66045

Program Rating

1	2	3	4	5	6	7
Applied Orientation			Equal Emphasis			Research Orientation

Contact Person: . . . . David Templin
Phone: 913.864.0778
Fax: 913.864.3343
Website: www.soe.ukans.edu/courses/hper892

Faculty and areas of interest

Jim LaPoint	Social psychology of sport
David Templin	Applied psychology of sport

Degrees offered
- MS
- EdD
- PhD

Approx. number of students in program
- 10 MS/10 PhD

Approx. number of students in each degree program
- 50% MS/50% PhD

Approx. number of students who apply to/are accepted by program annually
- 30 MS apply/10–15 MS accepted
- 20 PhD apply/3 PhD accepted

Admissions requirements
- MS: Undergraduate degree in physical education

- GPA of 3.00
- PhD: Undergraduate or master's degree in physical education
- Master's GPA of 3.50
- Undergraduate GPA of 3.00
- GRE verbal + quantitative > or = 1000
- Coaching or playing background in sport

The program has available for qualified students

- Teaching assistantships (PhD)

Assistantships

0%   Fellowships
0%   Research assistantships
25% Teaching assistantships
25% Tuition waivers
50% Other forms of financial aid

Internship possibility

- Yes (PhD)

Internship required for degree completion

- Yes (PhD)

Number of hours required for internship

- One season or semester required, 2 years possible

Description of typical internship experience

- Several options are available. First, the student can work as a sport psychology consultant for a high school district (with five high schools). Second, the student can spend consulting time in the University of Kansas Peak Performance Clinic, working with individual athletes and doing high school team seminars. Third, the student can work as a sport psychology consultant with one of the 16 teams at the university.

Comments

The program offers course work and opportunities that are applied in nature. Students are prepared in the doctoral program to pursue careers in higher education as applied sport psychologists or to work as applied sport psychology consultants in private practice. The program includes the Peak Performance Clinic and an internship program involving the University of Kansas Athletic Department and Kansas City High School athletic programs. Students who are accepted must have a strong sporting background (playing and/or coaching), a background in physical education or a related field, and strong interpersonal skills. An interview is suggested at the doctoral level. This program *does not* lead to licensure.

Lakehead
UNIVERSITY

Department of Physical Education

Lakehead University Fieldhouse
Lakehead University
Thunder Bay, Ontario,
Canada P7B 5E1

Program Rating

1	2	3	**4**	5	6	7
Applied Orientation			Equal Emphasis		Research Orientation	

Contact Person:	Jane Crossman
Phone:	807.343.8642
Fax:	807.343.8944
Email:	Jane.Crossman@lakeheadu.ca
Website:	www.lakeheadu.ca/ (Click Admissions, and then click Arts & Sciences.)

Faculty and areas of interest

Jane Crossman	Psychological rehabilitation from athletic injury, mental training
Jocelyn Farrell	Motivation and goal setting

Degrees offered
- MS

Approx. number of students in program
- 15

Approx. number of students who apply to/are accepted by program annually
- N/A apply/13–15 accepted

Admissions requirements
- Honors degree, minimum 70% standing
- If degree is not in physical education, a qualifying year may be necessary

The program has available for qualified students

- Fellowships
- Research assistantships
- Teaching assistantships
- Other forms of financial aid

Assistantships

0%   Fellowships
0%   Research assistantships
100%   Teaching assistantships
0%   Tuition waivers
0%   Other forms of financial aid

Internship possibility

- Yes—guaranteed

Internship required for degree completion

- Yes

Number of hours required for internship

- 10 hours per week

Description of typical internship experience

- Students may assist in the teaching of undergraduate courses or teach activity courses. Other possible tasks include assisting in research, supervising our microcomputer laboratory, or assisting with the coaching of our varsity teams.

Comments

Lakehead University provides the opportunity for qualified students to obtain an MS in applied sport science and coaching. The program of courses focuses on four areas in sport science: (1) psychology, (2) physiology, (3) biomechanics, and (4) sports medicine. The primary focus of the sport psychology course offerings involves the study of a variety of mental training procedures designed to improve athletic performance. Students are required to complete a master's thesis.

Leeds Metropolitan
UNIVERSITY

Carnegie School of Leisure and Sport Studies

Beckett Park Campus
Leeds, LS6 3QS
England

Program Rating

1	2	3	**4**	5	6	7
Applied Orientation			Equal Emphasis		Research Orientation	

Contact Person: . . . . Mark Nesti
Phone: 0113 2837566
Email: . . . . M.Nesti@lmu.ac.uk

Faculty and areas of interest

Mark Nesti	Existential psychology, anxiety and sport
Nikos Ntoumanis	Motivation, self-determination theory
Remco Polman	Motor control and learning

Degrees offered
- MSc (sport and exercise psychology)
- MPhil/PhD (sport and exercise psychology)

Approx. number of students in program
- 30

Approx. number of students in each degree program
- MSc 25
- MPhil/PhD 5

Approx. number of students who apply to/are accepted by program annually
- 30 apply/20 accepted

Admissions requirements

- Good undergraduate degree in related area (2:1 honors)

The program has available for qualified students

- None listed

Assistantships:

no financial assistance listed

Internship possibility

- No

Comments

The programme at Leeds Metropolitan University builds on the long-established and internationally respected work of Carnegie College in the area of PE, sport and leisure over the past 65 years. From such a solid foundation, the highly successful current course, which has been offered since 1993, has recently been redeveloped and improved to meet the changing needs of students and employers in sport and exercise as we enter the new millennium. This is reflected in a dynamic and flexible course structure that allows the student to pursue disciplined basic knowledge but does not overlook the need to provide opportunities to acquire vocationally relevant skills and professional competencies.

The core modules include Biomechanics: Theory and Measurement, Essentials of Exercise Physiology, Psychology and Sport, Research Methods, and Dissertation. The core module in Psychology and Sport will examine a broad range of sport psychology literature and research and will evaluate the contributions of mainstream psychology to the study of sport, as well as the contributions of sport to an understanding of psychology.

Manchester Metropolitan
UNIVERSITY

Crewe & Alsager Faculty

Manchester Metropolitan University
Hassall Road
Alsager ST 7 2HL, England

Program Rating

1	2	3	**4**	5	6	7
Applied Orientation			Equal Emphasis		Research Orientation	

Contact Person: . . . . Nick Smith
Phone: . . . . (44) 161-247-5455
Fax: . . . . (44) 161-247-6375
Email: . . . . N.C.SMITH@MMU.AC.UK
Website: . . . . www.mmu.ac.uk

Faculty and areas of interest

Keith Davids	Ecological psychology, motor control, and skill acquisition
Paul Holmes	Psychophysiology, imagery and modeling
Nick Smith	Psychophysiology, stress and coping, anxiety and cognition

Degrees offered
- MSc
- MPhil
- PhD

Approx. number of students in program
- 35

Approx. number of students in each degree program
- 5% MS/70% MPhil (with upgrade to PhD possible)/25% PhD

Approx. number of students who apply to/are accepted by program annually

- MSc 80 apply/25 accepted; PhD 30 apply/10 accepted

Admissions requirements

- Write for specifics. Decisions are based on profiles.

The program has available for qualified students

- 10% fellowships
- 20% research assistantships
- 10% teaching assistantships
- 5% tuition waivers
- 55% other forms of financial aid

Internship possibility

- No

Comments

The programme is a traditional British university model, with substantial emphasis on research, but placed within a vibrant and rapidly developing department. In addition, the department runs a full-time/part-time taught master's degree (much closer to the usual U.S. programme) in applied sport and exercise psychology. The department currently hosts over 25% of the government-funded sport science support programmes with elite athletes. Major projects in stress/performance, coach education, and match analysis are also features of the department's research portfolio.

UNIVERSITY OF
Manitoba

Department of Psychology

St. Paul's College
University of Manitoba
Winnipeg, Manitoba, Canada
R3T 2M6

or

Faculty of Physical Education and Recreation Studies

Frank Kennedy Building
University of Manitoba
Winnipeg, Manitoba, Canada
R3T 2N2

Program Rating

1	2	3	**4**	5	6	7

Applied Orientation   Equal Emphasis   Research Orientation

Contact Person: . . . . Garry Martin (Psychology)
. . . . Dennis Hrycaiko (Physical Education)
Phone: 204.474.8589
. . . . 204.474.8764
Fax: 204.275.5421
. . . . 204.474.7634
Website: . . . . www.UManitoba.ca/Faculties/Physed/

Faculty and areas of interest

Dennis Hrycaiko   Research/applied performance enhancement
Garry Martin   Research and applied, various aspects of sport performance enhancement

Degrees offered

- MA
- MSc
- PhD

Note: The MA and PhD degrees are in clinical psychology (an APA-approved program). Sport psychology is a subspecialty within clinical psychology. The MSc degree in physical education has a specialization in sport psychology.

Approx. number of students in program

- 55 in clinical psychology
- 37 in MSc in physical education

Approx. number of students in each degree program

- 30% MA/70% PhD in clinical psychology

- 6 students in sport psychology

Approx. number of students who apply to/are accepted by program annually
- 10 apply/1–2 accepted in clinical psychology
- 10 apply/5–6 accepted in sport psychology

Admissions requirements
- Must meet Department of Psychology requirements for clinical psychology program.
- Check with programs for specific admissions requirements.

The program has available for qualified students
- Teaching assistantships

Assistantships
5%   Fellowships
5%   Research assistantships
10%   Teaching assistantships
0%   Tuition waivers
0%   Other forms of financial aid

Internship possibility
- Yes

Internship required for degree completion
- Yes—PhD students in clinical psychology must complete an APA-approved internship in Canada or the USA.

Number of hours required for internship
- The APA-accredited internship is for one academic year (September to May) and does not specify a number of hours.

Description of typical internship experience
- Varies widely, but emphasis is clinical psychology.

Comments

Physical education offers a master of science degree program with the opportunity to specialize in sport psychology. The program has considerable flexibility and can be tailored to meet interests of individual students. In the clinical psychology program, students apply to 1 of 2 streams, a generalist stream or a behavior modification stream. Students who select the behavior modification stream have the option of receiving specialized training in sport psychology. Training includes readings; courses in sport psychology; thesis research in sport psychology; and sport psychology practica with Dr. Martin, working with a provincial sport team. Training is very behaviorally oriented.

Mankato State
UNIVERSITY

Department of Psychology/Clinical Psychology

Box 35
Mankato State University
Mankato, MN 56001

Contact Person: . . . . Wayne C. Harris
Phone: 507.389.1818

Faculty and areas of interest
Michael Fatis
Wayne C.Harris
Dan Sachan

Degrees offered
- MA (predoctoral in clinical psychology)
- MA (predoctoral in industrial/organizational psychology)

Approx. number of students in program
- 20 clinical/6I/O

Approx. number of students who apply to/are accepted by program annually
- 50 apply/15 accepted

Admissions requirements
- 3.0 undergraduate GPA
- GRE scores

The program has available for qualified students
- Fellowships (minority fellowship)
- Research assistantships (second-year student)
- Teaching assistantships
- Other forms of financial aid (work-study)

Internship possibility

• Yes

Internship required for degree completion

• Yes, required for the MA degree in clinical psychology

• In industrial/organizational, an internship is not required but is encouraged

Number of hours required for internship

• A minimum of 700 hours

Comments

Training in applied sport psychology is within the context of a predoctoral program in clinical psychology. The clinical program emphasizes behavior therapy/analysis and commitment to scientific psychology. Existing research programs can be found in the following areas: behavioral medicine, child behavior disorders, developmental disabilities, behavioral gerontology, and performance enhancement. Students are encouraged to participate in research and practice. Graduates of the program are regularly admitted to APA-approved doctoral programs in clinical psychology. Human performance is one emphasis area in the industrial/organizational MA Assessment of performance, training, and motivation are included in the human performance emphasis.

UNIVERSITY OF Maryland, COLLEGE PARK

Department of Kinesiology

HLHP Building
University of Maryland
College Park, MD 20742

Program Rating

1	2	3	4	5	**6**	7
Applied Orientation			Equal Emphasis		Research Orientation	

Contact Person: . . . . Brad D. Hatfield
Phone: 301.405.2489
. . . . 301.405.2450 (office)
Fax: 301.314.9167
Email: . . . . BH5@UMAIL.UMD.EDU

Faculty and areas of interest

Elizabeth Y. Brown   Sportvision
Brad D. Hatfield   Psychophysiology
Seppo Iso-Ahola   Social psychology and mental training

Degrees offered

- MA
- PhD

Approx. number of students in program

- 40

Approx. number of students in each degree program

- 20 MA (50%)/20 PhD (50%)

Admissions requirements

- 3.00 GPA
- GRE

The program has available for qualified students

• Teaching assistantships

Assistantships

10%	Fellowships
0%	Research assistantships
90%	Teaching assistantships
0%	Tuition waivers
0%	Other forms of financial aid

Internship possibility

• No

Comments

The program is oriented towards the social psychology and the psychophysiological aspects of exercise and sport psychology. There is collaborative laboratory support with the Exercise Physiology Lab at the University of Maryland as well as with other federal research institutions and the Naval Medical Research Institute at the Bethesda Naval Hospital. The clinical aspects of sport psychology are currently limited to academic coverage with the graduate course work.

McGill
UNIVERSITY

Department of Physical Education

McGill University
475 Pine Avenue West
Montréal, Québec, Canada H2W1S4

Program Rating

1	2	3	4	**5**	6	7

Applied Orientation   Equal Emphasis   Research Orientation

Note: Students may take an applied orientation, however, within or outside the thesis program.

Contact Person: . . . . Graham Neil
Phone: 514.398.4188
Fax: 514.398.4186
Email: . . . . Neil@EDUCATION.MCGILL.CA
Website: . . . . www.education.Mcgill.ca/phys_ed

Faculty and areas of interest

M. Downey	Psychology of motor learning/pedagogy
G. Bloom	Sport psychology and pedagogy
G. I. Neil	Social psychology of sport and physical activity

Degree offered

• MA with thesis
• MA without thesis

* Both are given in psychology of motor performance, sport psychology, or pedagogy.

Approx. number of students in program

• 15

Approx. number of students who apply to/are accepted by program annually

• 12 apply/6 accepted

94

Admissions requirements

- Undergraduate degree in physical education preferable; undergraduate in psychology accepted, but requires sport science courses.
- Cumulative GPA above a 3.00 on a 4.00 scale

The program has available for qualified students

- Fellowships
- Research assistantships
- Teaching assistantships
- Other forms of financial aid

Assistantships

10%   Fellowships
10%   Research assistantships
80%   Teaching assistantships
80%   Part-time work in PE or Athletics

Internship possibility

- No

UNIVERSITY OF
Memphis

Department of Human Movement Sciences and Education

Field House 1069
The University of Memphis
Memphis, TN 38152

Program Rating

1	2	3	4	5	**6**	7
Applied Orientation			Equal Emphasis		Research Orientation	

Contact Person:	Mary Fry
Phone:	901.678.4986
. . . .	901.678.4316 (department)
Fax:	901.678.3591
Email:	fry.mary@coe.memphis.edu
Website:	www.hmse.memphis.edu/gopher.hmse.memphis.edu

Faculty and areas of interest

Mary Fry	Motivation to participate in physical activity across the life span, developmental sport psychology, achievement motivation research, motivational climate
Tammy Schilling	Youth development

Degree offered

- MS in exercise and sport science

Approx. number of students in program

- 20–25

Approx. number of students who apply to/are accepted by program annually

- 50 apply/25 accepted

Admissions requirements

- GRE or MAT scores
- Undergraduate degree with acceptable GPA
- Letters of recommendation
- Application with written statement of goals

Assistantships

0%   Fellowships
20%   Research assistantships
80%   Teaching assistantships
100% Tuition waivers
10%   Other forms of financial aid

Internship possibility

- Yes

Internship required for degree completion

- No

UNIVERSITY OF
Memphis

Department of Psychology

University of Memphis
Memphis, TN 38152

Program Rating

1	2	3	4	5	**6**	7

Applied Orientation　　　　Equal Emphasis　　　　Research Orientation

Contact Person:	Andrew Meyers
Phone:	901.678.2146
Fax:	901.678.2579
Email:	AMEYERS@MEMPHIS.EDU
Website:	www.memphis.edu/psych.htm

Faculty and areas of interest

Robert Klesges	Health psychology, performance enhancement
Andrew Meyers	Performance enhancement, exercise and health
Robert Neimeyer	Exercise and mental health
James Whelan	Performance enhancement, ethics in sport psychology

Degrees offered
- MA
- MS
- PhD

Approx. number of students in program
- 65

Approx. number of students in each degree program
- 100% of clinical students in PhD

Approx. number of students who apply to/are accepted by program annually
- 200 apply/10 accepted

Admissions requirements

- 1100 GRE
- 3.00 GPA
- Average student scores are 1300 GRE and 3.50 GPA.

The program has available for qualified students

- Research assistantships
- Teaching assistantships
- Clinical placements

Assistantships

0%   Fellowships

60%   Research assistantships

20%   Teaching assistantships

100%   Tuition waivers (all students receive waiver of tuition and fees)

20%   Other forms of financial aid (clinical placements)

Internship possibility

- Possible. (All students must complete a one-year clinical internship for the PhD.)

Comments

No formal program in sport psychology is available. The department offers master's and PhD degrees in clinical, experimental, and school psychology, and a master's in general psychology. Within the clinical program there are behavioral medicine, child and family, and psychopathology and psychotherapy research specialties where sport psychology work can take place. The program is essentially a clinical one, with sport psychology as a subspecialty emphasis.

Miami
UNIVERSITY

663 miles 11 hrs

Department of Physical Education, Health, and Sport Studies

Phillips Hall
Miami University
Oxford, OH 45056

Program Rating

1	2	3	**4**	5	6	7
Applied Orientation			Equal Emphasis		Research Orientation	

Contact Person: . . . . Robert Weinberg
Phone: 513.529.2700
Fax: 513.529.5006
Email: . . . . WEINBER@MUOHIO.EDU
Website: . . . . www.muohio.edu/~phscwis/phs_program.html

Faculty and areas of interest

Thelma S. Horn	Children's perceived competence, coaching behavior, stress reactivity
Jay Kimiecik	Exercise psychology, motivation, peak experience
Robin S. Vealey	Anxiety, self-confidence, psychological skills training, coaching behavior
Robert Weinberg	Cognitive strategies, goal setting, anxiety, mental training

Degree offered
• MS

Approx. number of students in program
• 15

Approx. number of students who apply to/are accepted by program annually
• 30 apply/8 accepted

Admissions requirements
• 3.00 minimum undergraduate GPA

100

- Three letters of recommendation
- GRE

The program has available for qualified students
- Teaching assistantships

Assistantships
0%   Fellowships
10%   Research assistantships
50%   Teaching assistantships
0%   Tuition waivers
20%   Other forms of financial aid

Internship possibility
- Yes

Internship required for degree completion
- No

Description of typical internship experience
- Psychological skills intervention with university teams and individual athletes
- Collegiate, high school, and/or youth sport coaching
- Acting as an editorial assistant for sport psychology journals
- Academic counseling for university student-athletes
- Coaching education

Comments

Students may select either the thesis (30 total credits required) or nonthesis (34 total credits required) option. Nonthesis students may complete their degree in 1 calendar year. Thesis students should plan on 2 years to complete the degree. A comprehensive oral exit examination is required of all students. The curriculum is based on a crossdisciplinary perspective, with required course work in psychological, sociocultural, motoric, and physiological foundations of sport and/or exercise. Electives may include courses in counseling and psychology as well as independent study and research with faculty in the area. An ongoing sport and exercise psychology seminar is attended by students and faculty in which professional and research issues are discussed and group research projects are coordinated. The program emphasizes knowledge of theory, research, and practice in sport psychology. Opportunities for collaborative research with faculty and psychological intervention with athletes are available for students, and every attempt is made to match student interests with faculty expertise. Selected faculty research interests include goal setting, confidence, coaching behaviors, imagery, motivation, exercise motivation, and optimal experience. Both quantitative and qualitative methodologies are encouraged. The program has been successful in placing students in sport/exercise psychology doctoral programs as well as in coaching, academic counseling, and corporate fitness positions.

Michigan State
UNIVERSITY

Department of Kinesiology

201 IM Sports Circle
Michigan State University
East Lansing, MI 48824

Program Rating

1	2	3	4	**5**	6	7
Applied Orientation			Equal Emphasis		Research Orientation	

Contact Person: . . . . Martha Ewing
Phone: 517.353.4652
Fax: 517.353.2944
Website: . . . . www.educ.msu.edu/units/dept/kin

Faculty and areas of interest

Martha Ewing	Achievement motivation, anxiety, youth in sports, goal-setting
Deborah Feltz	Self-efficacy, collective efficacy

Degrees offered
- MS
- PhD

Approx. number of students in program
- 30

Approx. number of students in each degree program
- 60% MS/40% PhD

Approx. number of students who apply to/are accepted by program annually
- 10–15 apply/2–3 accepted

Admissions requirements

- Minimum score of 1000 on GRE (verbal + quantitative or verbal + analytic or quantitative +analytic)
- Major or minor in physical education
- Thesis in master's program

The program has available for qualified students

- Fellowships
- Research assistantships
- Teaching assistantships
- Other forms of financial aid (Dean's Scholars, Dissertation Grants, etc.)

Assistantships

20%   Fellowships
5%   Research assistantships
40%   Teaching assistantships
45%   Tuition waivers
5%   Other forms of financial aid

Internship possibility

- Yes

Practicum required for degree completion

- No

Number of hours required for practicum

- None required

Description of typical practicum experience

- Each doctoral student receives the opportunity to do applied work with a college, high school, or club sport team in a supervised experience.

Comments

An interdepartmental master's degree with urban studies is also available for interested students. Qualified students may complete a master's degree in counseling psychology.

UNIVERSITY OF
Minnesota

School of Kinesiology and Leisure Studies

220 Cooke Hall
University of Minnesota
Minneapolis, MN 55455

Program Rating

1	2	3	4	**5**	6	7

Applied Orientation   Equal Emphasis   Research Orientation

Contact Person:	Diane Wiese-Bjornstal
Phone:	612.625.6580
Fax:	612.626.7700
Email:	dwiese@TC.UMN.EDU
Website:	www.Kls.coled.umn.edu/

Faculty and areas of interest

Mary Jo Kane	Sport sociology, women in sport
March L. Krotee	Psychosocial dimensions, performance of elite athletes, systems management
Michael G. Wade	Performance effects, human factors
Diane Wiese-Bjornstal	Sport psychology, sport injury

Degrees offered
- MEd
- MA
- PhD

Approx. number of students in program
- 30

Approx. number of students in each degree program
- 50% master's/50% PhD

Approx. number of students who apply to/are accepted by program annually
- 30 apply/5 accepted

Admissions requirements

- GRE (500 verbal + 500 quantitative) or
- MAT (50, MA; 60, PhD)
- TOEFL (213 computer version or 550 paper version)
- GPA—3.00 undergraduate, 3.50 graduate

The program has available for qualified students

- Fellowships
- Research assistantships
- Teaching assistantships
- Other forms of financial aid (doctoral dissertation grants, graduate school scholarships, grants, and minority fellowships)

Assistantships

5%   Fellowships
10%   Research assistantships
65%   Teaching assistantships
10%   Tuition waivers
10%   Other forms of financial aid (Block grants)

Internship possibility

- Yes

Internship required for degree completion

- No

Number of hours required for internship

- Arranged; 1–6 semester credits (approx. 45 clock hours per credit)

Description of typical internship experience

- Self-directed and planned cooperatively between student, faculty, and participating unit, agency, or federation.

Comments

Psychology and Sociology of Sport at the University of Minnesota focuses on issues related to individual and institutional behavior and structure in sport. The emphasis areas include sport psychology, sport sociology, sport management, and international and comparative sport. In these subareas, students may explore such topics as the psychology of sport injury, women in sport and leisure, management issues in international sport, and comparative study of physical education programs across cultures. The Tucker Center for Research on Girls and Women in Sport (www.kls.coled.umn.edu/crgws/) has particular relevance for students interested in studying the psychology and sociology of sport. The academic focus of the program is social psychological in nature, with an emphasis on applied research. Graduate students in kinesiology largely develop their own programs of study by selecting courses from the school's science-based curriculum and from other disciplines throughout the university.

105

UNIVERSITY OF
Missouri
COLUMBIA

Department of Educational & Counseling Psychology

16 Hill Hall
University of Missouri, Columbia
Columbia, MO 65211

Program Rating

1	2	3	4	**5**	6	7
Applied Orientation			Equal Emphasis		Research Orientation	

Contact Person: . . . . Richard H. Cox
Phone: 573.882.7602
Fax: 573.884.5989
Email: . . . . coxrh@missouri.edu
Website: . . . . tiger.coe.missouri.edu/~ecp/

Faculty and areas of interest

Niels Beck   Clinical psychology
Richard H. Cox   Counseling sport psychology
Rick McGuire   Motivation and coaching

Degrees offered

- MA
- PhD

Approx. number of sport psychology students in program

- 10

Approx. number of students in each degree program

- MA, 4; PhD, 6

Approx. number of students who apply to/are accepted by program annually

- Admission into counseling psychology program is very competitive.

Admissions requirements

- GPA
- GRE
- Letters of support
- Research experience

The program has available for qualified students

- Research assistantships
- Teaching assistantships

Assistantships

Fellowships
Research assistantships
Teaching assistantships
Tuition waivers
Other forms of financial aid

Note: PhD candidates can expect some financial support in the form of an assistantship, a scholarship, and/or a fellowship, plus an academic fee waiver (in- and out-of-state).

Internship/practicum possibility

- Yes

Internship/practicum required for degree completion

- Yes

Number of hours required for internship/practicum

- 9 semester hours of practicum required for MA candidates
- 400 hours of practicum, and the full-time equivalent of one year of internship is required for PhD candidates.

Comments

The PhD program in counseling psychology at MU is APA approved and is consistently ranked among the top 3 programs nationally. Sport psychology is a subspecialty in counseling psychology, offered through the Department of Educational and Counseling Psychology. Counseling psychology students with a strong interest in sport psychology graduate with degrees in counseling psychology, with support work in sport psychology. The doctorate in counseling psychology, with a subspecialty in sport psychology, is designed to qualify the recipient to become a licensed counseling psychologist as well as an AAASP-certified applied counseling sport psychologist.

UNIVERSITY OF
Missouri
KANSAS CITY

Department of Physical Education

5100 Rockhill Road
University of Missouri, Kansas City
Kansas City, MO 64110-2499

Program Rating

1	2	3	4	5	6	**7**
Applied Orientation			Equal Emphasis		Research Orientation	

Contact Person: . . . . Joan Gallos
Phone: 816.235.2236
Fax: 816.235.5521
Email: . . . . Gallos@umkc.edu
Website: . . . . www.CCTR.UMKC.EDU/DEPT/PHYSED/

Degrees offered

- MA
- PhD (interdisciplinary)

Approx. number of students in program

- 20

Approx. number of students in each degree program

- 90% MA/10% PhD

Admissions requirements

- MA: Baccalaureate degree
- GPA of 2.75
- PhD: 1500 on GRE (500 verbal minimum + quantitative + specialized area)
  Other specified requirements identified by coordinating discipline and codiscipline

The program has available for qualified students

- Fellowships
- Teaching assistantships
- Other forms of financial aid

Assistantships

0%	Fellowships
10%	Research assistantships
0%	Teaching assistantships
15%	Tuition waivers
75%	Other forms of financial aid

Internship possibility

- Yes

Internship required for degree completion

- No

Number of hours required for internship

- 3–6 credit hours

Description of typical internship experience

- Working with intercollegiate, potential Olympic, high school, and mature athletes
- Working in a sports medicine setting
- Consulting with school districts on physical education and sport programs (interscholastic or youth)
- Working in fitness centers and exercise-testing situations

Comments

The MA and interdisciplinary PhD are designed to prepare students to become AAASP-certified sport psychology consultants. However, please note that the program is currently on hold. Please contact Dr. Joan Gallos for current information about the status of the program.

THE UNIVERSITY OF
Montana

2 393

Department of Health and Human Performance

McGill 220 A
The University of Montana
Missoula, MT 59812

Program Rating

1	2	3	**4***	5	6	7
Applied Orientation			Equal Emphasis		Research Orientation	

Program offers opportunities to pursue an applied orientation OR a research orientation (as opposed to equal emphasis of both).

Contact Person: . . . . Lewis A. Curry
Phone: 406.243.5242
Fax: 406.243.6252
Email: . . . . curry58@selway.umt.edu

Faculty and areas of interest

Lewis A. Curry — Applied exercise and sport psychology, optimal performance, life-skills training, and performance enhancement intervention and strategies

Degree offered

• MS
• EdD/PhD: Limited opportunities exist in counselor education or multidisciplined doctorate. Contact Lewis Curry for information.

Approx. number of students in program

• 6

Approx. number of students who apply to/are accepted by program annually

• 20–25 apply/10–12 accepted

110

Admissions requirements

- GRE 900 (verbal +quantitative)
- 3.00 GPA in health and human performance cr related field (such as psychology)
- Official copies of transcripts
- Three letters of recommendation

The program has available for qualified students

- Teaching assistantships
- One research assistantship beginning Fall 2000
- Other forms of financial aid

Assistantships

0%	Fellowships
25%	Research assistantships
50%	Teaching assistantships
0%	Tuition waivers
20%	Other forms of financial aid

Internship possibility

- Yes

Internship required for degree completion

- No

Number of hours required for internship

- 6 semester credits

Description of typical internship experience

- Flexible but limited, with some students having worked with athletic teams in high school/college settings. Internships/practicum experiences may be possible in the H.H.P Education Center, recently established to provide life-skills training and sport performance-enhancement consulting.

Comments

The University of Montana has a strong psychology program (PhD program); one strong point is that students take cognate courses in the psychology department.

Université de
Montréal

Département d'Education Physique

CP 6128, Succursale 'A'
Université de Montréal
Montréal, Québec
Canada H3C 3J7

Contact Person: . . . . Wayne R. Halliwell
Phone: 514.343.7008
Fax: 514.343.2181

Faculty and areas of interest

Claude Alain	Information processing, preparation to react
Wayne R. Halliwell	Motivation, mental preparation
Luc Proteau	Learning, movement control, individual differences
Claude Sarrazin	Decision making, intervention

Degrees offered
- MS
- PhD

Approx. number of students in program
- 40

Approx. number of students in each degree program
- 70% MS/30% PhD

Approx. number of students who apply to/are accepted by program annually
- 20 apply/10 accepted

Admissions requirements
- BA or BSc or BPE (usually in physical education or psychology)

The program has available for qualified students

- Research assistantships
- Teaching assistantships
- Other forms of financial aid

Internship possibility

- No

Comments

The program is currently an academically oriented, research program. However, a licensed psychologist is on staff and teaches two graduate courses in clinical psychology. Courses are given in French, but the majority of readings are in English and theses may be written in English.

Nanyang Technological

UNIVERSITY

National Institute of Education
School of Physical Education

469 Bukit Timah Road
Singapore 259756

Program Rating

1	2	3	**4***	5	6	7

Applied Orientation	Equal Emphasis	Research Orientation

This program has an equal emphasis between applied and research orientation.

Contact Person:	Daniel Smith
....	Harry Tan
....	Nick Aplin
Phone:	65-460-5368
....	65-460-5358
....	65-460-5364
Fax:	65-468-7506
....	65-468-7506
....	65-468-7506
Email:	desmith@nie.edu.sg
....	ekhtan@nie.edu.sg
....	ngaplin@nie.edu.sg
Website:	www.spe.ntu.edu.sg:8080/

Faculty and areas of interest

Nick Aplin	Values and pursuit of sports excellence in Singapore, with particular reference to the status of women during the post-war period and the period of national independence
Daniel Smith	Psychological skills training for performance enhancement with elite athletes, the use of psychological variables in predicting future success, crosscultural comparisons in elite athletes
Harry Tan	Psychological issues related to intervention programs for special populations such as obese adolescents and children, socialization of new physical education college students

Program Information

Degree(s) offered

- Master's by course work - 7 courses and a thesis
- Master's by research - 2 courses and a thesis
- PhD by research - 4 courses and a thesis

Approx. number of students in program

- 10 in the sport psychology graduate program

Approx. number of students in each degree program

- 50 in the school of PE graduate program

Admissions requirements

- Admission to the graduate programs requires application to NIE on pre-scribed forms available from the Student Affairs Division. The following documents must be submitted prior to final acceptance:
- Application for Admission as a Higher Degree Candidate
- Foreign students must submit their recent TOEFL and GRE scores. Additionally, an English Proficiency Test is administered by NIE during the first semester in attendance for students whose first language is not English. Some students may receive an English test in their home country prior to acceptance at NTU.
- Official transcripts of all undergraduate and graduate work taken at institutions other than NTU.
- Two Academic Referees Reports
- A written research proposal of the topic is required.
- An interview with the dean, the potential supervisor, and the graduate studies officer.

The program has available for qualified students

- A $1400 ($800 USD) per month scholarship is awarded to full-time masters-by-research students. A $1,500 ($900 USD)-per-month scholarship is awarded to all full-time PhD-by-research students.

Internship possibility

- Internships are available to implement psychological skills training programs with sports teams at a local high school. A few students, in the past, have also secured internships with the Singapore Sports Council, where they implemented psychological skills training programs with national team athletes and teams.

UNIVERSITY OF
New Hampshire

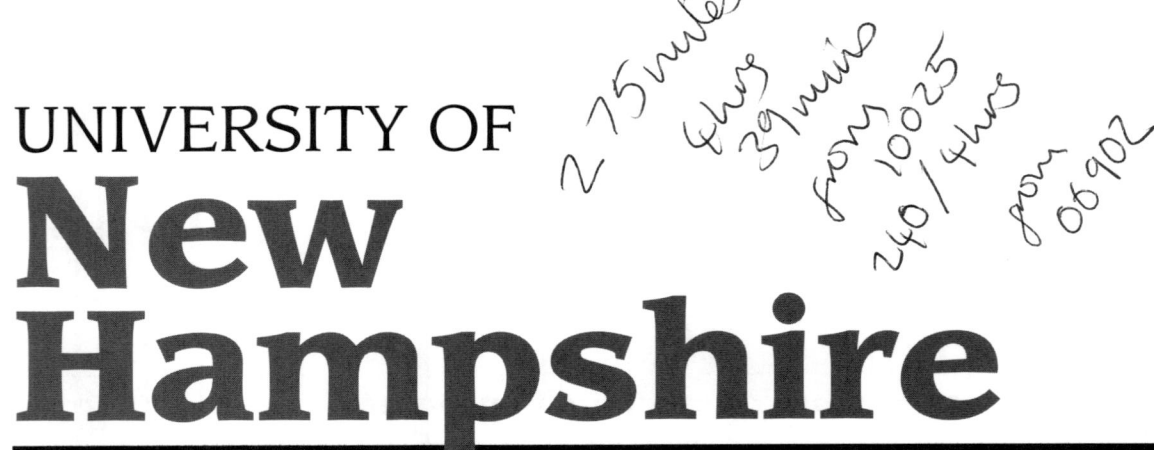

Department of Kinesiology

University of New Hampshire
209 New Hampshire Hall
Durham, NH 03824

Program Rating

1	2	3	**4**	5	6	7
Applied Orientation			Equal Emphasis		Research Orientation	

Contact Person:	Heather Barber
Phone:	603.862.2058
Fax:	603.862.0154
Email:	HB@CISUNIX.UNH.EDU
Website:	WWW.UNH.EDU

Faculty and areas of interest

Heather Barber	Motivation, coaching education
Ron Croce	Neuropsychology

Degree offered
• MS

Approx. number of students in program
• 7–10

Approx. number of students who apply to/are accepted by program annually
• 15 apply/8 accepted

Admissions requirements
• GRE (average student scores 1050)
• GPA (average student has 3.25 on 4.00 scale)

The program has available for qualified students

- Teaching assistantships
- Other forms of financial aid
- Coaching assistantships

Assistantships

0%	Fellowships
0%	Graduate assistantships
50%	Teaching assistantships/coaching assistantships
20%	Tuition waivers
10%	Other forms of financial aid

Internship possibility

- Yes

Internship required for degree completion

- No

Number of hours required for internship

- 8 credit hours

Description of typical internship experience

- Experiential learning in a setting appropriate to the student's objectives. Sport psychology students can either work on campus with the University of New Hampshire athletic program or off campus in approved sport organizations.

Comments

The University of New Hampshire offers a master of science in sport studies with a concentration in sport psychology. The concentration includes an optional internship with one of the university athletic teams, as well as required courses and a thesis.

THE UNIVERSITY OF
New Mexico

Department of Physical Performance and Development

University of New Mexico
Albuquerque, NM 87131

Program Rating

1	2	3	**4**	5	6	7
Applied Orientation			Equal Emphasis		Research Orientation	

Contact Person: . . . . Joy Griffin
Phone: 505.277.3534
Fax: 505.277.6227
Email: . . . . jgriffin@unm.edu
Website: . . . . WWW.UNM.EDU/~SPORTAD/

Faculty and areas of interest

Joy Griffin	Multicultural issues, performance enhancement
Vonda Long	Self-concept development, experiential learning *
Todd Seidler	Sport administration

* Dr. Long is the main contact person in the counselor education program.

Degrees offered

- MS
- PhD

Approx. number of students in program

- 80

Approx. number of students in each degree program

- 75% MS/25% Doctoral

Approx. number of students who apply to/are accepted by program annually

- 50–60 apply/20–25 accepted

Admissions requirements

- Bachelor's or master's degree in physical education, exercise science, health, psychology, or counseling (other degrees will be evaluated by department)
- Undergraduate GPA of 3.00 or better
- Three letters of recommendation
- Written statement of career goals and areas of interest
- History of prospective student's sport background
- Completed application form, including transcripts and official GRE scores

The program has available for qualified students

- Teaching assistantships

Assistantships

- Fellowships (1 official fellowship)
- Teaching assistantships (4–6 TAs)
- Coaching assistantships and sport administration assistance in athletics
- Tuition waivers (varies)
- Other forms of financial aid (varies)

Internship possibility

- Yes

Internship required for degree completion

- Yes

Number of hours required for internship

- 6 credit hours

Description of typical internship experience

- Internship experiences are available in work with high school, collegiate, semiprofessional and professional teams; other possibilities are available with faculty approval.

Comments

Our sport psychology program at UNM is designed to provide all of the criteria necessary for AAASP certification. Sport administration, physical education, and counselor education programs combine to provide an interdisciplinary approach that capitalizes on the strengths of several excellent programs to meet the current needs of the sport counselor. This program is ideal for professionals who wish to teach, conduct research, and work with athletes in an academic, athletic, or private organization. A bonus of our program is that the graduate (besides having the criteria for AAASP certification) also has expertise in sport administration and can be hired by an athletic department to be a sport counselor, and can also multitask.

The PhD graduate can teach in the sport psychology and sport administration fields. Budget constraints in academic and athletic departments may give the graduate student who is academically and experientially prepared to do many tasks an advantage in the hiring process. An applied orientation and/or a research orientation is tailored to the unique career needs and directions of each graduate student. The program is flexible, especially at the PhD level, to enable students to design their own course work (within the AAASP criteria mandates) to meet specific educational and employment objectives.

Program Mission Statement: Our mission is to prepare graduate students for a wide range of sport-related positions within organizations that are typically educational/professional in nature and scope. We strive to provide a superior educational experience to students by supporting our teaching with research in the areas of sport psychology, administration, and leadership. In addition, we provide service and program visibility through community involvement and representation in regional and national organizations. In congruence with this mission, we provide educational opportunities and experiences in the following areas: a) interscholastic and intercollegiate athletics, b) amateur and professional sport, c) public and private sport organizations, and d) the academic study of sport.

UNIVERSITY OF
North Carolina
GREENSBORO

Department of Exercise and Sport Science

University of North Carolina
Greensboro, NC 27412-5001

Program Rating

1	2	3	**4***	5	6	7
Applied Orientation			Equal Emphasis		Research Orientation	

* Program offers opportunities to pursue an applied orientation OR a research orientation (as opposed to an equal emphasis on both).

Contact Person: . . . . Diane L. Gill
. . . . Daniel Gould
. . . . Jeffrey Katula
Phone: 336.334.4683
. . . . 336.334.3037
. . . . 336.334.3271
. . . . 336.334.5573 (dept. main office)
Fax: 336.334.3238
Email: . . . . diane_gill@uncg.edu
. . . . drgould@uncg.edu
. . . . jakatula@uncg.edu
Website: . . . . www.uncg.edu/

Faculty and areas of interest

Diane L. Gill	Social psychology of sport and exercise
Daniel Gould	Applied sport psychology, youth sports
Jeffrey A. Katula	Exercise psychology

Degrees offered

- MS
- PhD

Approx. number of students in program
- 15

Approx. number of students in each degree program
- 60% MS/40% PhD

Approx. number of students who apply to/are accepted by program annually
- 60 apply/8 accepted

Admissions requirements
- Admission is based on previous academic performance (GPA).
- GRE scores
- Letters of reference
- Statement of career goals and objectives
- Past experience and accomplishments
- Visit to campus is strongly recommended for PhD candidates.

The program has available for qualified students
- Research assistantships
- Teaching assistantships

Assistantships
10%   Fellowships
25%   Research assistantships
25%   Teaching assistantships
50%   Tuition waivers (out-of-state waiver only, awarded with RA and TA)
0%   Other forms of financial aid

Internship possibility
- Yes

Internship required for degree completion
- No

Number of hours required for internship
- 3 credit hours

Description of typical internship experience
- Students serve as educational sport psychology specialists with university athletic teams. Both group presentations and individual athletic consultations are involved. Opportunities also exist for internships in nonuniversity sport and exercise programs.

Comments

The UNCG graduate program in sport and exercise psychology offers MS and PhD degrees and prepares students for careers as teachers, researchers, coaches, exercise leaders, or sport and exercise psychology consultants. The UNCG program is staffed by three full-time specialists with expertise in three complementary aspects of the field: social psychology, exercise psychology, and intervention/performance enhancement. This provides both depth and breadth of knowledge in sport and exercise psychology. Extensive research training and experience are provided, with the goal of developing top-flight sport and exercise psychology scholars. In addition, students have the opportunity to develop excellent applied sport and exercise psychology consulting competencies, based on a scientist-practitioner model, by working with athletic teams.

The PhD degree program enables students to pursue in-depth, research-oriented study in sport and exercise psychology, and the program is designed to meet each individual student's career goals and needs. A variety of graduate sport and exercise psychology courses are offered on a regular basis, including a graduate-level introduction to sport and exercise psychology; advanced courses in exercise psychology, social psychology, and applied sport psychology; and a consulting practicum. Also, special topics courses and independent studies are often offered. In addition to sport and exercise psychology courses, the department offers excellent support courses in exercise physiology, pedagogy, motor behavior, and sociocultural sport studies. Many students supplement their sport and exercise psychology programs with courses offered through the psychology and counseling departments.

UNIVERSITY OF
North Dakota

1523 miles

Department of Physical Education and Exercise Science

University Station, Box 8235
University of North Dakota
Grand Forks, ND 58202

Program Rating

1	2	3	**4**	5	6	7
Applied Orientation			Equal Emphasis		Research Orientation	

Contact Person: . . . . Sandra Short (Moritz)
Phone: 701.777.4325
Fax: 701.777.3531
Email: . . . . Sandra_Moritz@und.nodak.edu
Website: . . . . www.und.edu
(Our program website address is currently changing from HPER to PEXS)

Faculty and areas of interest

Sandra Short	Sport psychology—mental imagery and efficacy, golf team coaching
Jim Whitehead	Exercise psychology—motivation, physical self-perceptions

Degree offered

• MS

Approx. number of students in program

• 25

Approx. number of students who apply to/are accepted by program annually

• 20 apply/10 accepted

124

Admissions requirements

- GRE
- Undergraduate GPA 2.75 overall or 3.00 (last 2 years)
- Minimum of 20 credits in undergraduate physical education or equivalent
- TOEFL for applicants who are not native English-speakers (minimum 550 on paper or 213 on computer test)

The program has available for qualified students

- Teaching assistantships

Assistantships

0%	Fellowships
0%	Research assistantships
50%	Teaching assistantships
60%	Tuition waivers
30%	Graduate Student Assistantships with Athletics
0%	Other forms of financial aid

Internship possibility

- Yes

Internship required for degree completion

- No

Number of hours required for internship

- 3–6 credit hours

Description of typical internship experience

- Teaching undergraduate performance enhancement class, assisting in coaching minor program, supervising coaching practica, supervising fitness lab

UNIVERSITY OF
North Texas

Center for Sport Psychology and Performance Excellence

Department of Kinesiology
Health Promotion and Recreation
Box 13857

Department of Psychology, *
University of North Texas,
Box 311280,

University of North Texas
Denton, TX 76203

Program Rating: Program offers opportunities to pursue an applied orientation OR a research orientation (as opposed to an equal emphasis on both).

Contact Person:	Peggy Richardson
. . . .	Scott Martin
Phone:	817.565.3427
. . . .	817.565.3427
Fax:	817.565.4904
. . . .	817.565.4904
Email:	RCHRDSN@COEFS.COE.UNT.EDU
. . . .	SMARTIN@COEFS.COE.UNT.EDU
Website:	www.coe.unt.edu/

Faculty and areas of interest

Karen Cogan	Gender issues in sport and performance enhancement
Scott Martin	Sport and exercise psychology, goal attainment, attitudes and expectations about sport psychology, coaching behaviors
Trent Petrie	Eating disorders, athletic injuries, sport psychology counseling and life skills training
Peggy Richardson	Women in sport, motivation, sport psychology consulting, psychological momentum

Degrees offered

- MS in kinesiology
- PhD in counseling psychology

Approx. number of students in program

- 10–15 (master's)
- 10 (PhD) are admitted to the Department of Psychology (2–4 are interested in sport psychology).

Approx. number of students in each degree program

- 80% MS/20% PhD (from Department of Psychology, etc.)

Admissions requirements

- Master's—800 GRE (375 minimum on verbal and quantitative)
- PhD—1000 GRE (500 minimum on verbal and quantitative)
- MS—2.80 GPA; PhD—3.0 GPA

The program has available for qualified students

- Research assistantships
- Teaching assistantships
- Other forms of financial aid

Assistantships

15%	Fellowships/scholarships
15%	Research assistantships
40%	Teaching assistantships
15%	Tuition waivers (partial tuition waivers for out-of-state students)
60%	Other forms of financial aid

Internship possibility

- Yes

Internship required for degree completion

- No—MS; Yes—PhD

Number of hours required for internship

- 3–6 credit hours

Description of typical internship experience

- Develop a psychological skills intervention program with one of the university's teams.

Comments

The University of North Texas Center for Sport Psychology and Performance Excellence is a multidisciplinary center devoted to offering sport psychology interventions, research, and training. The MS is offered through kinesiology, health promotion, and recreation; the PhD degree is offered through the counseling psychology program (APA-approved program).

Contact persons for the Department of Psychology:

Karen Cogan
940.565.2671
Fax: 940.565.4682
COGAN@DSA.UNT.EDU

Trent Petrie
940.565.4718
Fax: 940.565.4682
PETRIET@UNT.EDU

127

UNIVERSITY OF
Northern
Colorado

175 + miles!

Department of Kinesiology

University of Northern Colorado
Greeley, CO 80639

Program Rating

1	2	3	4	5	**6**	7
Applied Orientation			Equal Emphasis		Research Orientation	

Contact Person: . . . . Robert Brustad
Phone: 303.351.1737
Fax: 303.351.1762
Email: . . . . bbrustad@hhs.UnivNorthCo.edu
Website: . . . . www.hhs.univnorthco.edu/

Faculty and areas of interest

Robert Brustad — Social psychology of sport, psychosocial aspects of children's sport and physical activity, exercise psychology, coaching effectiveness, motivation, physical activity promotion

Degrees offered
- MS
- EdD

Approx. number of students in program
- 10

Approx. number of students in each degree program
- 70% MS/30% EdD

Approx. number of students who apply to/are accepted by program annually
- MS: 10 apply/3 accepted
- EdD: 8 apply/1 accepted

Admissions requirements

- GPA and GRE scores operate on a sliding scale
- Minimum GPA of 3.00 for MS
- Minimum GPA of 3.50 for EdD
- GRE of 1500 for EdD (verbal + quantitative + analytical)

The program has available for qualified students

- Research assistantships
- Teaching assistantships
- Other forms of financial aid

Assistantships

20%   Fellowships
0%   Research assistantships
30%   Teaching assistantships
30%   Tuition waivers
10%   Other forms of financial aid

Internship possibility

- Yes

Internship required for degree completion

- No

Number of hours required for internship

- 6 credit hours

Description of typical internship experience

- Work with university athletic teams; work in health and exercise settings.

Comments

The program focus at the University of Northern Colorado is on the social psychology of sport and physical activity. It is expected that students will develop an excellent background in social psychological theory and will apply this knowledge to the study of sport and exercise behavior. Particular areas of interest of current faculty and students include the study of motivation, exercise behavior and adherence, children's sport and physical activity involvement, and coaching effectiveness. Master's and doctoral students are expected to supplement their departmental course work with courses from the departments of psychology and sociology. There is not a major emphasis on applied sport psychology in this program. However, some course work is available in the applied (intervention) area.

Northern Illinois

UNIVERSITY

Department of Physical Education

Northern Illinois University
Anderson Hall
DeKalb, IL 60115-2854

Program Rating

1	2	3	**4**	5	6	7
Applied Orientation			Equal Emphasis		Research Orientation	

Contact Person: . . . . Laurice Zittel
Phone: 815.753.1425
Fax: 815.753.1413
Website: . . . . www.niu.edu/acad/phed

Faculty and areas of interest

Judith Bischoff   Gender issues, sport governance

Lavon Williams   Motivation of youth sport participants and physical education students

Degree offered

• MSEd

Approx. number of students in program

• 75 (the entire graduate program)

Approx. number of students who apply to/are accepted by program annually

• 75 apply/25 accepted

Admissions requirements

- GPA of 2.75 (4.00 scale)
- GRE of 400 minimum each area (quantitative, verbal)
- Transcripts
- Two letters of recommendation
- Goal statement

The program has available for qualified students

- Fellowships
- Research assistantships
- Teaching assistantships
- Other forms of financial aid

Assistantships

0%   Fellowships
5%   Research assistantships
35%   Teaching assistantships
5%   Tuition waivers
        Other forms of financial aid

Internship possibility

- No

Comments

The MSEd. degree program offers specializations or options in sport and exercise psychology, exercise physiology/fitness leadership, adapted physical education, and coaching. Programs include work in exercise and health psychology. Students who wish to do so may be involved in ongoing research projects.

Oregon State
UNIVERSITY

Exercise and Sport Science Department

Langton Hall
Oregon State University
Corvallis, OR 97331

Program Rating

1	2	3	4	5	**6**	7

Applied Orientation   Equal Emphasis   Research Orientation

Contact Person:	Vicki Ebbeck
Phone:	541.737.6800 (office)
Fax:	541.737.2788
Email:	vicki.ebbeck@orst.edu
Website:	www.osu.orst.edu/hhp/exss

Faculty and areas of interest

Bradley J. Cardinal	Exercise psychology, exercise behavior change, professional issues
Vicki Ebbeck	Lifespan social psychology, motivation, self-concept development

Degrees offered
- MS
- PhD

Approx. number of students in program
- 12

Approx. number of students in each degree program
- 70% MS/30% PhD

Approx. number of students who apply to/are accepted by program annually
- 20 apply/1 PhD and 2 master's thesis are accepted. An open number of master's comprehensive-exam applicants are accepted.

Admissions requirements

- Letters of recommendation
- GRE scores
- Satisfactory GPA
- Transcripts
- Letter of intent

The program has available for qualified students

- Teaching assistantships
- Other forms of financial aid

Assistantships

0%	Fellowships
0%	Research assistantships
75%	Teaching assistantships (including a tuition waiver)
0%	Tuition waivers (via teaching assistantships)
0%	Other forms of financial aid

Internship possibility

- No

Comments

The sport and exercise psychology program at Oregon State University is research oriented with an emphasis in social psychology of physical activity. Recent research projects conducted in the department have investigated the exercise identity of older adults, the psychological outcomes for women "size 14 and over" who engage in a regular exercise program, a team-building intervention designed to enhance the self-conceptions of physical education students, as well as theoretical and applied strategies for enhancing physical activity behavior among diverse populations. The Sport and Exercise Psychology Lab is central to every phase of the research projects conducted by faculty and students. The lab is equipped with Macintosh and PC computers and printers, a scanner, transcribers, television monitors, and video equipment. In addition, an interview room adjoins the lab and allows for one-on-one data collections. In recent years, funding for research and related projects conducted through the Sport and Exercise Psychology Lab has been obtained from several sources, including the Association for the Advancement of Applied Sport Psychology, the John C. Erkkila Endowment for Health and Human Performance, and the National Institute on Disability and Rehabilitative Research of the U.S. Department of Education.

Comprehensive exam and thesis options are available for master's students. Both master's students completing theses and doctoral students are trained to conduct independent research, and doctoral students are exposed to additional experiences such as teaching sport and exercise psychology classes, publishing research articles, preparing grant proposals, and presenting at conferences. The three graduate sport and exercise psychology courses adopt a theory-to-practice approach that enables current research and theory to be applied to practical situations. Course work is supplemented with small-group or individual reading sessions designed to examine sport and exercise psychology topics in greater detail. All students benefit from informal as well as formal interactions with fellow students and program faculty. In addition, each academic program is carefully tailored to meet the professional needs and interests of the student. The overriding goal is to mentor students in their intellectual and professional development. More specifically, graduates of the program are able to enhance their existing careers or transition into new careers—be they in administration, coaching, the health-fitness industry, teaching, recreation services, or research—through their advanced study in sport and exercise psychology. While master's degree candidates are more broadly educated, doctoral candidates are specifically prepared for positions in higher education or government agencies, or for postdoctoral fellowships.

UNIVERSITY OF
Ottawa

School of Human Kinetics

University of Ottawa
125 University, Ottawa, Ontario
Canada KlN 6N5

Program Rating: Our nonthesis option in intervention and consulting has a strong applied orientation (1), whereas our thesis option has a strong research orientation (6).

Contact Person:	Lise O'Reilly
Phone:	613.562.5800 x5752
Fax:	613.562.5149
Email:	lcosa@uottawa.ca
Website:	www.health.uottawa.ca/hkgrad

Faculty and areas of interest

Michelle Fortier	Physical activity behavior, motivation. social influences, gender
Terry Orlick	Performance excellence, quality of life, mental training with children
John Salmela	Coach expertise, qualitative analysis
Diane Ste. Marie	Cognitive processes in judging, eating behaviors in athletes
Pierre Trudel	Coaching, intervention, qualitative methodology

Degrees offered
- MA
- PhD (possibility through the Faculties of Education and Psychology)

Approx. number of students in program
- 30 (20 thesis, 10 nonthesis)

Approx. number of students in each degree program
- 85% MA/15% PhD

Approx. number of students who apply to/are accepted by program annually
- 45 apply/25 accepted

Admissions requirements
- B+ in sport science or related area within education or psychology

The program has available for qualified students
- Research assistantships
- Teaching assistantships
- Other forms of financial aid
- Assistantships

Assistantships
5%   Fellowships
70%   Research assistantships
100%   Teaching assistantships
10%   Tuition waivers
0%   Other forms of financial aid

Internship possibility
- Yes

Internship required for degree completion
- Yes, for the nonthesis option

Number of hours required for internship
- 360 hours

Description of typical internship experience
- Intervention with university teams and individual athletes for performance enhancement
- Intervention with elementary and middle schools for student quality of life
- Intervention with inactive individuals to foster an active lifestyle
- Collaboration with other health professionals to intervene in hospital settings

Comments

The School of Human Kinetics, Faculty of Health Sciences, offers an MA in human kinetics with specialization in sport/exercise psychology and performance enhancement that is unique in the world. A multidisciplinary, research-based thesis program is offered in the overlapping fields of performance and life enhancement, which may continue to a doctoral level. A unique nonthesis program in consultation and intervention directed toward performance and life enhancement is also offered, which combines applied course work with supervised internships.

The school has a good assistantship program. First-year students are provided with teaching/research assistantships of a minimum of $3,500. Second year students may have teaching/research assistantship but will often receive support from their advisor's research grants. Students with a grade point average of 8.5 or better are eligible for an admission scholarship (tuition + $8,000).

Students can benefit from a large and diverse group of experienced sport, exercise, and performance psychology staff members who are bilingual, have numerous research grants, and have expertise in qualitative and quantitative research as well as applied fieldwork.

THE
Pennsylvania State
UNIVERSITY

242 miles / 4 hrs

Department of Kinesiology

146 Recreation Building
The Pennsylvania State University
University Park, PA 16802

Program Rating

1	2	3	4	**5**	**6**	7
Applied Orientation			Equal Emphasis		Research Orientation	

Contact Person:	David E. Conroy
. . . .	Sam Slobounov
. . . .	David Yukelson
Phone:	814.863.3451
. . . .	814.865.3146
. . . .	814.865.0407
. . . .	814.863.4493 (dept.)
Fax:	814.863.7360
. . . .	814.863.7360
. . . .	814.863.1539
Email:	David-Conroy@psu.edu
. . . .	SMS18@PSU.EDU
. . . .	Y39@PSU.EDU
Website:	www.personal.psu.edu/dept/kinesiology

Note: General information and application packets should be requested from the graduate program assistant in the Department of Kinesiology (Amy Bierly) at 814.863.0847. Ms. Bierly's email address is ALB1@PSU.EDU

Faculty and areas of interest

David E. Conroy*   Measurement, development and prevention of fears of failure; interpersonal influences on socioemotional development; consultation processes to facilitate performance and long-term achievement in sport

Sam Slobunov**   Psychology of diving, computer simulations, human postural dynamics, motor control

137

David Yukelson***   Applied sport psychology, group processes and team building, individual and group motivation, life-skill development and student-athlete welfare, psychology of injury

* David Conroy's website: www.personal.psu.edu/dec9/

** Sam Slobunov's website: www.personal.psu.edu/sms18/

*** Dr. Yukelson is an applied sport psychologist who works with all athletic teams at Penn State. Dr. Yukelson is also an affiliate assistant professor in the Department of Kinesiology where he teaches undergraduate courses in mental training, the psychology of coaching, and the social psychology of sport. In addition, he has graduate faculty status to serve on doctoral or thesis committees.

Degrees offered
- MS
- PhD

Approx. number of students in program
- 4

The program has available for qualified students
- Fellowships
- Research assistantships
- Teaching assistantships
- Other forms of financial aid

Assistantships

4%	Fellowships
74%	Graduate assistantships (teaching and research)
93%	Tuition waivers
15%	Other forms of financial aid (grants)

Internship possibility
- Yes

Internship required for degree completion
- No

Description of typical internship experience
- Possibilities exist for qualified students to work with Dr. Yukelson and the Academic Support Center for Student Athletes in an applied intercollegiate athletic setting. Dr. Conroy offers independent-study, supervised practica for graduate students.

Comments

The graduate program in the Department of Kinesiology is nationally and internationally prominent in several research areas within the broad field of kinesiology. This prominence is due to individual faculty excellence, the production and dissemination of quality research, and the mentoring and graduation of excellent graduate students. The program emphasizes research and scholarly activity in the chosen area of emphasis, typically interdisciplinary in nature.

Graduate study in kinesiology at Penn State is mentor based. Prospective students are strongly encouraged to identify and make contact with potential faculty mentors prior to the application process. Faculty do not necessarily accept students every year. Departmental policy requires, as an absolute *minimum*, a 3.0 GPA and a combined GRE (verbal and qualitative) score of 1000. Admission is competitive and admitted students typically have scores substantially above the stated minimum.

Students with an interest in consulting will have opportunities to take independent-study, supervised practica with Dr. Conroy; qualified students also may be eligible for an opportunity to complete a paid internship working with Penn State teams and individual athletes under the supervision of Dr. Yukelson.

Faculty have well-equipped laboratories, with a considerable range of computer-driven equipment that records online movement dynamics, EMG, ECG, EEG, and a variety of other biological and environmental aspects of motor behavior. Additionally, the department has a state-of-the-art computer video analysis system that facilitates behavioral observation research, such as the study of interpersonal processes in athletic or consulting environments.

Purdue
UNIVERSITY

Department of Health, Kinesiology, and Leisure Studies

Lambert 113
Purdue University
West Lafayette, IN 47907

Phone:	765.494.3172 or
. . . .	765.494.3178 or
. . . .	765.496.7551
Fax:	765.496.1239
Website:	www.purdue.edu/academic/hkls

Faculty and areas of interest

Melissa Chase	Sport and exercise psychology, self-efficacy
Alan Smith	Exercise and sport psychology
Lavon Williams	Exercise and sport psychology

Degrees offered

- MS
- PhD

Approx. number of students in program

- 8

Approx. number of students in each degree program

- 40% MS/60% PhD

Approx. number of students who apply to/are accepted by program annually

- 30 apply/1–2 accepted

The program has available for qualified students

- Research assistantships
- Teaching assistantships
- Other forms of financial aid

140

Internship possibility

- One-quarter appointment for a doctoral student with the Athletic Department. The department also offers course work/field experiences in health promotion, health psychology, marketing, and management, besides the other subdisciplines of kinesiology. The program has a research emphasis, but students do have applied experiences working with athletes and exercise groups.

Université du
Québec à Trois-Rivières

Département des Sciences de l'Activité-Physique

Université du Québec à Trois-Rivières
C.P 500, Trois-Rivières, Québec
Canada G9A 5H7

Contact Person: . . . . Pierre Lacoste
Phone: . . . . 819.376.5128, poste 3780
Fax: 819.376.5092

Faculty and areas of interest

Pierre Lacoste   Intervention strategies
Denis Methot   Training and performance

Degree offered

- MS

Approx. number of students in program

- 24

Approx. number of students who apply to/are accepted by program annually

- 23 apply/21 accepted

Admissions requirements

- Bachelor's degree
- 3.2 GPA

The program has available for qualified students

- Research assistantships
- Teaching assistantships

Internship possibility

- Yes

Internship required for degree completion

- No

Number of hours required for internship

- 45 hours (3 credits)

Comments

The program offers two options: (a) professional and (b) research.

Queen's UNIVERSITY

School of Physical and Health Education

Queen's University
Kingston, Ontario
Canada K7L 3N6

Contact Person:	John Albinson
Phone:	613.545.2666
Fax:	613.545.2009
Email:	ALBINSON@QUCDN.QUEENSU.CA

Faculty and areas of interest

John Albinson	Stress/hassles of elite athletes, eating disorders, athlete counseling, exercise counseling for nonathletes
Jean Côté	Exercise and sport psychology
David Pashevich	Collective efficacy, group cohesion, self-presentation

Degree offered

- MA

Approx. number of students in program

- 6

Approx. number of students who apply to/are accepted by program annually

- 12 apply/2–3 accepted

Admissions requirements

- Minimum high-B average from a 4-year degree in physical education/kinesiology, etc., or in psychology with a background in sport involvement
- TOEFL of 600 for students with English as a second language

The program has available for qualified students

- Fellowships
- Research assistantships
- Teaching assistantships

Internship possibility

* Yes

Internship required for degree completion

* No

Number of hours required for internship

* One-half course—3 semester hours

Description of typical internship experience

* Students may do a supervised internship/practicum with intercollegiate athletes (university has 46 varsity teams) or in exercise counseling.

Comments

The program offers the opportunity to focus on applied sport psychology both as it relates to consultation with elite athletes and as it relates to exercise counseling with nonelite populations. Students are expected to take a course in a cognate department, normally psychology, business (organizational behavior), or education (counseling). Students interested in exercise counseling may take courses from the Exercise Rehabilitation Program in the school. Normally, all students accepted will receive funding.

THE UNIVERSITY OF
Queensland

Schools of Human Movement Studies and Psychology

The University of Queensland
Queensland 4072
Australia

Program Rating

1	2	3	**4***	5	6	7
Applied Orientation			Equal Emphasis		Research Orientation	

* Program offers opportunities to pursue an applied orientation OR a research orientation (as opposed to an equal emphasis on both).

Contact Person:	Stephanie Hanrahan
Phone:	(61) 7-3365-6453
. . . .	(61) 7-3365-6240 (main office)
Fax:	(61) 7-3365-6877
Email:	Steph@hms.uq.edu.au
Website:	www.uq.edu.au/hms/
. . . .	psych.psy.uq.edu.au/

Faculty and areas of interest

Bruce Abernethy	Expertise, perception, and production of movement patterns, skill acquisition
Stephanie Hanrahan	Mental skills training, attributions/motivation, pedagogy in sport psychology
Victor Pendleton	Behaviour change as it relates to obesity and related chronic diseases, especially diabetes

Degrees offered

- Research Master's (Master of Arts; Master of Science)
- Master of Sport and Exercise Psychology (MSEP)—course work, research, and practica
- PhD

Approx. number of students in program

- 10–20

Approx. number of students in each degree program

- 5% Research Master's/65% MSEP/30% PhD

146

Approx. number of students who apply to/are accepted by program annually

- 25 apply/10 accepted

Admissions requirements

- Different requirements for different degrees
- MSEP requires a 4-year psychology degree.

The program has available for qualified students

- Research assistantships
- Teaching assistantships
- Other forms of financial aid

Assistantships

20%   Research assistantships
70%   Teaching assistantships
10%   Tuition waivers
10%   Other forms of financial aid

Internship possibility

- Yes, for MSEP

Internship required for degree completion

- Yes, for MSEP

Number of hours required for internship

- 1000 for MSEP

Description of typical internship experience

- University sports clubs/sport associations
- Working with private practitioners.
- Community/high school athletes, teams, coaches
- Opportunity to experience state academy or institute of sport program
- One non-sport placement (e.g., counseling, organizational, forensic, clinical)

Comments

The sport and exercise psychology programs are run jointly by the School of Human Movement Studies and the School of Psychology. Traditionally, master's and doctoral programs in Australia have been predominantly research based. The Master of Sport and Exercise Psychology offered at the University of Queensland is a professionally oriented training program and includes course work, research, and practicum (internship) components. The academic year coincides with the calendar year, with classes beginning in February.

San Diego State
UNIVERSITY

Department of Exercise and Nutritional Sciences

San Diego State University
San Diego, CA 92182

Program Rating

1	2	3	**4**	5	6	7
Applied Orientation			Equal Emphasis		Research Orientation	

Contact Person: . . . . Dennis J. Selder
Phone: 619.594.1920
Fax: 619.594.6553
Email: . . . . DSELDER@MAIL.SDSU.EDU
Website: . . . . www.rohan.sdsu.edu/~psyched

Faculty and areas of interest

Thomas L. McKenzie	Applied behavior analysis, performance enhancement
Robert Mechikoff	Psychology of coaching, social psychology
Brent Rushall	Performance enhancement, coach/athlete behavior, intentional effectiveness
Dennis J. Selder	Performance enhancement, motivation

Degree offered
- MA

Approx. number of students in program
- 18

Approx. number of students who apply to/are accepted by program annually
- 20 apply/15 accepted

Admissions requirements
- 950 GRE
- 3.00 GPA last 60 units

The program has available for qualified students
- Research assistantships
- Teaching assistantships
- Other forms of financial aid

Assistantships
0%   Fellowships
20%   Research assistantships
30%   Teaching assistantships
5%   Tuition waivers
0%   Other forms of financial aid

Internship possibility
- Yes

Internship required for degree completion
- Yes, for the MA

Number of hours required for internship
- Depends upon the student's situation

Description of typical internship experience
- Serve as consultant to intercollegiate teams, involving assessment, development of mental skills training programs, team building, research reports
- Serve as an intern to business and sport organizations

Comments

The study of the psychology of sport and physical activity ranges from theoretical sport psychology to applied sport psychology. Students are able to select their course of studies to reflect their own interests and backgrounds. A core of courses is required of all students so that they may appreciate the expanse of the area of study. Further courses are elected to meet each student's specific interests. The main strength of this sport psychology specialization is its emphasis on laboratory and practical experiences. It is designed to reflect the extensive resources in sport psychology that are available in the San Diego region.

An additional program of interest at San Diego State University is the joint PhD in behavioral medicine between the Department of Psychology at SDSU and the Department of Psychiatry at the University of California at San Diego.

San Diego
University for Integrative Studies

5703 Oberlin Drive, Suite 208
San Diego, California 92121

Contact Person:	Cristina Bortoni Versari
Phone:	858.638.1999
Fax:	858.638.1990
Email:	admissions@sduis.edu
....	cversari@sduis.edu (Cristina Bortoni Versari)
Website:	www.sdius.edu

Program Rating

1	**2**	3	4	5	6	7
Applied Orientation			Equal Emphasis		Research Orientation	

Faculty and areas of interest

Hilse Barbosa	Personal and career development, personality type, team building
Hans DeHaan	Clinical and sport psychology research, psychopharmacology
Roy Nasby	Nutrition and lifestyle management, Acupuncture, acupressure, and other alternative approaches to treating injured athletes
Sherry Newsham	Children's motivation for sport participation and performance enhancement, psychological characteristics of ultraendurance athletes
Bruce Ogilvie	Clinical approach to sport psychology and performance enhancement, applied sport psychology, psychology of coaching, children and sports
Walter Rutherford	Addictions and their effect on the team and family, Post Traumatic Stress Disorder (PTSD), meditation methods, clinical skills
James Sinclair	Business principles of sport psychology
Cristina Bortoni Versari	Career transition and athletic retirement, athletes and personality type, business principles of sport psychology, performance enhancement, distance learning education

150

Degrees offered

- MA in sport counseling
- PhD in sport psychology
- Certificate in sport psychology

Approx. number of students in program

- 32

Approx. number of students in each degree program

- 12 MA; 10 PhD; 10 Certificate

Approx. number of students who apply to/are accepted by program annually

- 20; Students who meet admissions requirements are accepted.

Admissions requirements

- MA in sport counseling – Undergraduate degree
- PhD in sport psychology – Master's degree and 35 units of graduate level psychology courses and 25 units of sport counseling courses
- Certificate in sport psychology – Undergraduate degree

Internship possibility

- Yes

Internship required for degree completion

- Yes, for PhD

Comments

The sport psychology program at the San Diego University for Integrative Studies consists of an 18-month degree in sports counseling and a 36–48-month PhD program in sport psychology. Both programs are designed to meet the needs of professionals dedicated to helping athletes and preparing them to be more effective in sports and in their personal lives during and after their athletic careers. A unique humanistic approach considering individual dimensions of mind, body, and spirit in their social, cultural, and environmental contexts is combined with personal development, technical, and professional skills.

Graduates in sport psychology consult with individual athletes, teams, athletic organizations, committees, and national and international governing bodies. Graduates are also able to effectively teach, coach, and develop programs tailored for this unique population. Through intensive training and internships, graduates enhance their competence and professional skills to better serve others. Individuals who wish to pursue licensing as an MFT or psychologist will have the opportunity to add courses that are required for the State of California licensing exam.

The faculty of the sport psychology program consists of experienced professionals who have proven results in applying psychology to such areas as performance enhancement, substance abuse, athletic career transition, retirement, testing and evaluation, individual and family counseling, crisis intervention, group techniques, communication and relationship skills, and gender issues. Leaders in the field of sport psychology enhance the quality of the program as guest lecturers; they guarantee the diversity of approaches in working with clients in the field of sports.

Courses are offered on a quarter system. All three programs are also available though a distance learning program.

MA in Sport Counseling: This program provides students with the theoretical and practical training needed to help athletes become more effective in sport and their personal lives. Emphasis is on practical counseling skills and innovative techniques for working with athletes and sport professionals to promote wellness and effectiveness in their endeavors.

PhD in Sport Psychology: The needs of athletes, coaches, fitness specialists, psychologists, and other professionals who specialize in sports have changed increasingly over the years. The challenges of understanding the dynamics of psychological changes and their relationships to athletic performance have become the focus of attention for professionals in sports. Students are trained in a variety of sport psychology approaches and techniques that prepare them to consult with athletes, teams, and athletic organizations. Students can also add courses that are required to become a licensed psychologist or MFT.

Certificate Program in Sport Counseling: This program is designed for the working professional who wishes to expand her/his skills and abilities in the areas of performance enhancement, sport counseling, and effective methods of working with athletes, coaches, and others in the expanding sports industry.

San Jose State
UNIVERSITY

Department of Human Performance

San Jose State University
One Washington Square
San Jose, CA 95192-0054

Program Rating

1	2	3	4	5	**6**	7
Applied Orientation			Equal Emphasis		Research Orientation	

Contact Person: . . . . David M. Furst
Phone: 408.924.3039
Fax: 408.924.3053
Email: . . . . furstd@email.sjsu.edu
Website: . . . . www.sjsu.edu/depts/casa/dept/hup.html

Faculty and areas of interest

Ted Butryn	Psychosocial impact of "cyborg sport," cognitions and mood states of endurance athletes, social justice issues related to applied sport psychology
David M. Furst	Endurance athletes, disabled athletes, association/ dissociation
Keith Johnsgard	Sensation seekers
Jill Steinberg	Women and sport

Degree offered
• MA

Approx. number of students in program
• 8

Approx. number of students who apply to/are accepted by program annually
• 3 apply/3 accepted

153

Admissions requirements (classified standing)

- Baccalaureate degree with a major or minor in physical education
- Minimum GPA of 3.00 in last 60 semester units (or minimum of 2.75 and on probation)
- No undergraduate course deficiencies
- Students are encouraged but not required to submit GRE scores.
- Non-PE majors can enter as "conditionally classified."

The program has available for qualified students

- Teaching assistantships
- Other forms of financial aid

Assistantships

0%	Fellowships
0%	Research assistantships
20%	Teaching assistantships
0%	Tuition waivers
30%	Other forms of financial aid
50%	No Financial Aid

Internship possibility

- Yes

Internship required for degree completion

- No

Description of typical internship experience

- Depending on the clinical/applied work being done with the various teams and athletic departments, the student will work with these teams under the direction of one of the clinical sport psychologists.

Comments

Professors at San Jose State University have been involved with sport psychology as long, or longer, than those at any other university in the United States. Emeritus professors Bruce Ogilvie and Thomas Tutko have achieved national and international recognition for their applied work with athletes on every level, from Olympic to professional to youth sport. Currently, the sport psychology program is housed within the Human Performance Department. Courses available to students are undergraduate and graduate sport psychology, exercise and mental health, motivation, psychology of coaching, cognition, personality, nutrition and sport, and others. Two of the four faculty involved in the applied sport psychology program have PhDs in clinical psychology.

Université de
Sherbrooke

Département de Kinanthropologie

Université de Sherbrooke
2500 Boulevard de l'Université
Sherbrooke, Québec, Canada JlK 2Rl

Program Rating

1	2	3	4	**5**	6	7

Applied Orientation	Equal Emphasis	Research Orientation

Contact Person:	Paul Deshaies
Phone:	819.821.8000, x3721
Fax:	819.821.7970
Email:	PDESHAIES@FEPS.USHERB.CA
Website:	www.usherb.ca/programmes/maitrise/ kinant.html

Faculty and areas of interest

Marc Belisle	Motives for involvement, stress management
Pierre Demers	Sociology of physical education
Paul Deshaies	Daily physical education for elementary schools, psychobiological analysis of performance
Georges B. Lemieux	Learning, observation

Degree offered
- MS

Approx. number of students in program
- 25

Approx. number of students who apply to/are accepted by program annually
- 20 apply/15 accepted

Admissions requirements
- Bachelor's degree in movement science, physical education, or equivalent

The program has available for qualified students
- Research assistantships
- Teaching assistantships
- Other forms of financial aid

Assistantships
10%	Fellowships
10%	Research assistantships
10%	Teaching assistantships
0%	Tuition waivers
60%	Other forms of financial aid

Internship possibility
- No

Comments

The programme is not specifically in applied sport psychology but in kinanthropology. The programme emphasizes a systematic approach applied to contexts such as athletic competition, physical fitness, and adapted physical activity. Within this framework, classes are offered in areas such as sport psychology, sport sociology, and environmental factors. Research activities count for 24 of the 45 credits required, and it is here that the student can concentrate on a specific area of interest.

Southeastern Louisiana
UNIVERSITY

Department of Kinesiology and Health Studies

Southeastern Louisiana University
Hammond, LA 70402

Program Rating

1	2	3	4	5	**6**	7

Applied Orientation	Equal Emphasis	Research Orientation

Contact Person: . . . . Dan Hollander
Phone: 504.549.3870
Fax: 504.549.5119
Email: . . . . dhollander@selu.edu
Website: . . . . www.selu.edu/

Faculty and areas of interest

Dan Hollander	Exercise and sport psychology
Eddie Hebert	Self-talk, videotape feedback, imagery
Marcus Kilpatrick	Exercise psychology

Degree Offered

- MA

Approx. number of students in program

- 2 in sport psychology
- 42 in overall program

Approx. number of students who apply/are accepted annually by program

- 1 applies/1 accepted in sport psychology program
- 15 apply/13 accepted in overall program

Admissions requirements

- Undergraduate GPA of 2.5 (or 3.0 in last 2 years)
- GRE of 800

Assistantships

50%   Fellowships (5% in overall program)

50%   Research assistantships (10% in overall program)

0%   Teaching assistantships (5% in overall program)

100% Tuition waivers (25% in overall program)

0%   Other forms of financial aid

Internship possibility

- Yes

Internship required for degree completion

- No

Number of hours required for internship

- Students concentrating in counseling have a greater opportunity to participate in internship experiences than do those concentrating in exercise science.

Description of typical internship experience

- Educational sport psychology with individual or team-sport athletes and various opportunities in the athletic training room with injured athletes.

UNIVERSITY OF
Southern California

Department of Exercise Science

University of Southern California
Los Angeles, CA 90089-0652

Program Rating

1	2	3	4	5	**6**	7

Applied Orientation   Equal Emphasis   Research Orientation

Contact Person: . . . . John Callaghan
Phone: 213.740.2971
Fax: 213.740.7909
Email: . . . . callagha@mizar.usc.edu
Website: . . . . www.usc.edu/dept/LAS/exsci/

Faculty and areas of interest

John Callaghan   Personality, motivation, attributions, perceived competence and anxiety, psychological skills

Degrees offered
- MA
- PhD

Approx. number of students in program
- 3–8

Approx. number of students in each degree program
- 50% MA/50% PhD

Approx. number of students who apply to/are accepted by program annually
- 2–3 accepted

Admissions requirements

- Undergraduate GPA of 3.00
- 1100 minimum GRE score (verbal + quantitative)

The program has available for qualified students

- Fellowships
- Research assistantships
- Teaching assistantships
- Other forms of financial aid

Assistantships

0%   Fellowships
40%   Research assistantships
40%   Teaching assistantships
0%   Tuition waivers
0%   Other forms of financial aid

Internship possibility

- No

Comments

The department has three tracks: exercise physiology, biomechanics, and sport psychology. These three specializations are at the graduate level. Sport psychology is offered for both MA and PhD degrees in the Department of Exercise Science.

Southern Connecticut
STATE UNIVERSITY

Human Performance Laboratory

Moore Fieldhouse
Southern Connecticut State University
501 Crescent Street
New Haven, CT 06515

Program Rating

1	2	3	**4**	5	6	7

Applied Orientation   Equal Emphasis   Research Orientation

Contact Person: . . . .   David S. Kemler
Phone: 203.392.6040
Fax: 203.392.6020
Email: . . . .   Kemler@scsu.ctstateu.edu
Website: . . . .   www.scsu.ctstateu.edu/

Faculty and areas of interest

Robert S. Axtell	Exercise physiology (graduate coordinator)
Joan A. Finn	Psychophysiology
David S. Kemler	Sport psychology, exercise psychology
David W. Martens	Biomechanics
Sharon Misasi	Sport psychology, social psychology
Karl F. Rinehardt	Exercise physiology
Jin Jin Yang	Motor learning

Degree offered
- MS (human performance)

Approx. number of students in program
- 70

Approx. number of students who apply to/are accepted by program annually
- 25 apply/15 accepted

161

Admissions requirements

- 2.50 GPA

The program has available for qualified students

- Graduate assistantships
- Other forms of financial aid

Assistantships

0%	Fellowships
4%	Research assistantships
0%	Teaching assistantships
0%	Tuition waivers
0%	Other forms of financial aid

Internship possibility

- Yes

Internship required for degree completion

- No

Number of hours required for internship

- 150 hours

Description of typical internship experience

- See comments

Comments

The sport psychology concentration is designed to offer the student in-depth study in the areas of health psychology, performance enhancement, social psychology, and intervention. This interdisciplinary approach presents 33 credits of course work from a variety of disciplines. Our program is an interdisciplinary program geared toward helping students to achieve their goals as they pursue fulfilling careers. The benefits of our program are twofold: First, we offer flexibility throughout the program, allowing students to select a wide range of options including emphases in performance enhancement, health psychology, and social psychology. Students are encouraged to take courses in psychology, public health, counseling and school psychology, and business, as well as marriage and family therapy. Second, because we are a rather small school (as compared with others in this field) we can offer students greater opportunities to integrate theory with application as they hone their skills in a supervised environment with athletic teams. Participating teams include the University of Connecticut and Yale University, as well as Southern Connecticut State University athletic departments. This background prepares students for advanced study, hospital wellness programs, corporate and commercial fitness centers, community agencies, coaching enhancement, or other related fields of study. Graduate assistantships are available for qualified applicants. Further information related to curriculum and research assistantships may be obtained by contacting Dr. David S. Kemler.

Southern Illinois
UNIVERSITY, CARBONDALE

Department of Physical Education

Southern Illinois University
Carbondale, IL 62901-4310

Program Rating

1	2	3	**4**	5	6	7
Applied Orientation			Equal Emphasis		Research Orientation	

Contact Person: . . . . Elaine Blinde
Phone: 618.453.3119
Fax: 618.453.3329
Email: . . . . blinde@SIU.EDU
Website: . . . . www.siu.edu/departments/coe/physed/

Faculty and areas of interest

Elaine M. Blinde — Gender dynamics in sport, sport retirement, disability dynamics, empowerment, homophobia

Sarah McCallister — Youth sports, teaching and coaching effectiveness, gender dynamics, disability issues, baseball

Degree offered
- MS

Approx. number of students in program
- 12 (social psychology of sport)

Approx. number of students who apply to/are accepted by program annually
- 12 apply/6 accepted

Admissions requirements
- GRE
- Three current letters of recommendation or evaluation forms
- Undergraduate and graduate transcripts

The program has available for qualified students

- Fellowships
- Research assistantships
- Teaching assistantships
- Other forms of financial aid

Assistantships

0%	Fellowships
10%	Research assistantships
40%	Teaching assistantships
80%	Tuition Waiver
50%	Other forms of Financial Aid

Internship possibility

- Yes, a full internship is available. Practicum experiences in applied sport psychology, working directly with athletes and/or exercisers, are available.

Description of typical practicum experience

- Individual and team consultation experiences, independent-study practica, practical experience through applied sport psychology graduate courses.

Comments

A wide range of teaching and research opportunities is available to graduate students through departmental assistantships and faculty grants. Students are provided opportunities to engage in both quantitative and qualitative research projects, as well as to teach classes in the applied sport psychology area (e.g., relaxation). In addition to the many courses offered by the Department of Physical Education in the social psychological domain, students are encouraged to take courses in counseling, psychology, and sociology. Excellent relationships have been established with related departments on campus. A sport psychology laboratory provides students with computers, office space, a seminar room, and facilities and equipment for consultation and interviewing.

Southern Illinois
UNIVERSITY, EDWARDSVILLE

Department of Kinesiology and Health Education

Box 1126
Vadalabene Center
Southern Illinois University Edwardsville
Edwardsville, IL 62026-1126

Program Rating

1	2	3	4	**5**	6	7
Applied Orientation			Equal Emphasis		Research Orientation	

Contact Person: . . . . Curt L. Lox
. . . . Brian Butki
Phone: 618.650.5961
. . . . 618.650.2306
Fax: 618.650.3369
. . . . 618.650.3369
Email: . . . . clox@siue.edu
. . . . bbutki@siue.edu
Website: . . . . www.siue.edu/HRPE/

Faculty and areas of interest

| Brian Butki | Sport and exercise psychology, exercise and mental health |
| Curt L. Lox | Exercise and sport psychology, behavioral medicine, coaching |

Degree Offered

- MSEd

Approx. number of students in program

- 15

Approx. number of students who apply/are accepted annually by program

- 15 apply/10 accepted

Admission requirements

- Undergraduate GPA of 2.5
- No standardized tests are required for either U.S. or international students.

Assistantships

5%   Fellowships
5%   Research assistantships
5%   Teaching assistantships
15% Tuition waivers
5%   Other forms of financial aid

Internship possibility

- Yes

Internship required for degree completion

- No

Number of hours required for internship

- 3 credit hours

Description of typical internship experience

- Working with university athletic teams. Opportunities also exist for internships in exercise, rehabilitation, and wellness settings.

Comments

The emphasis of the graduate sport and exercise psychology program is on research and academic sport and exercise psychology. Applied sport psychology issues are included, however, and opportunities exist for an individual to gain experience developing and implementing educational psychological skill programs. Opportunities also exist in exercise psychology settings for those individuals interested in corporate fitness, wellness, and rehabilitation.

The specific research interests of Curt Lox are exercise and special populations (e.g., AIDS, elderly), and motivational and affective aspects of exercise and mental health. Brian Butki examines the affective side of mental health and exercise including emotional and behavioral disorders in adolescents, fitness motivation, and anxiety management.

UNIVERSITY OF
Southern
Queensland

Faculty of Sciences, Department of Psychology

University of Southern Queensland
Toowoomba, Queensland 4350, Australia

Program Rating

1	2	3	4	5	6	**7**
Applied Orientation			Equal Emphasis			Research Orientation

The Master of Psychology has an applied orientation, while the MPhil and PhD programs are oriented toward research.

Contact Persons:	Gerry Fogarty
. . . .	Steven Christensen
. . . .	Andrea Lamont-Mills
Phone:	(GF) 61-7-46-31-2379
. . . .	(SC) 61-7-46-31-2707
. . . .	(ALM) 61-7-46-31-1703
Fax:	61-7-46-31-2721
Email:	fogarty@usq.edu.au
. . . .	christen@usq.edu.au
. . . .	lamontm@usq.edu.au
Website:	www.usq.edu.au/faculty/science/depts/ psych/psych.htm

Faculty and areas of interest

Steven Christensen	Applied issues, decision making, expertise
Gerry Fogarty	Intelligence, applied sport psychology
Andrea Lamont-Mills	Gender issues, discourse analysis, gifted young athletes

Degrees offered

- Master of Psychology (sport and exercise)
- MPhil (by research)
- Doctor of Sport and Exercise Psychology (PsyD)
- PhD

Approx. number of students in program

- 22

Approx. number of students in each degree program

- 70% master's/30% PsyD/PhD

Approx. number of students who apply/are accepted annually by program

- 27 apply/6 accepted

Admissions requirements

- 3 years plus honours for Australian students
- BA/BS for foreign students
- GPA
- References

Assistantships

0%	Fellowships
0%	Research assistantships
0%	Teaching assistantships
0%	Tuition waivers
0%	Other forms of financial aid

Internship possibility

- Yes

Internship required for degree completion

- Yes

Number of hours required for internship

- 1000+

Description of typical internship experience

- Sport psychology practica provide applied sport and personal development services to talented and elite athletes within regional/state institute/national institute programs. Exercise and health psychology practica provide applied health and behaviour-change services within community health clinics and corporate health and exercise settings.

Spalding
UNIVERSITY

706 notes)
12½ hrs

Department of Psychology

Spalding University
851 S. Fourth
Louisville, KY 40203

Program Rating

1	2	3	4	5	6	7

Applied Orientation   Equal Emphasis   Research Orientation

Contact Person: . . . . Thomas Titus (Chairman)
Phone: 502.585.9911
Fax: 502.585.7159
Website: . . . . www.spalding.edu

Faculty and areas of interest

Thomas Bergandi	Sport psychology
John James	Systems theory
John Kalafat	Crisis intervention, consultation
David Morgan	Learning
Thomas Titus	Learning, addictions
Barbara Williams	Supervision issues

Degrees offered

- MA
- PsyD

Approx. number of students in program

- 120

Approx. number of students in each degree program

- 20% MA/80% PsyD

Approx. number of students who apply to/are accepted by program annually

- 30 MA apply/5 MA accepted; 400 PsyD apply/25 PsyD accepted

169

Admissions requirements
- GRE—minimum for three tests: 1500 (MA), 1600 (PsyD)
- Three letters of recommendation
- Autobiography
- Professional/academic writing sample
- Personal interview for PsyD program

The program has available for qualified students
- Research assistantships
- Other forms of financial aid

Assistantships
0%	Fellowships
28%	Research assistantships
0%	Teaching assistantships
5%	Tuition waivers (scholarships)
100%	Other forms of financial aid (student loans)

Internship possibility
- Yes (may not be in applied sport psychology per se)

Internship required for degree completion
- Yes

Number of hours required for internship
- MA—650 hours/PsyD—2000 hours

Description of typical internship experience
- Numerous experiences are available for clinical training (e.g., hospitals, outpatient agencies, drug and alcohol agencies, correctional facilities, community mental health centers, etc.).

Springfield COLLEGE

School of Graduate Studies

Springfield College
Springfield, MA 01109

Program Rating

1	2	3	**4**	5	6	7

Applied Orientation	Equal Emphasis	Research Orientation

Contact Person:	Betty L. Mann
Phone:	413.748.3125
Fax:	413.748.3745
Website:	www.springfieldcollege.edu/

Faculty and areas of interest

Barbara Jensen	Measurement, research design, structural equation modeling
Betty L. Mann	Research advisement
Mimi Murray	Sport psychology

Degrees offered

- MS (thesis required)
- Doctor of Physical Education (DPE), specialization in sport psychology

Approx. number of students in program

- 12 MS
- 8 DPE in sport psychology

Approx. number of students in each degree program

- 60% MS/40% DPE

Approx. number of students who apply to/are accepted by program annually

- MS 15–20 apply/8–10 accepted
- DPE approximately 6 apply/ 2–3 accepted

Admissions requirements

- MS: GPA, references, applicant's statement of objectives
- DPE: GPA, GRE, references, applicant's statement of objectives

171

The program has available for qualified students

- Associateships (fellowships)
- Graduate assistantships
- Other forms of financial aid

Assistantships

20%   Fellowships (include all forms of research/teaching assistantships and tuition waivers)

0%   Research assistantships

0%   Teaching assistantships

0%   Tuition waivers

0%   Other forms of financial aid

Internship possibility

- Sport psychology consulting internship experience is required for students in the doctoral program.

Comments

The sport psychology concentration at the master's level is designed for students who have a scholarly interest in sport psychology and wish to pursue this interest further in doctoral programs of study. The intent of the program is to provide theoretical understanding of sport from a philosophical, sociological, psychological, and physiological perspective, particularly as this knowledge may be practically applied to helping athletes maximize sport performance. A thesis is required for the MS

The doctoral concentration in sport psychology has been designed to allow students, upon completion of the degree, to meet the requirements to apply for certification by AAASP In addition to theory-based and applied sport psychology course work, a series of seminars is offered that relates to current issues and research trends in the field, including youth sport, model building, behavior observation, cohesion/collective efficacy, race, gender, sport ethics, and motivation. Students also complete course work in athletic counseling and psychopathology, as well as in related areas of physical education, including motor learning/control and development, exercise physiology, and sociology.

Students in the department are working on a variety of research topics. Some of the current research includes the relationship between competitive orientation and goal-setting practices of collegiate athletes; self-perception of exercisers and nonexercisers; relationship between goal orientation and sources of self-confidence in high school and collegiate athletes; imagery and self-talk preferences and golf performance; a model to examine perceptions of psychological momentum; the development of a scale to measure coaching staff cohesion; parental influences on youth sport participation; behavioral observation of coaching behaviors and self-reported competence of youth soccer players; path analysis of perfectionism, attitudes toward eating, and mood states of ballet dancers; model building with team cohesion and collective efficacy; structural equation modeling of goal orientation and intrinsic/extrinsic motivation of women golfers; relationship between coaching behaviors and self-confidence of high school basketball players; and the development of a questionnaire to measure the sources of enjoyment in youth sport.

Springfield COLLEGE

Psychology Department

Springfield College
Springfield, MA 01109

2 hrs 23 mins from 10025
1 hr 48 from 06902

Program Rating

1	2	3	**4***	5	6	7

Applied Orientation   Equal Emphasis   Research Orientation

* Program offers opportunities to pursue an applied orientation OR a research orientation (as opposed to an equal emphasis on both).

Contact Person: . . . . Al Petitpas
Phone: 413.748.3325
Fax: 413.748.3854
Website: . . . . www.spfldcol.edu/

Faculty and areas of interest

Britton W. Brewer	Pain and injury in sport and exercise
John Brickner	Psychology of injury
Delight Champagne	Career development of athletes
Allen Cornelius	Research, statistics, humor
Burt Giges	Intervention skills, self-awareness
Al Petitpas	Personal and career development of athletes
Judy L. Van Raalte	Social psychology of sport and exercise (attributions, self-talk)

Degrees offered
- MEd
- MS
- CAS

Approx. number of students in program
- 24

Approx. number of students in each degree program
- 75% MS/25% MEd

Approx. number of students who apply to/are accepted by program annually

- 45 apply/12 accepted

Admissions requirements

- Psychology or physical education majors preferred
- Applied experience helpful
- Completed application
- Five letters of support
- Personal statement required

The program has available for qualified students

- Fellowships
- Research assistantships
- Teaching assistantships
- Other forms of financial aid

Assistantships

8%	Fellowships
36%	Research assistantships
16%	Teaching assistantships
8%	Tuition waivers
0%	Other forms of financial aid

Internship possibility

- Yes

Internship required for degree completion

- Yes, for all degrees

Number of hours required for internship

- Minimum of 300 hours required

Description of typical internship experience

- Academic/athletic counseling at colleges and universities, sports counseling in sport medicine clinics, career and personal development with athletes in sport agencies, work with college athletic teams.

Comments

The athletic counseling program offers course work in psychology, physical education, and counseling. The primary job market for graduates has been academic athletic counseling positions at major universities. Approximately 25% of graduates go directly into counseling psychology doctoral programs to gain the credentials necessary to develop independent practices in counseling with emphases in sport psychology.

Staffordshire
UNIVERSITY

Division of Sport, Health, and Exercise

Staffordshire University
Leek Road
Stoke-on-Trent ST4 2DF, United Kingdom

Program Rating

1	2	3	4	5*	6	7
Applied Orientation			Equal Emphasis		Research Orientation	

*Program offers opportunities to pursue an applied orientation OR a research orientation (as opposed to an equal emphasis on both).

Contact Person: . . . . Geoffrey Paull
Phone: . . . . (44) 1782-412515
Fax: . . . . (44) 1782-747167
Website: . . . . www.staffs.ac.uk/sands/scis/sport

Faculty and areas of interest

Basil Ashford	Sport psychology
Kim Buxton	Exercise psychology
Jo Doyle	Sport psychology
John Erskine	Motor learning/control
Nigel Gleeson	Exercise physiology
Tom Mercer	Exercise physiology
Jayne Mitchell	Exercise epidemiology, exercise psychology
Geoffrey Paull	Expertise in skilled behavior

Degrees offered
- MPhil, PhD
- MS (sport science)

Approx. number of students in program
- 10–20

Approx. number of students in each degree program
- 3–4 MPhil/6–10 MS/2–3 PhD

Approx. number of students who apply to/are accepted by program annually

- 12 accepted

Admissions requirements

- Undergraduate degree
- Marks/grades
- References

The program has available for qualified students

- Research assistantships
- Teaching assistantships

Assistantships

0%   Fellowships
25%   Research assistantships
0%   Teaching assistantships
0%   Tuition waivers
0%   Other forms of financial aid

Internship possibility

- Yes

Internship required for degree completion

- No

Description of typical internship experience

- Work with teams, work in leisure/fitness centers, work in performance center, work with individuals

UNIVERSITY OF
Stellenbosch

Department of Human Movement Studies

University of Stellenbosch
Private Bag X1
Matieland, Stellenbosch 7602
Republic of South Africa

Program Rating

1	2	3	4	5	**6**	7
Applied Orientation			Equal Emphasis		Research Orientation	

Contact Person: . . . . Justus R. Potgieter
Phone: . . . . (27) 21-8084915
Fax: . . . . (27) 21-8084817
Email: . . . . JRP@MATIES.SUN.AC.ZA

Faculty and areas of interest

Liz Bressan   Motor learning

Justus R. Potgieter   Performance enhancement, exercise psychology

Degrees offered

- Masters in human movement studies
- PhD

Approx. number of students in program

- 15 part-time students

Approx. number of students in each degree program

- 66% MHS/34% PhD

Approx. number of students who apply to/are accepted by program annually

- 10 apply/9 accepted

Admissions requirements

- Recognized honor's degree for master's degree
- Recognized master's degree for PhD

The program has available for qualified students

- Teaching assistantships (limited)

Assistantships

0%   Fellowships
0%   Research assistantships
25%   Teaching assistantships
0%   Tuition waivers
0%   Other forms of financial aid

Internship possibility

- No

Comments

Each student develops his or her own program of study. Emphasis is placed on the research dissertation.

Temple
UNIVERSITY

Department of Kinesiology, (048-00)
Temple University
Philadelphia, PA 19122

Contact Person:	Carole A. Oglesby
. . . .	Michael L. Sachs
Phone:	215.204.1948
. . . .	215.204.8718
Fax:	215.204.8705
. . . .	215.204.8705
Email:	REDS@ASTRO.TEMPLE.EDU
. . . .	MSACHS@NIMBUS.TEMPLE.EDU
Website:	www.temple.edu/education/PE

Program Rating

1	2	3	4	**5**	6	7

Applied Orientation	Equal Emphasis	Research Orientation

Faculty and areas of interest

Carole A. Oglesby	Family systems theory, gender and sexuality, psychological skills training
Marcella Ridenour	Perceptual motor, motor development
Michael L. Sachs	Exercise psychology, psychology of running, exercise addiction/dependence, professional and ethical issues, excusercise
Marianne Torbert	Psychosocial interactions in play

Degrees offered

- MS
- PhD

Approx. number of students in program

- 45 (majority are part time)

Approx. number of students in each degree program

- 40% MS/60% PhD

Approx. number of students who apply to/are accepted by program annually

- 25 apply/10 accepted

Admissions requirements

- Undergraduate GPA (2.80 or 3.00 last 2 years) and MAT or GRE for master's program (GRE for doctoral) required, but specific score not required for standardized tests
- Portfolio approach emphasized, wherein totality of student's academic, work, life, exercise/sport experiences are considered
- Telephone or personal interview required
- TOEFL required for students whose undergraduate degree was from an institution where the language of instruction was not English

The program has available for qualified students

- Fellowships (university-wide competition)
- Graduate assistantships
- Research assistantships

Assistantships:

0%	Fellowships
0%	Research assistantships
24%	Teaching assistantships (includes tuition waivers)
0%	Tuition waivers
4%	Other forms of financial aid

Internship possibility

- Yes

Internship required for degree completion

- Yes, for the doctoral degree; optional for the master's degree (please see note in comments below on Clinical Internship/Practicum option)

Number of hours required for internship

- At least 3 credit hours; usually 6 credit hours

Description of typical internship experience

- Quite varied and typically developed by the student—can include work with individuals or teams, ranging from youth to Olympic-level competitors, in exercise/wellness and sport psychology settings.

Comments

Each student develops as personal a program of study as is possible. There are some specific course requirements (especially at the doctoral level, where a core set of courses is required). The internship is "required" for each student's program of study at the doctoral level, and often is taken by students at the master's level as well. The master's program has four options: thesis, project, clinical internship/practicum, and comprehensive examinations. The clinical internship/practicum option is a 300 hour supervised internship experience designed to provide the student with a quality applied experience in exercise and sport psychology. Each student assists in selecting/obtaining an internship site. Students have worked, for example, at the Velodrome in Allentown, PA; with two gymnastics schools in PA and NJ; at a local tennis center; with national-level triathletes and swimmers; and with varsity teams at area colleges and Temple's fencing, field hockey, football, lacrosse, basketball, softball, volleyball, and tennis teams. There is also a research/discussion group—the Exercise and Sport Psychology (ESP) Division. The group has put on programs to advance public information about sport psychology (such as work at the Penn Relays). The group also critiques members' research efforts through help in preparing for upcoming conference presentations and providing a sounding board for research ideas. The Carole A. Oglesby Endowed Scholarship provides a significant level of financial support for graduate students interested in work on African-American women in sport. The graduate program attempts to offer students as much flexibility as possible in meeting their goals for graduate study. The doctoral program provides an opportunity to prepare for AAASP Certification if the student has this as one of her/his goals.

The graduate students are diverse in age, racial/cultural background and experience (athletic training, social work, counseling psychology, coaching, etc.), providing an enriching experience for students and faculty. The program has had an international flavor over the years, with students (some currently in program) from Australia, England, India, Indonesia, Israel, Greece, and several Caribbean nations. Temple University and Philadelphia provide an exciting experience for those who choose the Temple challenge!

UNIVERSITY OF
Tennessee
KNOXVILLE

Cultural Studies Program

31914 Andy Holt Avenue
University of Tennessee
Knoxville, TN 37996-2700

Program Rating

1	2	3	**4**	5	6	7
Applied Orientation			Equal Emphasis		Research Orientation	

Contact Person: . . . . Craig A. Wrisberg
Phone: 865.974.1283
Fax: 865.974.8981
Email: . . . . caw@utk.edu
Website: . . . . www.coe.utk.edu/units/cultural.html

Faculty and areas of interest

Joy De Sensi	Sociocultural aspects of gender, race, ethnicity, and multiculturalism in sport; leadership and ethics in sport management
Leslee Fisher	Gender role conflict in sport environments, sociocultural aspects of sport psychology. Moral development in youth sport
Craig Wrisberg	Performance enhancement, competition strategies, effects of augmented information on performance, sources of stress, quality of life of athletes

Degrees offered
- MS
- PhD

Approx. number of students in program
- 12–15

Approx. number of students in each degree program
- 60% MS/40% PhD

182

Approx. number of students who apply to/are accepted by program annually

- 40–50 apply/10–12 accepted (Not all accepted receive financial support, and therefore, some do not enroll.)

Admissions requirements

- MS: minimum 3.00 undergraduate GPA
- PhD: minimum 3.00 undergraduate and 3.25 graduate GPA
- Minimum 1000 GRE (sum of two highest areas)
- Both graduate degree levels require a writing sample and a specified number of recommendations from professionals.

The program has available for qualified students

- Graduate assistantships in athletics/sport psychology (doctoral students only)
- Research assistantships (only when faculty have grant money)
- Teaching assistantships

Assistantships

0%	Fellowships
0%	Research assistantships
60%	Teaching assistantships
10%	Athletics assistantships
70%	Tuition waivers (come with all assistantships)
15%	Other forms of financial aid

Internship possibility

- Yes

Internship required for degree completion

- Sometimes. The student's committee determines the specific requirements based on the student's past and present experiences and on the student's outcome objectives.

Number of hours required for internship

- 15 credit hours are possible, plus additional independent work and/or research

Description of typical internship experience

- Working with teams and/or individual athletes

Comments

Degree programs are individually tailored as much as possible to the career goals of students. Support for the program is also provided by faculty from programs in clinical and counseling psychology, and from personnel associated with the Department of Intercollegiate Athletics. While the primary emphasis is on performance enhancement, a strong interest in and commitment to research and scholarly activity are an expectation of all students. As part of a cultural studies program, faculty and students in sport psychology are also concerned about the impact of factors such as gender, race, sexual orientation, class, and power on sport participants.

Students are exposed to both quantitative and qualitative research methods and are encouraged to participate in projects using each form of analysis. The focus of faculty research in recent years has included the following topics: the relationship of life stress and recovery processes to the performance of athletes; the quality of life of intercollegiate athletes; the effect of performance reminders on subsequent sport performance; and athletes' perceptions of and preferences for different coach communication styles.

THE UNIVERSITY OF
Texas
AUSTIN

Department of Kinesiology and Health Education

Bellmont Hall 222
The University of Texas
Austin, TX 78712

Program Rating

1	2	3	4	5	**6**	7
Applied Orientation			Equal Emphasis		Research Orientation	

Contact Person: . . . . John B. Bartholomew
Phone: 512.471.4407
Fax: 512.471.0946
Email: . . . . john.bart@mail.utexas.edu

Faculty and areas of interest

John B. Bartholomew   Exercise and health psychology, stress reactivity, mood effects of aerobic and resistance exercise

Degrees Offered
- MA
- MEd
- PhD

Approx. number of students in program
6–10

Approx. number of students in each degree program
50% Master's/50% PhD

Admission requirements
- Minimum GPA of 3.00 (last 2 years)
- GRE scores of 1000

The program has available for qualified students

- Fellowships
- Research assistantships
- Teaching assistantships

Assistantships

0%   Fellowships
0%   Research assistantships
0%   Teaching assistantships

Internship possibility

- Yes, but there is no formal placement program

Internship required for degree completion

- No

Comments

The University of Texas at Austin offers an MA and an MEd in kinesiology with an area specialization in exercise and sport psychology. The PhD program is in health education with a specialization in health psychology. The program is primarily focused on research in health and exercise psychology. The student is strongly encouraged to seek out collaborative experiences both within the department (e.g., exercise physiology, health behavior, physical development and aging), and outside the department (e.g., psychology and educational psychology). As a result, students develop their own programs from psychophysiological, social-psychological, or behavior-change perspectives as best fits their research interests. There is not a major focus on applied sport psychology within the program.

Texas Christian UNIVERSITY

Department of Kinesiology

TCU Box 297730
Texas Christian University
Fort Worth, TX 76129

Program Rating

1	2	3	4	5	**6**	7

Applied Orientation   Equal Emphasis   Research Orientation

Contact Person: . . . . Gloria B. Solomon
Phone: 817.257.6866
Fax: 817.257.7702
Email: . . . . G.SOLOMON@TCU.EDU
Website: . . . . www.tcu.edu/

Faculty and areas of interest

Gloria B. Solomon   Sociomoral development, coach education, youth sport

Degree Offered

• MS

Approx. number of students in program

• 5

Admissions requirements

• Undergraduate GPA of 3.00
• GRE
• Two letters of recommendation
• Purpose/goal statement

Assistantships

0%   Fellowships
20%   Research assistantships

30%   Teaching assistantships
100% Tuition waivers
50%   Other forms of financial aid (graduate coaching assistantships)

Internship possibility

- Yes

Internship required for degree completion

- No

Number of hours required for internship

- 3 credit hours

Description of typical internship experience

- An internship might consist of serving as a consultant with campus athletic teams with supervision and specialized training. Other internship opportunities include teaching elementary physical education in a lab school focusing on sociomoral skill development.

Comments

This program offers a master's degree in kinesiology. It includes broadbased course work in kinesiology with an emphasis in sport psychology. Opportunities for internships are available for second-year master's-level students.

The program of study for each student is personalized to meet professional interests and build on academic limitations. Students coming from an exercise science background are offered more course work in psychology; students coming from a psychology background take more courses in the exercise sciences. A sport psychology lab offers opportunities to engage in ongoing research projects. The graduate students are diverse in age and background. Approximately 50% are planning to pursue doctoral-level work.

Texas Tech
UNIVERSITY

Health, Physical Education, and Recreation

PO Box 43011
Texas Tech University
Lubbock, TX 79409-3011

Program Rating

1	2	3	4	5	**6**	7

Applied Orientation   Equal Emphasis   Research Orientation

Contact Person: . . . . Lanie Dornier
Phone: 806.742.3371
Fax: 806.742.1688
Email: . . . . LANIE@TTU.EDU
Website: . . . . www.ttu.edu/~hper/

Degrees offered
- MS
- EdD (interdisciplinary through the College of Education)

Approx. number of students in program
- 10

Admissions requirements
- Must take GRE; sliding scale is applied using GRE score and last 60 hours GPA

The program has available for qualified students
- Research assistantships
- Teaching assistantships
- Other forms of financial aid

Assistantships
0%	Fellowships
10%	Research assistantships
50%	Teaching assistantships
50%	Tuition waivers
50%	Other forms of financial aid

Internship possibility

• Yes

Internship required for degree completion

• No

Number of hours required for internship

• Three-hour course requiring 120 hours of contact on site

Description of typical internship experience

• Athletes from various teams within the university routinely receive training in psychological skills. Internship possibilities are available with these athletes.

Comments

An interdisciplinary area of emphasis in applied sport psychology is available within the MS program and within the EdD program through the College of Education. It is designed on an individual basis according to the student's background and career goals. Courses in physical education, psychology, and educational and counseling psychology may typically be included in the area of emphasis.

Utah State
UNIVERSITY

Department of Health, Physical Education, and Recreation

Utah State University
Logan, UT 84322-7000

Program Rating

1	2	**3***	4	5	6	7

Applied Orientation   Equal Emphasis   Research Orientation

*Program offers opportunities to pursue an applied orientation OR a research orientation (as opposed to an equal emphasis on both).

Contact Person: . . . . Richard Gordin
Phone: 435.797.1506
Fax: 435.797.3759
Email: . . . . gordin@cc.usu.edu
Website: . . . . www.usu.edu/

Faculty and areas of interest

Richard Gordin   Intervention/performance enhancement

Degree offered

- MS

Approx. number of students in program

- 2–5

Approx. number of students who apply to/are accepted by program annually

- 2–5 apply/2 accepted

Admissions requirements

- 3.00 GPA (undergraduate)
- 43 MAT or minimum of 40th percentile on GRE
- Three strong letters of recommendation

The program has available for qualified students

- Research assistantships
- Teaching assistantships

Assistantships

0%	Fellowships
50%	Research assistantships
50%	Teaching assistantships
0%	Tuition waivers
0%	Other forms of financial aid

Internship possibility

- Yes

Internship required for degree completion

- No

Number of hours required for internship

- Depends on opportunity; however, we will attempt to amass the 400 hours required for AAASP certification.

Description of typical internship experience

- The student will usually interact with an athlete or a team in a consulting relationship under the guidance of a certified consultant or will interact with the teams while collecting data for the thesis. The area of emphasis in research is usually intervention/performance enhancement. This is an applied program.

UNIVERSITY OF
Utah

Exercise and Sport Science Department

University of Utah
Salt Lake City, UT 84112

Contact Person:	. . . .	Keith Henschen
Phone:	. . . .	801.581.7558 (department office)
Fax:	. . . .	801.585.3992
Website:	. . . .	www.utah.edu

Faculty and areas of interest

Keith Henschen	Performance enhancement
Maria Newton	
Barry Shultz	Motor learning

Degrees offered

- MS
- PhD

Approx. number of students in program

- 20

Approx. number of students in each degree program

- 50% MS/50% PhD

Approx. number of students who apply to/are accepted by program annually

- 30 apply/10 accepted

Admissions requirements

- MS: 3.00 GPA
  Two letters of reference
- PhD: 3.30 GPA
  51 on MAT or 1000 GRE
  Three letters of recommendation

The program has available for qualified students

- Fellowships
- Teaching assistantships

Internship possibility

- Yes

Internship required for degree completion

- Yes, for the PhD

Number of hours required for internship

- 10 quarter hours

Victoria
UNIVERSITY

Department of Human Movement, Recreation, and Performance

Flinders Street Campus
PO Box 14428
Melbourne Mail Centre, Melbourne
Victoria 8001, Australia

* Program offers opportunities to pursue an applied orientation OR a research orientation (as opposed to an equal emphasis on both). The MAP is an applied program and the MAS and Phd are research oriented.

Contact Person: . . . . Daryl Marchant (PhD/MAS)
. . . . Mark Andersen (MAP)
Phone: 61 3 9248 1135
. . . . 61 3 9248 1132
Fax: 61 3 9248 1124
. . . . 61 3 9248 1110
Email: . . . . daryl.marchant@vu.edu.au
. . . . mark.andersen@vu.edu.au
Website: . . . . www.vu.edu.au/

Faculty and areas of interest

Mark Andersen   Health psychology, athletic injury, supervision, counselling
Daryl Marchant   Anxiety, PST, counselling, assessment and psychometrics
Tony Morris   PST, transitions, motivation, counselling, imagery
Terry Seedsman   Development, gerontology, exercise benefits
Harriet Speed   Injury prevention, athlete career education, quantitative methods

Degrees offered

- MAP (Master of Applied Psychology) by course work
- MAS (Master of Applied Science) by research
- PhD by research

Approx. number of students in program

- 12 MAP/30 MAS/PhD

Approx. number of students in each degree program

- 28.5% MAP/71.5% MAS/PhD

Approx. number of students who apply to/are accepted by program annually

- 25 apply/12 accepted

Admissions requirements

- MAP: 4 years of APS Accredited Psychology (Australian Psychological Society—national equivalents should be accepted, e.g., APA, BPS)
- MAS: Undergraduate degree in any relevant area (MAS candidates can transfer to PhD subject to satisfactory progress—usually first study successfully completed.)
- PhD: Undergraduate degree and honours year or equivalent

The program has available for qualified students*

- Research assistantships
- Teaching assistantships
- Other forms of financial aid

Assistantships

20%	Fellowships/scholarships
0%	Research assistantships
10%	Teaching assistantships
25–40%	Tuition waivers (Approximately 25% of MAS students and 40% of PhD students receive tuition waivers.)
0%	Other forms of financial aid

Internship possibility

- Yes

Internship required for degree completion

- Yes, for MAP only; not required for MAS or PhD

Number of hours required for internship

- Approximately 1000 hours total, spread over several practica/internships

Description of typical internship experience

- Students are required to complete one general practicum not in sport psychology (these are very varied—potentially, at least), and one or *more* practica in sport psychology. The latter are also potentially varied, including work in our own clinic; work with private practitioners; work at the Australian Institute of Sport, the Victorian Institute of Sport, and other state institutions; work in sports clubs or with teams; and work in exercise settings such as rehabilitation centres and sports medicine clinics.

* Only available for PhD and MAS Research students, and are rather limited, but plans for further opportunities are in development

Comments

Master of Applied Psychology

This is a program offered in conjunction with the Department of Psychology (by Physical Education) to ensure accreditation within the new Australian system for accrediting sport psychology professional training courses. It is one of only four such programs in Australia. The program consists of a core of professional skills in psychology, taught with specialists in other areas and including assessment, ethical issues, research methods, counseling practice, and health and organizational psychology. Four specialist subjects in sport psychology cover theory, applications, practice issues, and practice organization. In addition, there is the practicum and a substantial thesis on an applied topic. The thesis topic is largely up to the student to select, provided it has an applied focus. Students are also free to negotiate their own practicum placements, but help is available if needed.

Doctoral/Master's Research Program

The only required course work for research students in Australia, at VU at least, is a research design course (exception if equivalent can be demonstrated). Students may choose or be advised to sit subjects relevant to their research/career aims if not experienced in those areas. Students work closely with a principal supervisor, backed up by the sport psych team and a range of other specialists. They select and develop their own research areas under guidance. The department has a vast network of local and national connections in all aspects of sport to offer opportunities for field experiences and research. A sport psychology research group offers opportunities to communicate research plans, results, and conclusions in a friendly atmosphere, and to hear and discuss the ideas of staff and other research students on projects and on one another's work. This also offers good practice for conference presentations. There are also area-specific research groups on such issues as imagery, career transitions, motivation, and sports injuries, where sufficient staff and student research interest is focused.

UNIVERSITY OF
Virginia

Department of Human Services—Kinesiology

201 Memorial Gymnasium
University of Virginia
Charlottesville, VA 22903

Program Rating

1	2	3	4	5	**6**	7
Applied Orientation			Equal Emphasis		Research Orientation	

Contact Person: . . . . Maureen Weiss
Phone: 804.924.7860
Fax: 804.924.1389
Email: . . . . mrw5d@virginia.edu
Website: . . . . curry.edschool.virginia.edu/curry/dept/edbs/ hlthpel/sprtpsy/

Faculty and areas of interest

Linda K. Bunker — Motor learning, youth sport, women in sport

Maureen R. Weiss — Developmental issues related to self-perceptions, motivation, modeling, moral development

Diane E. Whaley — Self-identity in middle and older adult exercisers; gender issues

Degrees offered
- MEd
- PhD

Approx. number of students in program
- 7–8 MEd/4 PhD

Approx. number of students in each degree program
- 75% MEd/25% PhD

Approx. number of students who apply to/are accepted by program annually
- 30 MEd apply/5 MEd accepted
- 20 PhD apply/1 PhD accepted

198

Admissions requirements

- Minimum 1500 on 3 GRE scores, 1000 on 2 GRE scores
- 3.00 GPA
- Two letters of recommendation
- Admissions decisions made by April 1 for fall
- Fall admissions only

The program has available for qualified students

- Fellowships
- Research assistantships
- Teaching assistantships
- Other forms of financial aid

Assistantships

PhD:

100% Fellowships
100% Research assistantships
100% Teaching assistantships
100% Tuition diferentials
100% Other forms of financial aid

MEd:

50%   Fellowships
50%   Research assistantships
50%   Teaching assistantships
0%   Tuition differentials
100% Other forms of financial aid

Internship possibility

- Yes

Internship required for degree completion

- No

Description of typical internship experience

- Public schools, community agencies, athletics

Comments

The area of sport and exercise psychology addresses the social influences and individual factors related to participation and performance. Two major categories of questions comprise the focus of this field: (a) How does participation in sport and exercise contribute to the personal development of participants? And (b) how do psychological factors influence participation and performance in sport and exercise? The first category includes topics such as self-esteem, character development, intrinsic motivation, and ability to cope with anxiety and stress. Topics under the second category include social support; motivation; self-confidence; and methods such as goal setting, arousal control, and mental imagery.

The research program will specialize in "developmental sport and exercise psychology," an area that investigates age-related patterns in social and psychological factors related to participation in physical activity across the lifespan. Central topics will include determinants of self-esteem (i.e., perceptions of competence, social factors); motivational actors related to participation and performance (i.e., contextual and individual factors); and social influences on participation and performance (i.e., parents, peers, coaches). The applied aspect of the program entails opportunities for translating theory and practice to a variety of practical settings, such as athletics, exercise and fitness management, sport management, and youth organizations.

The sport and exercise psychology program is committed to providing graduate students with the knowledge, skills, and experiences that will prepare them with the theoretical and practical background to be marketable for desired careers in athletics, health, or fitness, or for continued graduate training. Students who pursue a terminal master's degree will be prepared for positions as teachers, coaches, or professionals in fitness or athletic clubs. Students will also be well prepared to go on to PhD programs to pursue research and teaching careers in higher education. Students in the doctoral program will be excellently prepared for careers in academe through their study of the breadth and depth of the field, as well as through ample opportunities to engage in research, teaching, mentoring students, collaborating in grant writing, and professional service activities.

Virginia Commonwealth
UNIVERSITY

(handwritten: 3 45 miles / 5 hrs 41 / from 10025)

Department of Psychology
Box 2018
Virginia Commonwealth University
Richmond, VA 23284

Program Rating

1	2	3	4	**5**	6	7

Applied Orientation   Equal Emphasis   Research Orientation

Contact Person: . . . . Steven J. Danish
Phone: 804.828.4384
Fax: 804.828.0239
Email: . . . . sdanish@saturn.vcu.edu
Website: www.has.vcu.edu/psy/cans97.html

Faculty and areas of interest

Steven J. Danish   Life skills, youth sports, performance enhancement

Degree offered

- PhD

Approx. number of students in program

- 2 sport psychology (total of 150 graduate students in psychology, with 35 graduate students in counseling psychology)

Approx. number of students who apply to/are accepted by program annually

- 240 apply/8 accepted (counseling psychology program)

Admissions requirements

- There are no minimum GRE or GPA scores.
- Interested applicants are sent profiles of typical students accepted.
- Because admission is so competitive, GRE scores, GPA scores, human services and research experiences, the number of psychology courses taken, and references rank as important criteria.

201

The program has available for qualified students

- Fellowships
- Research assistantships
- Teaching assistantships
- Other forms of financial aid

Assistantships (during the first three years)

10%	Fellowships
30%	Research assistantships
60%	Teaching assistantships
0%	Tuition waivers
0%	Other forms of financial aid

Internship possibility (paid)

- Yes

Internship required for degree completion

- Yes

Number of hours required for internship

- 2000 hours required (APA-approved program)

Description of typical internship experience

- Internships in psychology are not done on campus and are a competitive process in themselves. They may have nothing to do with sport psychology. Assistantships may have opportunities associated with one of the life-skills and youth-sport programs, doing research/training.

Comments

There are no formal courses in sport psychology within the department or the counseling program. The focus of the training and research opportunities is with children and adolescents through the Life Skills Center directed by Dr. Danish. Some of the center programs use sport as a metaphor for teaching life skills; other programs use sport as a vehicle to teach life skills. Sport psychology within the program is defined very broadly: It involves the use of sport to enhance competence and to promote human development throughout the life span. Given this definition, sport psychologists are as concerned about life development as they are about athletic development. Students who pursue subspecialties in sport psychology or performance excellence have the opportunity to be supervised.

In 1995, *The Counseling Psychologist* published research by Hanish, Horan, Keen, St. Peter, Ceperich, and Beasley, that ranked VCU second in citations among counseling psychology programs nationwide and fourth in articles listed in PsychLit.

UNIVERSITY OF
Waterloo

Department of Kinesiology
University of Waterloo
Waterloo, Ontario,
Canada N2L 3Gl

Program Rating

1	2	3	**4**	5	6	7

Applied Orientation	Equal Emphasis	Research Orientation

Contact Person: . . . . L. R. Brawley
Phone: 519.885.1211 x3153
Fax: 519.746.6776
Email: . . . . lrbrawle@healthy.uwaterloo.ca
Website: . . . . www.ahs.uwaterloo.ca/kin/kinhome.html

Faculty and areas of interest

F. Allard — Cognitive factors in movement performance, expert/novice differences

L.R. Brawley — Applied social psychology, sport psychology, group cohesion, collective efficacy, self-efficacy, attitude change, health and exercise in normal and diseased populations.

K. DuCharme* — Motivation; goal setting; self-efficacy; adherence in exercise, health, and sport

W. Neil Widmeyer* — Group cohesion, group dynamics, collective efficacy, aggression in sport, team building in groups

* Adjunct faculty

Degrees offered
- MSc
- PhD

Approx. number of students currently in program
- 14 full- and part-time in psychomotor behavior/social psychology
- Five of these students are supervised by faculty listed above

Approx. number of students in each degree program
- 45% MSc/55% PhD

Approx. number of students who apply to/are accepted by program annually

- MSc: 36 apply/10 accepted
- PhD: 16 apply/7 accepted

Admissions requirements

- Minimum B+ average in undergraduate (for MS) or graduate (PhD) work
- Three letters of reference
- Copy of recent term paper (MS) or master's thesis (PhD)
- Letter explaining interest in graduate program
- GRE scores (verbal, quantitative, analytical)

The program has available for qualified students

- Research assistantships
- Teaching assistantships
- Other forms of financial aid

Assistantships

50%   Fellowships (from major granting agencies only)
100%   Research assistantships
100%   Teaching assistantships
N/A   Tuition waivers
75%   Other forms of financial aid

Note: These percentages apply only to full-time students studying social and sport psychology.

Internship possibility

- Yes, for PhD only

Internship required for degree completion

- No

Number of hours required for internship

- Dependent on internship available

Description of typical internship experience

- Specific to the PhD program developed and is appropriate to the needs of the PhD student.

Comments

Sport psychology interests can be satisfied through the area in kinesiology called psychomotor behavior. Sport psychology is offered at the MSc and PhD levels in psychomotor behavior, which divides into three areas: (a) psychological and social psychological approaches to examining motor behavior, health, exercise, and rehabilitation; (b) motor control; and (c) motor learning and skill acquisition. Applicants with sport psychology interests apply in the first area in psychomotor behavior. Students can undertake problems incorporating interventions, but these must be examined in a research framework. For example, a problem must include a treatment and control group to examine intervention effects. International authorities in psychology at Waterloo include Donald Meichenbaum (adjunct faculty in clinical psychology) and Mark Zanna (attitudes).

The kinesiology program emphasizes a range of basic and applied research problems of human movement, including topics in sport, health, exercise, ergonomics, rehabilitation, and leisure. The student whose sport psychology interests are health related will find close ties between the Department of Kinesiology and Department of Health Studies and Gerontology. Dr. Brawley is a cross-appointed professor to both departments, where the faculty of applied health science is housed.

Dr. Brawley is a past president of AAASP and serves on the editorial boards of the *Journal of Sport and Exercise Psychology* and the *Journal of Applied Sport Psychology*. He is currently the associate chair of graduate studies for the Department of Kinesiology.

All PhD graduates of the program in the last 5 years have been placed in faculty positions in universities in Canada and the U.S.A.

Wayne State
UNIVERSITY

Division of Health, Physical Education, and Recreation

Matthaei Building
Wayne State University
Detroit, MI 48202

Program Rating

1	2	3	4	5	6	**7**
Applied Orientation			Equal Emphasis			Research Orientation

Contact Person: . . . . Jeff Martin
Phone: 313.577.1381
Fax: 313.577.5999
Email . . . . 993975@wayne.edu
Website: . . . . www.hpr.wayne.edu

Faculty and areas of interest

Jeffrey J. Martin   Exercise and sport psychology, motivation, self-efficacy, disability sport

Degree offered

- MEd

Approx. number of students in program

- <10 (almost all part time)

Approx. number of students who apply to/are accepted by program annually

- This is a new program.

Admissions requirements

- Regular admisssion—3.00 GPA
- Degree in related area
- GRE
- Qualified admission—Write for details.

The program has available for qualified students (all on a competitive basis)

- Fellowships
- Research assistantships
- Teaching assistantships
- Other forms of financial aid

Assistantships

0%	Fellowships
5–10%	Research assistantships
5–10%	Teaching assistantships
5–10%	Tuition waivers (part of assistantships)
0%	Other forms of financial aid

Internship possibility

- Yes

Internship required for degree completion

- No

Number of hours required for internship

- 3 credits

Description of typical internship experience

- New program

School of Physical Education—Sport Psychology Program

268 Coliseum
Morgantown, WV 26506-6116

Program Rating

1	2	3	4	**5**	6	7
Applied Orientation			Equal Emphasis		Research Orientation	

Contact Person: . . . . Andrew Ostrow
Phone: 304.293.3295 x268
Fax: 304.293.4641
Email: . . . . aostrow2@wvu.edu
Website: . . . . www.wvu.edu/~physed/sportpsych/
spmain.htm

Faculty and areas of interest

Dana Brooks	Leadership, cohesion, African-American athlete
Edward Etzel	Counseling college student-athletes, ethical issues, sport injury
Nancy Martin:	Health/exercise psychology, self-efficacy, anxiety, sport injury
Andrew Ostrow	Sport psychological testing, older adult populations
Sam Zizzi	Performance enhancement, exercise/lifestyle interventions, assessment

Degree offered

- EdD

Approx. number of students in program

- 12–15

Approx. number of students who apply to/are accepted by program annually

- 50-60 apply/2–3 accepted

208

Admissions requirements

- 3.00 undergraduate GPA (minimum)
- 1050 GRE OR 55 MAT (minimum)
- Three letters of reference
- Interview
- Written professional goals statement
- January 15 deadlines for receipt of all credentials

The program has available for all students

- Fellowships
- Teaching assistantships
- Other forms of financial aid

Comments

The graduate program in sport psychology has positioned itself as one of the leading programs in applied sport psychology in the country. The program, while housed in the School of Physical Education, employs four full-time faculty members, two of whom are licensed psychologists with expertise in counseling athletes, performance enhancement interventions, and exercise/health psychology. These two psychologists supervise all student practicum and internship experiences. In fact, one licensed psychologist is a former Olympic gold medalist in shooting and is also the psychologist for the WVU Department of Intercollegiate Athletics. The Sport Psychology Graduate Student Club promotes close professional and personal relationships among students enrolled in the program. The graduate program in sport psychology has very close ties with the Department of Counseling, Counseling Psychology, and Rehabilitation Psychology, with faculty holding adjunct appointments between departments. There is a strong commitment to interdisciplinary graduate education. Further, graduate students pursue rewarding internal or external internships in applied sport and exercise psychology. The program prides itself on having an excellent balance between research training and opportunities for developing applied skills.

What makes the graduate program in sport psychology at West Virginia University unique? First, while there is not a master's degree program track, students can be admitted to the doctoral program with either a baccalaureate or master's degree. Second, students admitted to the doctoral program in sport psychology are also admitted concurrently to the master's degree program in counseling. Thus, graduates of the program can sit for the licensure examination to become a professional counselor. Check out our 50+ page doctoral program in sport psychology website, which provides extensive details from admission criteria (including online application) to an explanation of all requirements for completing the degree.

UNIVERSITY OF
Western Australia

Sport Psychology Laboratory

Department of Human Movement
The University of Western Australia
Nedlands, Western Australia
Australia 6907

Program Rating

1	2	3	**4**	5	6	7
Applied Orientation			Equal Emphasis		Research Orientation	

Contact Person:	J. Robert Grove
. . . .	Sandy Gordon
Phone:	(61-8) 9380-2361
. . . .	(61-8) 9380-2361
Fax:	(61-8) 9380-1039
. . . .	(61-8) 9380-1039
Email:	Bob.Grove@uwa.edu.au
. . . .	sgordon@cyllene.uwa.edu.au
Website:	www.general.uwa.edu.au/~hmweb/

Faculty and areas of interest

Robert C. Eklund	Social psychology of sport, exercise and health psychology
Sandy Gordon	Social psychology of sport, performance enhancement
J. Robert Grove	Social psychology of sport, exercise and health psychology

Degrees offered

• MSc
• PhD

Approx. number of students in program

• 15

Approx. number of students in each degree program

- 67% Master's/33% PhD

Approx. number of students who apply to/are accepted by program annually

- 12–15 apply/4–5 accepted

Admissions requirements

- Master's: background in sport science and psychology at the undergraduate level
- PhD: completion of research thesis at honours or master's level

The program has available for qualified students

- Fellowships
- Research assistantships
- The financial aid is university-wide rather than specific to the department. It is competitive and based on a ranking of all candidates being considered.

Assistantships

0%	Fellowships
20%	Research assistantships
10%	Teaching assistantships
0%	Tuition waivers
10%	Other forms of financial aid

Internship possibility

- Yes

Internship required for degree completion

- Recommended but not required for PhD
- Available and selective for MSc

Number of hours required for internship

- 1000 hours (consistent with Australian Psychological Society guidelines for approved degree programs)

Description of typical internship experience

- Course credit is available for hands-on work with sport teams and/or with individual athletes. Experiences vary but usually include working with teams and/or players for a 6–9-month period under the supervision of a faculty member. Activities undertaken include needs assessment, intervention, and evaluation of treatment effects.

Comments

The MSc includes course work in social psychology of sport, applied sport psychology, and exercise psychology. Supervised internships can be taken as electives within the MSc program.

The PhD is research based, with course work required only if the student's background is considered deficient in relevant areas. PhD candidates are expected to spend 2–4 years conducting and publishing research in a specific area within exercise and sport psychology. We recommend, but do not require, that doctoral students take part in both a teaching internship and a field internship. PhD candidates are also encouraged to pursue external grants to support their research.

Western Illinois
UNIVERSITY

Department of Physical Education

Brophy Hall
Western Illinois University
Macomb, IL 61455

Contact Person:	Laura Finch
Phone:	309.298.2350 (office)
	309.298.1981 (department)
Fax:	309.298.2981
Email:	LM-Finch@wiu.edu
Website:	www.wiu.edu/users/mipe/

Faculty and areas of interest

Laura Finch	Applied sport psychology, sport sociology, coping strategies, performance enhancement, youth sport
Letty Foutch	Coaching pedagogy
Donna Phillips	Coaching pedagogy

Degrees offered

- MS in physical education
- MS in physical education/sport management

Approx. number of students in program

- 60 full-time students in the department; about 5–6 per year in sport psychology program

Approx. number of students in each degree program

- 50% MS in PE/50% MS in PE/sport management

Approx. number of students who apply to/are accepted by program annually

- 100 apply/50 accepted in department; about 12–16 apply, 8–12 accepted in sport psychology program

Admissions requirements

- 3.00 undergraduate GPA (cumulative); lower GPAs admitted on probation
- 3.20 GPA in last 2 years
- No GRE scores required

The program has available for qualified students

- Fellowships (university based)
- Research assistantships
- Teaching assistantships
- Other forms of financial aid (university based, e.g., athletics, University Union, campus recreation)

Assistantships

0%	Fellowships
33%	Research assistantships
33%	Teaching assistantships
100%	Tuition waivers (All students with assistantships receive tuition waivers.)
33%	Other forms of financial aid

Internship possibility

- Yes

Internship required for degree completion

- Recommended for sport psychology specialization
- Recommended for coaching/teaching specialization
- Required for sport management specialization

Number of hours required for internship

- 4–6 semester hours

Description of typical internship experience

- Individual and team experiences ranging from youth to college- and master's-level athletes in competitive sport environments as well as exercise and wellness settings. The internship is designed to enrich the student's academic and career goals, so the internship experience varies depending on the student.

Comment

The program at Western Illinois is new and looking for motivated students. The public university enrolls about 12,000 students and is located in a rural community in west central Illinois. Most students begin the program in the fall, but January enrollment is possible. The goal of the graduate specialization in sport and exercise psychology is twofold: (a) to prepare future professionals in the field of sport and exercise psychology (i.e., doctoral study) and (b) to provide teachers, coaches, and sport, exercise, and fitness professionals with specialized study in sport and exercise psychology to complement their existing knowledge base and careers.

The emphasis at WIU is on flexibility so that the student's goals are met. Students design their own programs around a departmental core. Course work options in sport psychology are available, including traditional classes, seminars, and workshops, as well as independent studies and research projects. Some summer school is also available. Supporting departmental course work is available in coaching, pedagogy, sport sociology, fitness and wellness, exercise science, adapted physical education, and sport management.

The sport psychology program recognizes the contributions of both research and application to sport psychology; the flexibility of the program allows students to pursue either option after the core course work has been successfully completed. Supervised internship/practica opportunities can be arranged with faculty (AAASP-certified consultant) for additional experiences in sport psychology. Both thesis and nonthesis degree options are available. The program takes 1–2 years to complete, depending on course work choices, thesis option selected, and summer school. Strong ties exist with the psychology department; thus, possibilities for interdisciplinary work are numerous. The program is small enough to allow for one-on-one contact with faculty, yet large enough to allow students to learn from each other in a team approach as well. Students can gain practical experience through teaching opportunities, joint research projects with faculty, and supervised consulting and workshop experiences.

UNIVERSITY OF
Western
Ontario

School of Kinesiology

Faculty of Health Sciences
University of Western Ontario
London, Ontario
Canada N6A 3K7

Program Rating

1	2	3	4	5	**6**	7
Applied Orientation			Equal Emphasis		Research Orientation	

Contact Person: . . . . Craig R. Hall
Phone: 519.679.2111 x88388
Fax: 519.661.2008
Email: . . . . CHALL@JULIAN.UWO.CA
Website: . . . . www.uwo.ca/kinesiology/

Faculty and areas of interest

Albert V. Carron   Group dynamics, home advantage
Craig R. Hall   Imagery, psychological intervention

Degrees offered

- MA
- PhD

Approx. number of students in program

- 75

Approx. number of students in each degree program

- 60% MA/40% PhD

Approx. number of students who apply to/are accepted by program annually

- 100 apply/15–20 accepted

Admissions requirements

- Master's: Honors BA or equivalent in kinesiology, mid-B average
- PhD: MA/MS in kinesiology

The program has available for qualified students

- Research assistantships
- Teaching assistantships
- Other forms of financial aid

Assistantships

25%   Fellowships
20%   Research assistantships
50%   Teaching assistantships
0%   Tuition waivers
5%   Other forms of financial aid

Internship possibility

- Yes

Description of typical internship experience

- Developing psychological intervention programs for varsity athletes

UNIVERSITY OF
Western
Sydney

Department of Sport Studies

University of Western Sydney, MacArthur
P.O. Box 555
Campbelltown, NSW 2560
Australia

Contact Person:	Patsy Tremayne
Phone:	62-2-9772-6568
Fax:	62-2-9772-1017
Email:	p.tremayne@uws.edu.au
Website:	www.macarthur.uws.edu.au/

Faculty and areas of interest

John Gross	Motivations and attributions of mature age sports participants, coaching behaviors. John Gross is a national executive member of the State College of Sport Psychologists.
Jacqueline Savis	Sleep and human performance, psychological skills training, emotional intelligence and sport, chronobiology. Jacqueline Savis is a committee member of the State College of Sport Psychologists.
Patsy Tremayne	Psychophysiology, attention and arousal, performance enhancement in diverse populations. Patsy Tremayne is the chairperson of the State College of Sport Psychologists.

Degree offered

- MPsych

Approx. number of students in program

- 10 students/year maximum

Admissions requirements

- 4-year degree in psychology*

Internship required for degree completion

- Yes

Number of hours required for internship

- 100 hours placement in the field

Description of typical internship experience

- Placements can include institutes of sport, performing arts schools, and drug and alcohol rehabilitation centres.

Comments

Admissions Information: The MPsych award provides professional training of sport psychologists at a postgraduate level to meet the requirements of the NSW Psychologists Registration Board's certification to practice and the Australian Psychological Society for full membership. The MPsych is a fulltime, fee-paying course over two years, by coursework and major thesis.

The philosophy of the sport psychology specialization within the Award is to produce students who are both professional sport psychologists and researchers who will advance the profession. Skills cover areas of professional psychological practice, sport and exercise psychology, and sports sciences. A specific philosophical commitment is that these professionals will be oriented not only towards the needs of the elite and recreational athletes, but also towards people in the community who need performance enhancement skills in diverse areas such as fitness and exercise, sports injury, pain control, rehabilitation, dance, opera, music, public speaking, examination preparation, and presentations within the corporate world.

* For those students who have a three-year degree in psychology, we also offer an accredited 4th year postgraduate diploma in applied sport psychology. Graduates from this one-year course are given first preference into the MPsych (sport psychology).

Western Washington
UNIVERSITY

Physical Education, Health, and Recreation

Mail Stop 9067
Western Washington University
Bellingham, WA 98225

Program Rating

1	2	3	**4**	5	6	7
Applied Orientation			Equal Emphasis		Research Orientation	

Contact Person: . . . . Ralph A. Vernacchia
Phone: 360.650.3514
Fax: 360.650.7447
Email: . . . . anthony@cc.wwu.edu
Website: . . . . www.ac.www.edu/~pehr/gradbroc.html

Faculty and areas of interest

Ralph A. Vernacchia — Psychology of coaching, mental skills training, mental imagery/practice

Degree offered

- MS

Approx. number of students in program

- 10–15

Approx. number of students who apply/are accepted annually (every other year) by program

- 10 apply/3–5 accepted

Admissions requirements

- 3.00 GPA in last 90 quarter or 60 semester hours
- Three letters of recommendation
- GRE scores
- Undergraduate degree appropriate to individual field of study

The program has available for qualified students

- Teaching assistantships
- Other forms of financial aid

Assistantships

0%	Fellowships
5%	Research assistantships
25%	Teaching assistantships
10%	Tuition waivers
25%	Other forms of financial aid

Internship possibility

- Yes

Internship required for degree completion

- Yes

Number of hours required for internship

- 6 quarter credits under advisement

Description of typical internship experience

- Internships available with Western Washington University athletic teams, the Adult Fitness Program, and Western Washington University Athletic Training Program

Comments

Program emphasis is on the educational, behavioral, and applied orientations of psychology to sport/athletic/exercise settings.

UNIVERSITY OF
Wisconsin
MILWAUKEE

Department of Human Kinetics

Enderis Hall, PO Box 413
University of Wisconsin, Milwaukee
Milwaukee, WI 53201

Program Rating

1	2	3	4	**5**	6	7
Applied Orientation			Equal Emphasis		Research Orientation	

Contact Person: . . . . Barbara B. Meyer
Phone: 414.229.4591
Fax: 414.906.3942
Email: . . . . bbmeyer@uwm.edu
Website: . . . . www.uwm.edu/SAHP/gp/hk/ghkmenu.htm

Faculty and Areas of Interest

Margaret C. Duncan	Media representations of female athletes and women's sport, women's body culture, narrative sociology, qualitative methodology
Cynthia A. Hasbrook	Sociology of physical activity
Barbara B. Meyer	Adventure education (ropes and challenge courses), performance enhancement, social psychology

Degree offered

- MS

Approx. number of students in program

- 25

Admissions requirements

- Undergraduate GPA of 2.75 or better
- GRE total score (verbal + quantitative) = 1000

The program has available for qualified students

- Research assistantships (dependent upon extramural funding)
- Teaching assistantships
- Other forms of financial aid (including fellowships and nonresident tuition remission)

Assistantships

5%   Fellowships

15%   Research assistantships

25%   Teaching assistantships

0%   Tuition waivers

0%   Other forms of financial aid

Approximately 40% of students are employed full time in related fields and, therefore, do not seek financial aid of any sort.

Internship possibility

- Yes, interdisciplinary internships may be arranged in conjunction with other campus disciplines, such as psychology or counseling psychology.

Internship required for degree completion

- No

Description of typical internship experience

- Dependent upon student interest and faculty availability.

Comments

The Department of Human Kinetics at the University of Wisconsin, Milwaukee, offers a master of science degree program emphasizing applied research in the human movement sciences. The program provides instruction and research opportunities for students interested in studying the biopsychosocial aspects of human movement. The thrust of the curriculum is the integration of the body of knowledge fundamental to the science of human movement through study in at least three of the five subdisciplines represented by the faculty in the program (psychological aspects of physical activity, sociological aspects of physical activity, motor control, exercise physiology, and biomechanics). The integrative nature of the human kinetics degree provides an excellent background for continued education in the movement sciences. The psychology-of-physical-activity emphasis at the University of Wisconsin-Milwaukee utilizes a broad-based perspective to focus on psychological issues related to physical activity in general, including but not limited to organized sport, athletic training, fitness and wellness, physical therapy, and cardiac rehabilitation. Students are encouraged to participate in ongoing research and consulting projects, and they are guided to pursue their own interests in these areas.

York
UNIVERSITY

Graduate Programme in Exercise and Health Science

York University
344 Bethune College
4700 Keele Street
North York, Ontario
Canada M3J 1P3

Program Rating

1	2	3	4	5	6	**7**
Applied Orientation			Equal Emphasis			Research Orientation

Contact Person: . . . . Barry Fowler
(director, graduate programme)
Phone: 416.736.5728
Fax: 416.736.5892
Email: . . . . EAHS@YORKU.CA
Website: . . . . www.yorku.ca/academics/bfowler/

Faculty and Areas of Interest

Health Psychology

B. Cheung	Mechanism of spatial disorientation
M. Cowles	Individual differences, psychophysiology
C. Davis	Personality, health, and exercise psychology
L. Fillion	Stress, health behaviours, psychoneuroimmunology
B. Fowler	Stressors and performance, electrophysiological indices of stress and performance
K. Helmers	Personality, stress, and cardiovascular disease
S. H. Kennedy*	Psychobiology of mood, anxiety, and wellness

Exercise Physiology

F. Buick*	Aerospace physiology
E. Cafarelli	Neuromuscular physiology/muscle sensory processes
N. Gledhill	Cardiovascular/respiratory physiology and fitness
L. S. Goodman*	Cardiovascular physiology
D. Hood	Biochemistry and molecular biology of skeletal muscle adaptations and cardiac hypertrophy

J. C. McDermott	Regulation of muscle gene expression/skeletal muscle regeneration
T. M. McLellan*	Heat strain of protective clothing: influence of heat acclimation, hydration, and fitness
M. P. Olmsted*	Eating disorders

* Adjunct faculty

** Although there is presently no applied sport psychologist in the programme, we are in the process of hiring one.

Degrees offered

- MS in exercise physiology
- MA in health psychology

Approx. number of students in program

- 24

Approx. number of students in each degree program

- 50% MS/50% MA

Approx. number of students who apply to/are accepted by program annually

- 43 apply/12 accepted

The program has available for qualified students

- Research assistantships
- Teaching assistantships
- Other forms of financial Aid

  All students accepted into the program are funded to a minimum level of $10,000 per year for 2 years

Assistantships

0%	Fellowships
100%	Research assistantships
100%	Teaching assistantships
0%	Tuition waivers
10%	Other forms of financial aid

Internship possibility

- Yes

Internship required for degree completion

- No

Number of hours required for internship
- Two courses (see below)

Description of typical internship experience
- There are two practicum courses involving laboratory work under the students' supervisors (10 hours per week, minimum).

Comments

The programme takes 2 years and is experimentally oriented. The standard for the thesis is that it should be of publishable quality in a refereed journal.

Guide to Appendices

There are 18 appendices in this directory. The appendices are designed to facilitate your use of the information in the directory, as well as to provide other resources for you to use to your advantage in learning more about applied sport psychology and in considering the various programs. A brief description of each appendix follows.

Appendix A: Additions, Deletions, and Changes to Directory Entries indicates the programs that have been added to this sixth edition of the directory, those that have been deleted from the fifth edition, and changes in program entries (i.e., movement from one department to another). These lists may be particularly useful for those familiar with earlier editions of the directory.

Appendix B: Other Programs provides information on searching for other programs relevant to applied sport psychology, in addition to (or instead of) those available in this directory.

Appendix C: A Word About Internships provides information about internships. Many students are interested in finding internships or learning more about them.

Appendix D: Doctoral Programs in Clinical/Counseling Psychology provides information about doctoral programs in clinical/counseling psychology that are not listed in this directory but may still be of interest to students with a passion for applied sport psychology.

Appendix E: Graduate Training and Career Possibilities provides a copy of the graduate training and career possibilities brochure published jointly by Division 47 (Exercise and Sport Psychology) of the APA (American Psychological Association), the AAASP (Association for the Advancement of Applied Sport Psychology), and the NASPSPA (North American Society for the Psychology of Sport and Physical Activity). This brochure is very valuable background reading for students interested in applied sport psychology.

Appendix F: Ethical Principles and Standards of the Association for the Advancement of Applied Sport Psychology provides a copy of the ethical principles and standards of the AAASP.

Appendix G: Texts in Applied Sport Psychology provides a list of texts in applied sport psychology that readers may wish to consider for valuable background reading in the field.

Appendix H: References in Applied Sport Psychology: Professional & Ethical Issues provides a list of references in applied sport psychology, focusing on professional and ethical issues; readers may wish to consider the list for valuable background reading in the field.

Appendix I: Reading List in Applied Sport Psychology: Psychological Skills Training provides a list of books in applied sport psychology, focusing particularly on psychological skills training; readers may wish to consider for valuable background reading in the field.

Appendix J: Reference List of Mental Training/Sport Psychology Videos provides a list of mental training/sport psychology videos that readers may wish to consider for valuable background information in the field or for current use.

Appendix K: Geographical List of Graduate Programs provides a geographical list, by country, of programs in the directory.

Appendix L: Contact Persons provides a list of contact persons, alphabetically, for programs in the directory.

Appendix M: Telephone Number List of Contact Persons provides a list of telephone numbers for contact persons, numerically by area code within each country, for programs in the directory.

Appendix N: Email List for Contact Persons provides a list of email addresses for contact persons, alphabetically by program and by individual, for programs in the directory.

Appendix O: Surfing the Net: Using the Internet for Success provides information on using the internet in your work in exercise and sport psychology.

Appendix P: Websites for Programs provides a list of websites for the programs included in the directory.

Appendix Q: Location of Graduate Programs: Physical Education and Psychology, Master's and Doctoral Levels provides information on whether programs listed in the directory are in physical education, kinesiology, exercise and sport sciences, or psychology, and whether they offer master's and/or doctoral programs.

Appendix R: Quick Chart of Program Information: Degrees Offered, Program-Emphasis Rating, and Internship Possibility provides an alphabetical list of programs with the information indicated by the title.

Appendix A
Additions, Deletions, and Changes to Directory Entries

Twelve programs have been deleted from those listed in the fifth edition of the directory, primarily due to programmatic changes, faculty transferring to other universities, and faculty retiring. Deletions with (school) indicate a request from the school to be removed. Deletions with (editor) indicate removal by editorial decision (generally due to no response from school and knowledge of faculty and/or programmatic changes). Six programs have been added to this sixth edition of the directory. Other programs have changed the department or university name. The specific changes are as follows.

Deleted: Auburn University (editor)

Brooklyn College, City University of New York (school)

University of California, Berkeley (editor)

University of Colorado (editor)

University of North Carolina, Chapel Hill (school)

San Francisco State University (editor)

Texas Christian University (school)

Virginia Polytechnic Institute and State University (school)

University of Washington (school)

University of Wollongong (editor)

University of Wyoming (editor)

Xavier University (school)

Added: Arizona School of Professional Psychology

California State University, Fresno

University of Edinburgh

Leeds Metropolitan University

Nanyang Technological University

University of Western Sydney

Changes: Boise State University (from Department of Health, Physical Education, and Recreation to Department of Kinesiology)

Iowa State University (from Department of Physical Education and Leisure Studies to Department of Health and Human Performance)

Michigan State University (from Department of Physical Education and Exercise Science to Department of Kinesiology)

The University of New Mexico (from Department of Health, Physical Education, and Recreation to Department of Physical Performance and Development)

University of North Dakota (from Department of Health, Physical Education and Recreation to Department of Physical Education and Exercise Science)

The University of Queensland (from Departments of Human Movement Studies and Psychology to Schools of Human Movement Studies and Psychology)

San Diego University for Integrative Studies (from The University for Humanistic Studies)

Southern Illinois University, Edwardsville (from Department of Health, Recreation, and Physical Education to Department of Kinesiology and Health Education)

Temple University (from Department of Physical Education to Department of Kinesiology)

University of Tennessee, Knoxville (from Cultural Studies Unit to Cultural Studies Program)

Texas Christian University (from Department of Kinesiology and Physical Education to Department of Kinesiology)

Victoria University (from Victoria University of Technology)

University of Virginia (from Department of Human Services—Health and Physical Education to Department of Human Services—Kinesiology)

Appendix B
Other Programs

A number of universities and other sites have selected courses, certificate programs, interest groups, or other links with applied sport psychology. Readers are encouraged to check with area colleges and universities for courses, workshops, etc., that may be available, even if a "program" per se is not offered. One example is the following:

University of California, Irvine
Extension/Health Services
PO Box 6050
Irvine, CA 92616-6050

Contact person:	Mickie Shapiro
Phone:	714.751.1792
Fax:	714.725.2090
Email:	ironmickie@aol.com

A certificate program in fitness instruction upon completion of 18 units is available for nurses and health fitness specialists. The program includes courses on exercise physiology, exercise psychology, nutrition, anatomy, athletic injuries, and teaching of fitness programs. The 10-week, 30-hour quarter course taught by Mickie Shapiro, "The Psychology of Exercise," includes the following areas: adherence, personality, and choice of fitness activity; gender/cultural/aging/youth sport issues; addiction, motivation; psychological implications of injury/decrease in performance; anxiety/competition; healthy lifestyle; cognitive therapy; and procrastination/burnout. The course is a general overview, introducing students to the research and clinical issues of sport psychology.

Late-Breaking Programs

The Optimal Performance Institute (MA, PhD)
The Optimal Performance Institute
520 S. Murphy Ave., Suite #256
Sunnyvale, CA 94086

Contact Person:	Mitchell Flaum
Phone:	212.352.9532
Fax:	212.352.9516
Website:	www.chelseapiers.com

Note: This is a new program that is by correspondence.

Appendix C
A Word About Internships

Michael L. Sachs and Lois A. Butcher, Temple University
Shelley A. Wiechman, University of Washington

Supervised field experiences are an important component of sport psychology training. A number of institutions in this directory list internships as part of their sport psychology programs. It is imperative that you regard these internship opportunities as vehicles toward practical application of course work and as part of the process for qualification as a certified consultant. Please remember, though, the differences (qualitative and quantitative) between practicum experiences and internships noted in the introduction to this directory and be sure you are informed about what is required of you and what experiences you may gain.

There are some cautions for the prospective student, and once again, as a consumer of the goods and services provided by the institution of your choice, you must make sure you get what you have bargained for. The expectations of a master's student may be quite different from those of a doctoral student or a postdoctoral individual who needs supervised hours to become a certified consultant. Commitment of time is critical! You need to decide if you are able to work independently and if you have enough financial support to get through the entire endeavor. Flexibility is essential. Your ideas about interning may not match the reality of the opportunities offered. For example, if you desire to work with elite athletes only, or to deal with one specific, high-level team, you may not get what you want. It is important to be open to experiences at clubs, schools, YMCAs, etc.

Be aware that if an institution states that it provides internships for its graduate students, only a small number of students in the program may be able to get them. Supervision is another issue. It may be nonexistent, minimal, or not what you expect. Check Appendix H for a list of references that include some issues regarding supervision.

Some programs have internships already identified for students and simply place students in those "slots." Other programs provide networking opportunities and encourage students to find internships on their own. This has a real-world advantage in that it requires students to make connections, develop relationships, and secure their own opportunities, as many will be required to do after completing their degree work. Clearly, you need to ask questions of faculty and current students, investigate options, and gather additional information to assist you in choosing a school and in avoiding potential problems and disappointments in your program.

Many of the institutions in this directory list internship opportunities for their students. There are many internship opportunities that are not listed within the program information. The United States Olympic Committee internship opportunity is one of these. The Sport Science and Technology Division of the United States Olympic Committee, which includes a sport psychology department, has one clinical research assistant position open every year. The position is open to students with a master's degree and is 2 calendar years in length. It includes consultation with athletes as well as opportunities to present educational sport psychology information to athletes and coaches and the chance to participate in applied sport psychology research projects. For further information contact Dr. Sean McCann, Mental Training and Counseling Program, United States Olympic Committee, 1 Olympic Plaza, Colorado Springs, CO 80909.

Internships in exercise and sport psychology, as well as APA-approved predoctoral internships, may not be clearly identified within the program listings; a listing of those known to the authors as of July 1, 1997, follows. Complete information on one such internship (Washington State University) is provided as well. Another internship opportunity that is not connected with any program listed in this directory is offered by the Lewis-Gale Clinic in Roanoke, VA; information concerning that program follows at the end of this appendix.

It is important to remember, though, the individual nature of each internship experience and of the facilities provided by or connected to each school. It is critical that, as a prospective student, you dig for information, especially if your interests and goals require some practical background experiences. Whether you are in an applied or research area, you must know certain things about what to expect regarding to your time, energy, and resources, and how to best utilize them. A few questions may help you with your search for a fulfilling internship experience:

1. Is the internship a requirement for degree completion?

2. If your interests are research oriented, will you gain practical lab/research experience?

3. If you are a hands-on, applied person, will the internship allow you be able to work with the populations that interest you (e.g., young children, individuals with eating disorders), or will it require you to work only with the teams/athletes at your school?

4. Are internships made available to you through your department or advisor? If so, how many are available for someone with your particular interest or focus? (It helps to know if you must compete for the spot.)

5. Is it up to you to create your own internship or to seek out an experience? Are contact lists provided to aid you in your search?

6. Will you be able to work independently, or would you have to work in tandem with your supervisor and/or another (perhaps more advanced) student-intern as an assistant?

7. If you do work independently, how much supervision will you have? Is supervision available or required for the internship? Who will be your supervisor?

8. Will you receive course credit for your internship work?

9. Are paid internship possible, or is the internship volunteer based? If it is a volunteer position, will you have the financial resources to support yourself during the internship period?

10. How much time are you willing and able to commit to your internship? Don't forget all the details that go into the work of a sport psychologist: Notes must be recorded; records must be kept; meetings with coaches, athletes, and your supervisor need to be arranged; etc. Keeping this information is also important if you decide to apply for certified consultant status (certification currently requires 400 hours of supervised experience; keep good records!).

To gain especially valuable information on internships, talk to students who have done them. They can tell you what to expect in terms of time and effort, the effects on your personal life, and the impact on your other school- and course-work, as well as what the supervisors are like, etc. The student representatives for Division 47 (Exercise and Sport Psychology) of the American Psychological Association and for the AAASP

(Association for the Advancement of Applied Sport Psychology) are also good sources of information.

Remember, internships are a critical means of honing your skills in sport psychology. An internship experience with appropriate supervision will give you important feedback that will allow you to refine your good points, improve your weak areas, and form a solid base for future reference with clients after you've left the cocoon of school and entered the real world.

Sport Psychology Internships

Exercise and Sport Sciences

Many programs provide applied experiences for their own graduate students. These programs are listed in the directory. The following programs provide internships for students separate from their graduate programs:

United States Olympic Committee—two-year clinical research assistantship, 719.578.4810

The Pennsylvania State University—Department of Intercollegiate Athletics (contact Dr. David Yukelson—see PSU entry)

APA-Approved Predoctoral Internships

The following are APA-approved internships through university counseling centers. They either offer a rotation through the athletic department or are willing to work with the intern in providing experiences with athletes. We recommend that you call the internship director at each site for more details. The telephone numbers listed for the contact person at each internship site were correct as of July 1, 1997. (Ask for the contact person for the internship; we have not provided a given person's name, because that may change from year to year.)

Arizona State University, 602.965.6147

UCLA, 310.794.7950

University of Delaware, 302.831.8107

George Washington University, 202.994.6550

Indiana University, 812.855.5711

Iowa State University, 515.294.5056

Lewis-Gale Clinic (Salem, VA—not a counseling center), 703.982.2463, x2930

Kansas State University, 913.532.6927

University of Memphis, 901.678.2067

University of Missouri, Columbia, 314.882.6601

University of Nebraska, Lincoln, 402.472.6208

University of New Hampshire, 603.862.2090

Notre Dame University, 219.631.7336

Ohio State University (also offers a postdoctoral fellowship), 614.293.2440

University of Oregon, 503.346.3227

The Pennsylvania State University, 814.863.0395

University of Tennessee, 615.974.2196

Virginia Commonwealth University, 804.828.3964

Virginia Polytechnic Institute and State University

Virginia Tech (not yet APA approved) 540.231.6557

Washington State University, 509.335.3792

West Virginia University, 304.293.4431

Psychological Medicine Department
Lewis-Gale Clinic
4910 Valley View Boulevard
Roanoke, VA 24012

Contact Person:	John Heil
Phone:	703.265.1605
. . . .	703.772.3485
Fax:	703.366.7353

Faculty

Lola Byrd, PhD

John Heil, DA

Rob Lanahan, PsyD

Samuel Rogers, PhD

Bruce Sellars, PsyD

Comments

Lewis-Gale clinic provides elective training rotations as part of a Veteran's Administration Medical Center, APA-approved, predoctoral psychology internship. The clinic is a multispecialty physician-group practice with approximately 130 physicians representing a wide range of medical specialties. The Psychological Medicine Department has 16 staff members. The department offers a broad range of assessment and treatment approaches to a variety of inpatient and outpatient populations. All interns can elect to serve up to 8 hours per week at the Lewis-Gale Clinic for the training year. Different training experiences are available according to the intern's interests. Supervision for the sport psychology experience is provided by Dr. John Heil.

Sport Psychology. The sport psychology rotation has two distinct foci: enhancing performance and psychological well-being in athletes (and others who perform in highly demanding environments); and the use of sport, exercise, and performance enhancement techniques in the treatment of medical problems.

Training in the use of sport, exercise, and performance-enhancement methods with general medical populations is centered in the Lewis-Gale Hospital Pain Center.

Applications include consultation with rehabilitation staff in the design and monitoring of aerobic and therapeutic exercise programs focusing on goal setting, pacing, motivation, and compliance; resumption of lost recreational activities; use of performance-anxiety treatment protocols; and use of activity-based muscular biofeedback.

Work with athletes and other performers may include participation in educational programs for coaches and parents; consultation with sports teams, sport organizations, and health professionals; and individual consultation and therapy with athletes. Direct work with athletes is contingent on prior training and sport experience. Interns undergo personal mental training for application in performance settings (e.g., sport, music, public speaking).

Washington State University
Department of Intercollegiate Athletics
Washington State University
Pullman, WA 99164-1610

Contact Person:	Mark Summerson (sport psychology and performance-enhancement services)
Phone:	509.335.0267
Fax:	509.335.0328
Email:	mtsummer@wsu.edu

Predoctoral Psychology Internship (July 1–June 30)

- Fully approved American Psychological Association Internship Center
- Rotation in sport psychology
- 3–5 hours/week—Athletics; approximately 35 hours/week—Counseling Center
- Stipend and benefits provided by WSU Counseling Center
- intern position, one-year internship

Application timeframe/requirements

- Application deadline: typically the first week in December
- Counseling/clinical PhD and PsyD candidates only
- Applications submitted to WSU Counseling and Testing Services
- Application procedures pursuant to internship and postdoctoral programs in professional psychology (Association of Psychology Postdoctoral and Internship Centers)

Predoctoral/master's sport psychology/consultant internship

- 9-month practicum/internship (August–May)
- 15–18 hours/week
- Small stipend available (sport psychology funding)

Appendix D

Doctoral Programs in Clinical and Counseling Psychology

Now that you have examined the offerings of the 103 graduate programs in applied sport psychology that are listed in this directory, you may be feeling a bit overwhelmed. The programs outlined in the directory display a range of interests, applications, and orientations that demonstrate the breadth of the field of applied sport psychology. An additional aspect of your graduate program search to consider is programs in clinical and counseling psychology. While only a few of these programs offer a specialization in sport psychology per se, others offer specialties that relate directly to athletes and exercise/sport/physical activity.

Decisions regarding graduate programs require one vitally important consideration: What do you want at the end of it all? Do you want to work with people? Are your skills strongest in research? Do you enjoy working from a particular theoretical perspective? Will your talents be put to the best possible use through the program you have chosen? Often, the best possible match of a program to a person's goals and talents may be in a clinical/counseling program with sport psychology as a component, rather than as a primary focus. With this in mind, you need to think about where you want to fit in as a professional and where you will best be able to do "your thing" once you have left the cocoon of graduate school. Be sure to read "Taking the Next Step: What to Ask as You Review the Directory," by Patricia Latham Bach, found just after the introduction to this directory.

It is critical that you understand several important points about clinical/counseling programs, including how they are presented in this directory:

1. The programs listed in the specialty categories table *are not* applied sport psychology programs. They are clinical/counseling psychology programs. Please do not contact these programs for information about their sport psychology specializations; they do not have any! Rather, ask them about their clinical/counseling psychology specializations and follow up with questions about work in exercise and sport. Be sure to talk with the person(s) on the faculty interested in exercise and sport.

2. If the institution you choose offers sport psychology courses, you may be able to take them as electives within your clinical/counseling program of study. Again, be sure to talk with faculty who have an interest in sport and exercise.

3. A number of schools have both a clinical/counseling program and a doctoral program in physical education (or kinesiology, exercise and sport sciences, or a related name). In these cases you might get the best of both worlds. If the two programs have good relations, collaborative work may be more likely than at a school that does not offer both programs. It takes some effort to check out institutions with both programs, but the end result may be exactly what you want or need.

A resource that will prove to be an important tool in your decision-making process is the *Insider's Guide to Graduate Programs in Clinical and Counseling Psychology* (2000/2001 edition, published 2000) by Tracy J. Mayne, John C. Norcross, and Michael A. Sayette (The Guilford Press, 72 Spring Street, New York, New York 10012; also available in bookstores).

The *Insider's Guide* provides the prospective student with a wealth of information, from how to choose programs that might make a good match to how to work through the application and interview processes. It offers a visual means of determining the research to application orientations of each program and lists the basic entrance requirements and program prerequisites, the specialty areas of each program, and research/grant funding for those areas.

Sport psychology specialties within clinical psychology programs are indicated for the following institutions:

Illinois Institute of Technology

University of Manitoba (listed in this directory)

University of Washington

The following institutions are listed as having faculty with sport psychology research interests:

Illinois Institute of Technology

University of Manitoba

University of Missouri, Kansas City

University of North Texas

Oklahoma State University

Spalding University

University of Washington

West Virginia University

Note that three of these programs (University of Manitoba, University of North Texas, Spalding University) are listed in this directory. Additionally, two of these programs (University of Missouri, Kansas City and West Virginia University) are located at universities where programs in kinesiology/physical education/exercise and sport sciences are available and are listed in this directory.

Additional program areas listed related to sport and exercise in the directory include behavioral medicine; biofeedback/relaxation; eating disorders; gender roles/sex differences; health psychology; hypnosis; minority/crosscultural psychology; pain; and substance abuse/addictive behaviors.

Other resources that may help you decide on a program are available through the American Psychological Association (APA), which offers a helpful booklet titled *Graduate Training and Career Possibilities in Exercise and Sport Psychology* (see Appendix E). The APA also publishes the *Graduate Study in Psychology* volume, which is updated regularly. The 2000 edition (635 pages) was published earlier this year. It should be noted, however, that the *Index of Programs by Area of Study Offered* indicates only two programs under "Sports"—Arizona School of Professional Psychology and Springfield College (both of which are listed in this directory). The APA guide may be especially helpful if you are interested in programs in kinesiology/physical education/exercise and sport sciences and check whether there are clinical and/or counseling psychology programs on campus (or in close geographical proximity, such as the same city). The APA website may be found at <www.apa.org>.

Contacting Division 47 (Exercise and Sport Psychology) of APA is another good idea; the address of their website is <www.psyc.unt.edu/apadiv47>.

Appendix E

Graduate Training & Career Possibilities In Exercise & Sport Psychology

Sponsored by:

American Psychological Association
Division of Exercise and Sport
Psychology (APA Division 47)

Association for the Advancement of
Applied Sport Psychology (AAASP)

North American Society for the
Psychology of Sport and Physical
Activity (NASPSPA)

Table Of Contents

CONSIDERATIONS IN SELECTING
EXERCISE AND SPORT PSYCHOLOGY
CAREERS   1

CAREER TRACK I:
TEACHING/RESEARCH IN SPORT
SCIENCES AND WORK WITH ATHLETES
ON PERFORMANCE ENHANCEMENT   3

CAREER TRACK II:
TEACHING/RESEARCH IN PSYCHOLOGY
AND ALSO INTERESTED IN WORKING
WITH ATHLETES   5

CAREER TRACK III:
PROVIDE CLINICAL/COUNSELING
SERVICES TO VARIOUS POPULATIONS,
INCLUDING ATHLETES   6

CAREER TRACK IV:
HEALTH PROMOTION AND WORKING
WITH ATHLETES BUT NOT NECESSARILY
DIRECTLY IN SPORT PSYCHOLOGY   8

ADDITIONAL SUGGESTIONS   10

SUGGESTED REFERENCES   12

Graduate Training and Career Possibilities In Exercise and Sport Psychology

As interest has grown in exercise and sport psychology, requests from students and prospective students for information about graduate training and career possibilities have increased. This booklet addresses some of the commonly asked questions about careers and academic preparation in the field of exercise and sport psychology. The answers reflect the current state of the field, not necessarily the ideal state.

CONSIDERATIONS IN SELECTING EXERCISE AND SPORT PSYCHOLOGY CAREERS

What roles do exercise and sport psychologists perform?

Exercise and sport psychologists typically perform three primary roles: 1) teaching, 2) research, and 3) practice. Career opportunities in exercise and sport psychology may emphasize various aspects or combinations of these roles. Careful selection of a career track will guide you in determining the type of graduate training needed to qualify for career opportunities available in the field of exercise and sport psychology, hereafter referred to as sport psychology.

What sort of education do I need to become involved in sport psychology?

Sport psychology has traditionally been an interdisciplinary field and, therefore, academic training can come from departments of physical education, psychology, or counseling. Many departments of physical education have changed their emphases and now call themselves Exercise and Sport Sciences, Kinesiology, Movement Sciences, Human Performance, or some similar variation (hereafter referred to as sport sciences). The career track that you select will determine the type of academic preparation needed, and will ultimately influence the career opportunities for which you optimally qualify.

Whatever degree you choose to obtain (masters or doctorate), and whether the degree comes from a department of sport sciences or psychology, you should take supplemental course work from the allied discipline not represented by your home department. For instance, both the U. S. Olympic Committee (USOC) Sport Psychology Registry and the Association for the Advancement of Applied Sport Psychology (AAASP) "Certification Criteria" recommend that psychology majors take sport psychology classes and supplemental course work in sport sciences (e.g., biomechanics, exercise physiology, motor development/learning/ control, and sport sociology). Likewise, sport sciences graduate students specializing in sport psychology should take undergraduate and graduate courses in departments of psychology or counseling psychology (e.g., abnormal psychology, principles of counseling, psychopathology, personality, and social psychology). Further information about the specific coursework requirements for becoming an AAASP certified consultant is available from AAASP.

A well-integrated graduate program would combine traditional psychology, sport sciences, and sport psychology; however, few such formal programs exist. Often students must seek courses as well as research and applied mentoring from professionals in different disciplines/departments.

How much training will I need?

Most of the professional employment opportunities in sport psychology require doctoral degrees from accredited colleges and universities. In addition, students in counseling or clinical psychology doctoral programs usually complete post-graduate internships (normally not in sport psychology) as part of their education. Even if students with a masters degree complete sport psychology internships, these graduates compete at a distinct disadvantage for the limited number of full-time positions available in sport psychology.

Because of the limited number of full-time positions, many individuals work in the sport psychology field on a part-time basis. Whether you want a part- or full-time position in the field is a salient consideration in selecting a graduate program. Depending upon the area you wish to pursue within the field (i.e., teaching, research, and/or practice), there are four possible career tracks that are discussed below. Three of the career tracks (academic sport sciences, academic psychology, clinical/ counseling sport psychology) require doctoral degrees while one rather diverse track (e.g., academic athletic counseling, health promotion, or coaching) requires at least a masters degree.

2

TRACK I

TEACHING/RESEARCH IN SPORT SCIENCES AND WORK WITH ATHLETES ON PERFORMANCE ENHANCEMENT

Educational Requirements for Track I

• Doctoral Degree in Sport Sciences with a Specialization in Sport Psychology and a Significant Proportion of Course Work in Psychology or Counseling.

Primary Employment for Track I

• Academic Position in College/University

• Researcher in Research Institute or Medical Research Laboratory

• Coaching Educator for College/University or Sport Organization

Opportunities with the above may include part-time consulting with amateur and professional athletes and teams and on *rare* occasions, full-time consulting

If you decide that you want a job that primarily involves teaching and research in sport psychology as well as the possibility of providing performance enhancement techniques to athletes (e.g., relaxation, imagery, goal setting), a doctoral degree from a graduate program in sport sciences is the safest possibility because, with very few exceptions, the academic positions (mostly tenure track) in sport psychology exist in sport sciences departments. (College or university positions are often tenure-track. A person who receives tenure is assured some job security. Job termination cannot occur without "just cause" [e.g., demonstrated incompetence, substantial neglect of assigned duties, or substantial physical or mental incapacity]).

Individuals trained in sport psychology through sport sciences departments also can provide performance enhancement skills to athletes, but training in recognizing psychopathology is crucial. When athletes experience emotional difficulties such as depression, substance abuse, or eating disorders, individuals consulting with teams/athletes should have the competence to recognize these disorders and refer athletes to licensed clinical/ counseling psychologists.

Because sport sciences departments monopolize the academic job market in sport psychology, applicants for these positions usually need formal academic course work in sport science core areas such as exercise physiology, biomechanics, motor development, motor learning/control, and sport sociology, in addition to specialized training in sport psychology.

Obtaining a job usually depends more on the applicants' research and teaching records in sport psychology than their ability to provide athletes with performance enhancement and consultation. Having a license to provide counseling or clinical services to athletes is not a prerequisite and may even be a liability if it prevents the applicant from developing competence in the research and teaching aspects of the field. Thus, if you want to stress teaching and research in a relatively secure academic environment, a doctoral degree in sport sciences is the most logical route to obtain academic or research positions that deal exclusively with exercise and sport.

On rare occasions (see the last paragraph of Track III), individuals with the preceding training may work full-time primarily consulting with athletes. We cannot emphasize strongly enough, however, how rarely these opportunities occur. When these full-time sport psychology consulting positions do occur, they normally go to individuals with extensive post-doctoral experience working with athletes.

TRACK II

TEACHING/RESEARCH IN PSYCHOLOGY AND ALSO INTERESTED IN WORKING WITH ATHLETES

Educational Requirements for Track II

- Doctoral Degree in Psychological Field with a Significant Proportion of Course Work in Exercise and Sport Science.

Primary Employment for Track II

- Academic Psychology Position in College/University
- Researcher in Research Institute or Medical Research Laboratory

Opportunities with the above may include part-time consulting with amateur and professional athletes and teams and on *rare* occasions, full-time consulting.

This is an appropriate track if your interest lies more in a career in which you teach and conduct psychological research on a variety of topics (including sport psychology) and consult with athletes. Some positions exist each year in research institutes, medical research laboratories, and college or university departments of psychology, counseling psychology, or educational psychology. Applicants usually are hired for their teaching and research competence in traditional subject matter areas of psychology (e.g., counseling psychology, group procedures, learning and motivation, psychotherapy, social psychology) rather than experience in sport psychology. Sometimes, these faculty may offer a sport psychology course, consult with athletes/athletic teams, or conduct research in this area.

To prepare for an academic or research position in psychology, you should attempt to enter a doctoral program in psychology, counseling, or educational psychology. Since these departments typically do not offer training in sport psychology, look for a psychology program that at least permits students to take graduate classes in sport psychology and courses in other relevant areas from a sport sciences department.

TRACK III

PROVIDE CLINICAL/COUNSELING SERVICES TO VARIOUS POPULATIONS, INCLUDING ATHLETES

Educational Requirements for Track III

• Doctoral Degree in an American Psychological Association (APA) Accredited Clinical/Counseling Psychology Program with a Significant Proportion of Course Work in Sport Psychology and Related Sport Sciences.

> **Primary Employment for Track III**
>
> • Private Psychology Practice
> • Clinical/Counseling Psychologist in University Counseling Center
> • University Health Education Psychologist
> • Sports Medicine Clinic Psychological Consultant
> • University Substance Abuse Specialist
> • Career Specialist
>
> Many of the above may include part-time consulting with amateur and professional athletes and teams and on *rare* occasions, full-time consulting.

If you would like a career in which you work with athletes as well as non-athletes (e.g., business people, college students, hospital patients, or the general population) there are several reasons for pursuing a doctoral degree in an APA accredited clinical or counseling psychology program.

First, various career opportunities working with clinical problems *require* a doctoral degree in clinical or counseling psychology from an APA accredited program that includes a 1-year APA approved internship. There are laws that govern the practice of psychology such that, in most states, these positions typically require applicants to have a state license or certificate to practice (see AAASP certified consultant criteria for guidance regarding recommended training for working with athletes). People receiving traditional graduate training from sport sciences departments that are not APA accredited will rarely qualify for these positions. Thus, if you want to provide psychological services for people in general (of whom a percentage may be athletes), this track has the distinct advantage of providing the greatest variety of career opportunities as well as the best chance for you to obtain employment upon completion of a doctoral degree and internship.

Second, very few sport psychologists earn most of their income working full-time with competitive athletes. Those professionals who consult with athletes on a part-time basis usually have other employment, such as academic positions, or more traditional clinical or counseling practices in which they earn most of their income. Over the past 3-5 years, only one or two *full-time* positions occurred each year for people to work with collegiate, Olympic, or professional athletes, or athletes attending private sport academies.

Typically, these positions are filled by people with extensive post-doctoral experience working with athletes. Not only are these positions few in number with no dramatic increase in sight, but they generally offer less job security than other positions. At present, staking your hopes on full-time work with elite athletes appears a risky venture.

TRACK IV

HEALTH PROMOTION AND WORKING WITH ATHLETES BUT NOT NECESSARILY DIRECTLY IN SPORT PSYCHOLOGY

Educational Requirements for Track IV

• Masters Degree in Clinical/Counseling Psychology Program with a Significant Proportion of Course Work in Exercise and Sport Science or Masters Degree in Sport Sciences Department with a Significant Proportion of Course Work in Psychology (some colleges, universities, and health centers look for doctoral degrees)

Primary Employment for Track IV

• College or University Academic Athletic Advisor
• Health Promotion Worker
• Coach

If you would like to provide general support services to and work closely with athletes and/or exercisers, you may decide to pursue a career in academic athletic counseling or coaching. Sport psychology programs that have considerable emphasis in the area of exercise/ health psychology may provide opportunities for their graduates to seek careers in health promotion and rehabilitation.

In terms of academic athletic counseling, the vast majority of positions are at Division I colleges and universities. Academic athletic counselors often organize academic tutoring services, monitor academic progress, assist in academic scheduling, and provide other support services for college student-athletes. In larger universities, academic athletic counselors may be assigned to work with a specific team on academic, personal, or sport performance issues, and/or may provide specialized services, such as career development, new student orientation, substance abuse prevention, learning disabilities assessment, or life skills development. In selecting graduate programs that might best prepare you for an academic athletic counseling position, it is imperative to find programs that can offer you fieldwork placements working directly with college student-athletes. Specific course work in counseling, college student development, career development, and sport psychology are particularly relevant. Job opportunities in academic athletic counseling have continued to grow at a slow but steady pace over the last decade.

Health care settings may offer opportunities for people interested in working in health promotion and rehabilitation settings such as employee wellness programs, HMOs, rehabilitation programs, and sports medicine clinics. Although a recent study found that only 2.8% of sports medicine clinics currently have counselors working with injured athletes on psychological factors associated with injury and rehabilitation, it seems likely that employment opportunities in this and other health promotion areas will increase. To maximize your chances in these areas, it is imperative to find a program that permits internships in health promotion. You also may want to seek certification by the American College of Sports Medicine when appropriate to do so.

For individuals interested in coaching, a degree in sport psychology may make you an outstanding candidate for positions at the college or university level. Your degree work should be complemented by coaching experience and knowledge of NCAA guidelines. Certification by the American Coaching Effectiveness Program (ACEP) may increase your marketability if you are considering youth sport jobs.

ADDITIONAL SUGGESTIONS

How can I obtain information about graduate programs in sport psychology?

The Association for the Advancement of Applied Sport Psychology (AAASP) publishes the *Directory of Graduate Programs in Applied Sport Psychology*. The *Directory* describes each graduate program and lists a contact person. The North American Society for the Psychology of Sport and Physical Activity (NASPSPA) publishes a list of graduate programs in sport psychology in its newsletter. The American Psychological Association (APA) also publishes some information about sport psychology graduate programs in its *Graduate Study in Psychology*, but has a focus on programs in psychology departments.

Once you have an idea of what colleges or universities interest you, you can ask them to send you a description of their programs, degrees, and faculty. The types of degrees and specific requirements for a particular degree differ from school to school. Degrees may be available in counseling psychology, clinical psychology, or sport psychology. Departments of education, counseling, psychology, and sports sciences may offer M.A., M.S., M.Ed., Ph.D., Ed.D., or Psy.D. degrees. The Psy.D. is a relatively new degree which is comparable to the Ph.D., and is designed for people who are primarily interested in applied psychology practice with less emphasis on research.

What else should I ask?

Make sure the program offers the career track and degree you desire. Investigate the reputation of the faculty and program in terms of the opportunities and emphasis in sport psychology, the average time taken by students to complete the program, the funding for graduate students, and the success of graduates in obtaining the kind of sport psychology positions you desire.

Next, check to see if appropriate interdisciplinary course work exists and is an accepted part of the program of study. Opportunities for sport psychology research and graduate sport psychology internship/practica experiences also vary across programs. Give careful consideration to the research and/or clinical/practice focus of the program to ensure that the faculty conducts research on topics of interest to you and is qualified to supervise internship/practica experiences.

For the most thorough information, you should talk to both faculty and students at the programs you have selected. Consideration of the preceding factors can lead to better quality training, which ultimately should make you more competitive for part- or full-time sport psychology positions.

SUGGESTED REFERENCES

For further information on graduate training and career possibilities, and the field of sport psychology in general, the following references may be helpful:

Association for the Advancement of Applied Sport Psychology (1990). Certification criteria. *AAASP Newsletter, 5,* (Winter).

Clark, K. S. (1984). The U.S.O.C. sport psychology registry: A clarification. *Journal of Sport Psychology, 6,* 365-366.

Dishman, R. K. (1983). Identity crisis in North American sport psychology: Academics in professional issues. *Journal of Sport Psychology, 5,* 123-134.

Heyman, S. R. (1984). The development of models for sport psychology: Examining the U.S.O.C. guidelines. *Journal of Sport Psychology, 6,* 125-132.

Sachs, M. L. (1991). Reading list in applied sport psychology: Psychological skills training. *The Sport Psychologist, 5,* 88-91.

Sachs, M. L., Burke, K. L., Salitsky, P. B. (1992). *Directory of graduate programs in applied sport psychology* (3rd ed.). Boise, ID: Association for the Advancement of Applied Sport Psychology.

Taylor, J. (1991). Career direction, development, and opportunities in applied sport psychology. *The Sport Psychologist, 5,* 266-280.

Revised June 1994 by:

Judy L. Van Raalte, Ph.D. &
Jean M. Williams, Ph.D.

Appendix F

Ethical Principles and Standards of the Association for the Advancement of Applied Sport Psychology

Considering Ethics

AAASP Ethics Committee

In 1987 AAASP established an ethics committee. After considerable deliberation, this committee recommended that the association temporarily adopt the American Psychological Association's (APA) 1981 Ethics Standards for Psychologists. One reason for this recommendation was the APA tradition for maintaining high standards for practice, research, and teaching. Another reason was that this code addressed many issues that AAASP members appeared to face.

After certification passed, however, the idea of an ethics code for the AAASP membership. In 1990 the chairman of the Ethics Committee, Al Petitpas, addressed this issue with a study of AAASP members' experiences and attitudes about various ethical problems. The results of this survey revealed the advantages and disadvantages of the continued reliance on the APA Ethics code. These results were published in the *Journal of Applied Sport Psychology* in 1994.

With these results in hand, the 1993 Ethics Committee co-chairs, Andy Meyers and Dan Gould, were asked to develop a new code of ethics written specifically for the association. This charge was completed in two steps. The first was the development of a set of ethics principles, or statements of ethical aspirations that should guide members' decision making. These principles were discussed and adopted by the association at the 1994 convention. The second step was to articulate a set of specific ethics guidelines that could be use as rules for specific professional situations. After being approved by the AAASP board, these guidelines were discussed and adopted by the AAASP during the 1996 convention.

Introduction

AAASP is dedicated to the development and professionalization of the field of sport psychology. As we establish ourselves as a profession, we must attend to both the privileges and responsibilities of a profession. Privileges derive from society's agreement to accept our designation as a group of trained individuals possessing specialized knowledge and, therefore, the power implicit in this knowledge. Our responsibilities, in turn, result from the society's trust that the profession will regulate itself to do no harm, and to govern itself to ensure the dignity and welfare of individuals we serve and the public. To maintain this status, professional organizations must develop and enforce guidelines that regulate their members' professional conduct. A code of ethical principles and standards is one such set of self-regulatory guidelines. This code guides professionals to act responsibly as they employ the privileges granted by society. A profession's inability to regulate itself violates the public's trust and undermines the profession's potential to be of service to society.

Ethical codes of conduct that professions adopt are based in the values of the society. Consequently, these values include the balance between the rights and privacy of the individual and the general welfare of society. Each profession must determine its values and social function. The profession must then develop and adopt an ethics code which guides professional conduct. While no set of guidelines can anticipate all situations, a useful code should provide guidance when problems or dilemmas arise. This code should also proactively direct the actions of its members in work-related settings. If this is accomplished, the code will ensure society's trust in the profession.

The Association for the Advancement of Applied Sport Psychology's (AAASP) Ethical Principles and Standards (hereinafter referred to as the Ethics Code) is presented here and consists of this Introduction, a Preamble, six general Principles, and 25 Standards. The Intro-duction discusses the intent and organizational considerations of the Ethics Code. The Preamble and General Principles are intended to guide AAASP members toward the highest ideals of the profession. The Standards more precisely specify the boundaries of ethical conduct. Although the Preamble and the General Principles are not themselves enforceable rules, they should be considered by AAASP members in arriving at an ethical course of action. Ethical Standards are enforceable rules that mandate behavioral choices.

Membership in the AAASP commits members to adhere to the AAASP Ethics Code. AAASP members should be aware that, in many situations, additional ethical and legal codes may be applied to them by other professional organizations or public bodies. In the process of making decisions regarding their professional behavior, AAASP members must consider this Ethics Code, in addition to other ethical guidelines or legal codes. If the Ethics Code suggests a higher standard of conduct than is required by legal codes or other ethical guidelines, AAASP members should meet the higher ethical standard. If the Ethics Code standard appears to conflict with the requirements of law, then AAASP members must make known their commitment to the Ethics Code and take steps to resolve the conflict in a responsible manner. If neither law nor the Ethics Code resolves an issue, AAASP members should consider other professional materials (e.g., guidelines and standards that have been adopted or endorsed by other professional physical education, sport science, and social science organizations), the dictates of their own conscience, and consultation with others within the field when this is practical.[1]

Preamble

AAASP members may fulfill many roles based on their professional training and competence. In these roles they may work to develop a valid and reliable body of scientific knowledge based on research; they may apply that knowledge to human behavior in a variety of sport, exercise, physical activity, and health contexts. Their goals are to broaden knowledge of this behavior and, where appropriate, to apply it pragmatically to improve the condition of both the individual and society. AAASP members respect the central importance of freedom of inquiry and expression in research, teaching, and consulting. They also strive to help the public to develop informed judgments and choices concerning sport, exercise, physical activity, and health behavior. This Ethics Code provides a common set of values upon which AAASP members build their professional and scientific work.

---

1. This Ethics Code is based in large part on the American Psychological Association's Ethical Principles of Psychologists and Code of Conduct (*American Psychologist,* 1992, V.47, #12, pp. 1597–1611.). Over 50 other organizational ethics codes, including the code of the American College of Sports Medicine, were also examined and many influenced this document. We wish to thank all of these organizations.

This Code is intended to provide the general principles and specific ethical standards for managing many situations encountered by AAASP members. It has as its primary goal the welfare and protection of the individuals and groups with whom AAASP members work. It is the individual responsibility of each AAASP member to aspire to the highest possible standards of conduct. AAASP members respect and protect human and civil rights, and do not knowingly participate in or condone unfair discriminatory practices.

The development of a dynamic ethical code for an AAASP member's work-related conduct requires a personal commitment to a lifelong effort to act ethically; to encourage ethical behavior by students, supervisees, employees, and colleagues, as appropriate; and to consult with others, as needed, concerning ethical problems. Each AAASP member supplements, but does not violate, the Ethics Code's values, on the basis of guidance drawn from personal values, culture, and experience.

General Principles

Principle A: Competence

AAASP members maintain the highest standards of competence in their work. They recognize the boundaries of their professional competencies and the limitations of their expertise. They maintain knowledge related to the services they render, and they recognize the need for ongoing education AAASP members make appropriate use of scientific, professional, technical, and administrative resources. They provide only those services and use only those techniques for which they are qualified by education, training, or experience. AAASP members are cognizant of the fact that the competencies required in serving, teaching, and/or studying groups of people vary with the distinctive characteristics of those groups. In those areas in which recognized professional standards do not yet exist. AAASP members exercise careful judgment and take appropriate precautions to protect the welfare of those with whom they work.

Principle B: Integrity

AAASP members promote integrity in the science, teaching, and practice of their profession. In these activities AAASP members are honest and fair. When describing or reporting their qualifications, services, products, fees, research, or teaching, they do not make statements that are false, misleading, or deceptive. They clarify for relevant parties the roles they are performing and the obligations they adopt. They function appropriately in accordance with those roles and obligations. AAASP members avoid improper and potentially harmful dual relationships.

Principle C: Professional and Scientific Responsibility

AAASP members are responsible for safeguarding the public and AAASP from members who are deficient in ethical conduct. They uphold professional standards of conduct and accept appropriate responsibility for their behavior. AAASP members consult with, refer to, or cooperate with other professionals and institutions to the extent needed to serve the best interests of the recipients of their services. AAASP members' moral standards and conduct are personal matters to the same degree as is true for any other person, except as their conduct may compromise their professional responsibilities or reduce the public's trust in the profession and the organization. AAASP members are concerned about the ethical compliance of their colleagues' scientific and professional conduct. When appropriate, they consult with colleagues in order to prevent, avoid, or terminate unethical conduct.

Principle D: Respect for People's Rights and Dignity

AAASP members accord appropriate respect to the fundamental rights, dignity, and worth of all people. They respect the rights of individuals to privacy, confidentiality, self-determination, and autonomy, mindful that legal and other obligations may lead to inconsistency and conflict with the exercise of these rights. AAASP members are aware of cultural, individual, and role differences, including those due to age, gender, race, ethnicity, national origin, religion, sexual orientation, disability, language, and socioeconomic status. AAASP members try to eliminate the effect on their work of biases based on those factors, and they do not knowingly participate in or condone unfair discriminatory practices.

Principle E: Concern for Others' Welfare

AAASP members seek to contribute to the welfare of those with whom they interact professionally. When conflicts occur among AAASP members' obligations or concerns, they attempt to resolve those conflicts and to perform those roles in a responsible fashion that avoids or minimizes harm. AAASP members are sensitive to real and ascribed differences in power between themselves and others. They do not exploit or mislead other people during or after professional relationships.

Principle F: Social Responsibility

AAASP members are aware of their professional and scientific responsibilities to the community and the society in which they work and live. They apply and make public their knowledge in order to contribute to human welfare. When undertaking research, AAASP members strive to advance human welfare and their profession while always protecting the rights of the participants. AAASP members try to avoid misuse of their work, and they comply with the law.

General Ethical Standards

These General Standards are applicable to AAASP members across all their professional roles and in all their professional interactions and communications.

1. **Professional and Scientific Relationship**

   AAASP members provide diagnostic, therapeutic, teaching, research, educational, supervisory, or other consultative services only in the context of a defined professional or scientific relationship or role.

2. **Boundaries of Competence**

   (a) AAASP members represent diverse academic and professional backgrounds. These different training histories provide different competencies. Those trained in clinical and counseling psychology must be aware of potential limitations in their sport science competencies. AAASP members trained in the sport sciences must be aware of their limitations in clinical and counseling psychology. Individuals from different training backgrounds must deliver services, teach, and conduct research only within the boundaries of their competence.

(b) AAASP members provide services, teach, or conduct research in new areas only after taking the necessary actions to guarantee a high level of competence in those areas.

(c) AAASP members who engage in assessment, therapy, teaching, research, organ-izational consulting, or other professional activities maintain a reasonable level of awareness of current scientific and professional information in their fields of activity, and undertake ongoing efforts to maintain competence in the skills they use.

(d) AAASP members are aware of the limitations of their scientific work and do not make claims or take actions that exceed these limitations.

3. Human Differences

(a) AAASP members recognize that differences of age, gender, race, ethnicity, national origin, religion, sexual orientation, disability, language, or socioeconomic status can significantly affect their work. AAASP members working with specific populations have the responsibility to develop the necessary skills to be competent with these populations, or they make appropriate referrals.

(b) AAASP members do not engage in unfair discrimination based on age, gender, race, ethnicity, national origin, religion, sexual orientation, disability, socioeconomic status, or any basis proscribed by law.

4. Exploitation and Harassment

(a) AAASP members do not exploit persons over whom they have supervisory, evaluative, or other authority, such as students, supervisees, employees, research participants, and clients or patients.

(b) AAASP members do not engage in behavior that is harassing or demeaning to persons with whom they interact in their work.

(c) AAASP members do not solicit testimonials from current psychotherapy clients or patients or other persons who because of their particular circumstances are vulnerable to undue influence.

5. Personal Problems and Conflicts

(a) AAASP members recognize that personal problems, including addictions, and personal conflicts may interfere with their effectiveness. Accordingly, they refrain from undertaking an activity when their personal problems may harm others to whom they may owe a professional or scientific obligation.

(b) AAASP members are aware that the extreme visibility and notoriety of some of the clients and organizations that they work with may compromise their professional objectivity and competence. In such situations, it is the AAASP member's responsibility to take corrective action, including consultation with other professionals and termination and referral if necessary.

(c) In their professional roles AAASP members may obtain privileged information about clients or client organizations. AAASP members do not use this information for personal gain.

6. Avoiding Harm

AAASP members take reasonable steps to avoid harming their patients or clients, research participants, students, and others with whom they work, and to minimize harm where it is foreseeable and unavoidable.

7. Misuse of AAASP Members' Influence

Because AAASP members' scientific and professional judgments and actions may affect the lives of others, they are alert to and guard against personal, financial, social, organizational, or political factors that might lead to misuse of their influence.

8. Misuse of AAASP Members' Work

AAASP members do not participate in activities in which it appears likely that their skills or products will be misused by others. If AAASP members learn of misuse or misrepresentation of their work, they take reasonable steps to correct or minimize the misuse or misrepresentation.

9. Multiple Relationships

(a) AAASP members must always be sensitive to the potential harmful if unintended effects of social or other nonprofessional contacts on their work and on those persons with whom they deal. Such multiple relationships might impair the AAASP member's objectivity or might harm or exploit the other party.

(b) An AAASP member refrains from taking on professional or scientific obligations when preexisting relationships would create a risk of such harm.

(c) AAASP members do not engage in sexual relationships with students, supervisees, and clients over whom the AAASP member has evaluative, direct, or indirect authority, because such relationships are so likely to impair judgment or be exploitative.

(d) AAASP members avoid personal, scientific, professional, financial, or other relationships with family members of minor clients because such relationships are so likely to impair judgment or be exploitative.

(e) If an AAASP member finds that, due to unforeseen factors, a potentially harmful multiple relationship has arisen, the AAASP member attempts to resolve it with due regard for the best interests of the affected person and maximal compliance with the Ethics Code.

10. Barter (with Patients or Clients)

AAASP members refrain from accepting goods, services, or other nonmonetary remuneration from patients, clients, students, supervisees, or research subjects in return for services, because such arrangements create inherent potential for conflicts, exploitation, and distortion of the professional relationship. In certain circumstances AAASP members may receive tokens of appreciation from clients or client organizations. In these situations it is the AAASP member's responsibility to determine that the gifts are appropriate for the setting, not exploitative, and that the gifts do not serve as payment for services.

11. Consultations and Referrals

(a) AAASP members arrange for appropriate consultations and referrals based principally on the best interests of their patients or clients, with appropriate consent and subject to other relevant considerations, including applicable law and contractual obligations.

(b) AAASP members cooperate with other professionals in order to serve their patients or clients effectively and appropriately.

12. Third-Party Requests for Services

(a) When an AAASP member agrees to provide services to a person or entity at the request of a third party, the AAASP member clarifies, at the outset of the service, the nature of the relationship with each party. This clarification includes the role of the AAASP member, the probable uses of the services provided or the information obtained, and the fact that there may be limits to confidentiality.

(b) If there is a foreseeable risk of the AAASP member's being called upon to perform conflicting roles because of the involvement of a third party, the AAASP member clarifies the nature and direction of his or her responsibilities, keeps all parties appropriately informed as matters develop, and resolves the situation in accordance with the Ethics Code.

13. Delegation to and Supervision of Subordinates

(a) AAASP members delegate to their employees, supervisees, and research assistants only those responsibilities that such persons can reasonably be expected to perform competently.

(b) AAASP members provide proper training and supervision to their employees or supervisees and take reasonable steps to see that such persons perform services responsibly, competently, and ethically.

14. Documentation of Professional and Scientific Work

AAASP members appropriately document their professional and scientific work in order to facilitate provision of services later by them or by other professionals, to ensure accountability, and to meet other requirements of institutions or the law.

15. Fees and Financial Arrangements

(a) As early as is feasible in a professional or scientific relationship, the AAASP member and the patient, client, or other appropriate recipient of services reach an agreement clearly specifying the compensation and the billing arrangements.

(b) AAASP members do not exploit recipients of services or payers with respect to fees.

(c) If limitations to services can be anticipated because of limitations in financing, this is discussed with the patient, client, or other appropriate recipient of services as early as is feasible.

(d) AAASP members do not deliver services for future remuneration based on the client's future achievements nor do they accept testimonials in place of fees for services.

16. Definition of Public Statements

AAASP members are responsible for the clarity and honesty of public statements about their work made to students, clients, colleagues, or the public, by themselves or others representing them. If AAASP members learn of deceptive statements about their work made by others, AAASP members make reasonable efforts to correct such statements.

17. Informed Consent to Practice

(a) AAASP members obtain appropriate informed consent to educational and counseling procedures, using language that is reasonably understandable to participants. The content of informed consent will vary depending on circumstances. However, informed consent generally implies that the person (1) has the capacity to consent, (2) has been informed of significant information concerning the procedure, (3) has freely and without undue influence expressed consent, and (4) consent has been appropriately documented.

(b) When persons are legally incapable of giving informed consent, AAASP members obtain informed permission from a legally authorized person, if such substitute consent is permitted by law.

(c) In addition, AAASP members (1) inform those persons who are legally incapable of giving informed consent about the proposed interventions in a manner commensurate with the persons' psychological capacities, (2) seek their assent to those interventions, and (3) consider such persons' preferences and best interests.

18. Maintaining Confidentiality

(a) AAASP members have a primary obligation to uphold and take reasonable precautions to respect the confidentiality rights of those with whom they work or consult, recognizing that confidentiality may be established by law, institutional rules, and/or professional or scientific relationships.

(b) AAASP members discuss with persons and organizations with whom they work (1) the relevant limitations on confidentiality, including limitations where applicable in group, marital, and family counseling or in organizational consulting, and (2) the foreseeable uses of the information generated through their services.

(c) AAASP members do not disclose in their writings, lectures, or other public media, confidential, personally identifiable information concerning their patients, individual or organizational clients, students, research participants, or other recipients of their services that they obtained during the course of their work, unless the person or organization has consented in writing or unless there is other ethical or legal authorization for doing so.

19. Informed Consent to Research

(a) Prior to conducting research (except research involving only anonymous surveys, naturalistic observations, or similar methods where the risk of harm is minimal), AAASP members enter into an agreement with participants that clarifies the nature of the research and the responsibilities of each party.

(b) AAASP members use language that is reasonably understandable to research participants in obtaining their appropriate informed consent. Such informed consent is appropriately documented.

(c) Using language that is reasonably understandable to participants, AAASP members inform participants of the nature of the research; they inform participants that they are free to participate or to decline to participate or to withdraw from the research; they explain the foreseeable consequences of declining or withdrawing; they inform participants of significant factors that may be expected to influence their willingness to participate (such as risks, discomfort, adverse effects, or limitations on confidentiality); and they explain other aspects about which the prospective participants inquire.

(d) When AAASP members conduct research with individuals such as students or sub-ordinates, AAASP members take special care to protect the prospective participants from adverse consequences of declining or withdrawing from participation.

(e) When research participation is a course or team requirement or opportunity for extra course credit, the prospective participant is given the choice of equitable alternative activities.

(f) For persons who are legally incapable of giving informed consent, AAASP members nevertheless (1) provide an appropriate explanation, (2) where possible, obtain the participant's assent, and (3) obtain appropriate permission from a legally authorized person, if such substitute consent is permitted by law.

20. Conduct of Research

(a) AAASP members design, conduct, and report research in accordance with recognized standards of scientific competence and ethical research.

(b) AAASP members plan their research so as to minimize the possibility that results will be misleading.

(c) AAASP members take reasonable steps to implement appropriate protections for the rights and welfare of human participants, other persons affected by the research, and the welfare of animal subjects.

(d) AAASP members obtain from host institutions or organizations appropriate approval prior to conducting research, and they provide accurate information about their research proposals. They conduct the research in accordance with the approved research protocol.

(e) AAASP members do not offer excessive or inappropriate financial or other inducements to obtain research participants, particularly when it might tend to coerce participation.

21. Deception in Research

(a) AAASP members do not conduct a study involving deception unless they have determined that the use of deceptive techniques is justified by the study's prospective scientific, educational, or applied value, will not harm the participant, and that equally effective alternative procedures that do not use deception are not feasible.

(b) AAASP members never deceive research participants about significant aspects that would affect their willingness to participate, such as physical risks, discomfort, or unpleasant emotional experiences.

(c) Any other deception that is an integral feature of the design and conduct of an experiment must be explained to participants as early as is feasible, preferably at the conclusion of their participation, but no later than at the conclusion of the research. If scientific or humane values justify delaying or withholding this information, AAASP members take reasonable measures to reduce the risk of harm.

22. Minimizing Invasiveness

In conducting research, AAASP members interfere with the participants or milieu from which data are collected only in a manner that is warranted by an appropriate research design and that is consistent with AAASP members' roles as scientific investigators.

23. Honesty in Research

(a) AAASP members do not fabricate data or falsify results in their publications.

(b) If AAASP members discover errors in their published data, they take reasonable steps to correct such errors in a correction, retraction, erratum, or other appropriate publication means.

(c) AAASP members do not present substantial portions or elements of another's work or data as their own, even if the other work or data source is cited occasionally. AAASP members only accept publication and other credit for work that they have created or performed.

24. Conflicts between Ethics and Organizational Demands

If the demands of an organization with which AAASP members are affiliated conflict with the Ethics Code, members clarify the nature of the conflict, make known their commitment to the Ethics Code, and to the extent feasible, seek to resolve the conflict in a way that permits the fullest adherence to the Ethics Code.

25. Resolution of Ethical Conflicts

The successful implementation of an ethics code requires a personal commitment to act ethically, encourage ethical behavior by others, and consult with others concerning ethical problems. When applying the code of ethical conduct, AAASP members may encounter problems in identifying unethical conduct or in resolving ethical conflict. When faced with significant ethical concerns, one should consider the following courses of action.

- Before any action is taken, one may benefit from advice from uninvolved and objective advisors or peers familiar with ethical issues.

- When members believes that there may have been an ethical violation by another member, they may attempt to clarify and resolve the issue by bringing the matter to the attention of the other involved parties if such an informal resolution appears appropriate and the intervention does not violate any confidentiality rights that may be involved.

- Discuss ethical problems with your immediate supervisor except when it appears that the supervisor is involved in the ethical issue, in which case the problem should be presented to the next higher administrative level. If satisfactory resolution cannot be achieved when the problem is initially presented, the issue should be submitted to the next higher administrative level.

- Contact with levels above the immediate administrator should be initiated only with the administrator's knowledge, assuming that the administrator is not involved.

- If the ethical problem or conflict still exists after exhausting all levels of internal review, support from appropriate professional organizations should be obtained.

It is important for AAASP members to understand that unethical conduct is a serious matter. However, the primary aims of these ethical principles are to inform and motivate the highest standards of conduct among AAASP members as we serve our clients, our professions, and our community.

(Submitted by Dr. James Whelan, University of Memphis, on behalf of the AAASP Ethics Committee)

Appendix G
Texts in Applied Sport Psychology

There are numerous texts or key reference works in applied sport psychology that may interest you. Mary Beth Allen's 1994 article in *The Sport Psychologist* (vol. 8, pp. 94–99), entitled "Authorship in Sport Psychology: A Reference List," provides an excellent reference list in this area.

You may find the following books to be particularly helpful.

Anshel, M. H. (2000). *Sport psychology: From theory to practice* (4th ed.). Scottsdale, AZ: Gorsuch Scarisbrick.

Cox, R. H. (1999). *Sport psychology: Concepts and applications* (4th ed.). Dubuque, IA: Wm. C. Brown.

Gill, D. L. (1986). *Psychological dynamics of sport.* Champaign, IL: Human Kinetics. (Currently being revised)

Horn, T. S. (Ed.). (1992). *Advances in sport psychology.* Champaign, IL: Human Kinetics.

Kremer, J. M., & Scully, D. (1994). *Psychology in sport.* Bristol, PA: Taylor & Francis, Inc.

LeUnes, A. D., & Nation, J. R. (1998). *Sport psychology: An introduction* (2nd ed.) Chicago: Nelson-Hall.

Morris, T., & Summers, J. (Eds.). *Sport psychology: Theory, applications and issues.* Brisbane, Australia: John Wiley & Sons.

Murphy, S. M. (Ed.). (1995). *Sport psychology interventions.* Champaign, IL: Human Kinetics.

Pargman, D. (1998). *Understanding sport behavior.* Upper Saddle River, NJ: Prentice-Hall.

Rotella, R., Boyce, A. B., Allyson, B., & Savis, J. (1997). *Case studies in sport psychology.* Boston, MA: Jones and Bartlett Publishers.

Silva, J. M., & Weinberg, Robert S. (1984). *Psychological foundations of sport.* Champaign, IL: Human Kinetics.

Wann, D. L. (1997). Sport psychology. Upper Saddle River, NJ: Prentice Hall.

Weinberg, R. S., & Gould, D. (2000). *Foundations of sport and exercise psychology* (2 ed.). Champaign, IL: Human Kinetics.

Williams, J. M. (Ed.). (1997). *Applied sport psychology: Personal growth to peak performance* (3rd ed.). Mountain View, CA: Mayfield Publishing Company.

Texts in Exercise Psychology

Berger, B. G., & Pargman, D. (in press). *Exercise psychology.* Morgantown, WV: Fitness Information Technology, Inc.

Hays, K. F. *Working it out: Using exercise in psychotherapy.* Washington, DC: American Psychological Association Press.

Willis, Joe D., & Campbell, L. F. (1992). *Exercise psychology.* Champaign, IL: Human Kinetics.

General/Other References

Begel, D., & Burton, R. W. (Eds.). (2000). *Sport psychiatry: Theory and practice.* New York: W. W. Norton & Company.
—Current, definitive edited work in this area.

Carron, A. V., & Hausenblas, H. A. (1998). *Group dynamics in sports* (2 ed.). Morgantown, WV: Fitness Information Technology, Inc.
—Overview of work on groups in sport settings.

Duda, J. L. (Ed.). (1998). *Advances in sport and exercise psychology measurement.* Morgantown, WV: Fitness Information Technology, Inc.
—Comprehensive review of measurement issues and information on many instruments used in exercise and sport psychology.

Salmela, J. H. (1992). *The world sport psychology sourcebook.* (2nd ed.). Champaign, IL: Human Kinetics.
—Excellent publication with background information and a comprehensive Who's Who in the world of sport psychology.

Singer, R. N., Murphey, M., & Tennant, L. K. (1993). *Handbook of research on sport psychology.* New York: Macmillan Publishing Company. (Currently being revised.)
—This is the definitive reference work in sport psychology, with 44 chapters (984 pages).

Skinner, J. S., Corbin, C. B., Landers, D. M., Martin, P. E., & Wells, C. L. (Eds.). (1989). *Future directions in exercise and sport science research.* Champaign, IL: Human Kinetics.
—This volume contains numerous excellent chapters in the exercise and sport sciences in general, with sport psychology chapters written by Deborah Feltz, Daniel Landers, William Morgan, Glyn Roberts, Ronald Smith, and Richard Suinn.

Van Raalte, J. L., & Brewer, B. W. (Eds.). (1996). *Exploring sport and exercise psychology.* Washington, DC: American Psychological Association. (Currently being updated.)
—An excellent resource with 21 chapters in sections on performance enhancement, promoting well-being, clinical issues, working with specific populations, and professional issues.

Appendix H

References in Applied Sport Psychology: Professional and Ethical Issues

There are numerous references in applied sport psychology that deal with professional and ethical issues that may interest you. You can find an excellent list in Vincent Granito and Betty Wenz's 1995 article in *The Sport Psychologist* (vol. 9, pp. 96–103) entitled "Reading List for Professional Issues in Applied Sport Psychology." The following list represents an updated version of the list provided in previous editions of this directory. You may wish to review both this list and the Granito and Wenz list.

Allen, M. B. (1994). Authorship in sport psychology: A reference list. *The Sport Psychologist, 8*, 94–99.

American Psychological Association. (1987). *Casebook on ethical principles of psychologists*. Washington, DC: Author.

American Psychological Association. (1990). Ethical principles of psychologists (Amended June 2, 1989). *American Psychologist, 45*, 390–395.

Andersen, M. B. (1994). Ethical considerations in the supervision of applied sport psychology graduate students. *Journal of Applied Sport Psychology, 6*, 152–167.

Andersen, M. B., & Williams-Rice, B. T. (1996). Supervision in the education and training of sport psychology service providers. *Journal of Applied Sport Psychology, 10*, 278–290.

Andersen, M. B., Van Raalte, J. L., & Brewer, B. W. (1994). Assessing the skills of sport psychology supervisors. *The Sport Psychologist, 8*, 238–247.

Anshel, M. H. (1990). Perceptions of black intercollegiate football players: Implications for the sport psychology consultant. *The Sport Psychologist, 4*, 235–248.

Anshel, M. H. (1992). The case against the certification of sport psychologists: In search of the phantom expert. *The Sport Psychologist, 6*, 265–286.

Anshel, M. H. (1993). Against the certification of sport psychology consultants: A response to Zaichkowsky and Perna. *The Sport Psychologist, 7*, 344–353.

Barney, S. T., Andersen, M. B., & Riggs, C. A. (1996). Supervision in sport psychology: Some recommendations for practicum training. *Journal of Applied Sport Psychology, 8*, 200–217.

Brown, J. M. (1982). Are sport psychologists really psychologists? *Journal of Sport Psychology, 4*, 13–18.

Brustad, R. J., & Ritter-Taylor, M. (1997). Applying social psychological perspectives to the sport psychology consulting process. *The Sport Psychologist, 11*, 107–119.

Buceta, J. M. (1993). The sport psychologist/athletic coach dual role: Advantages, difficulties, and ethical considerations. *Journal of Applied Sport Psychology, 5*, 64–77.

Burke, K. L., & Johnson, J. J. (1992). The sport psychologist-coach dual role position: A rebuttal to Ellickson and Brown (1990). *Journal of Applied Sport Psychology, 4*, 51–55.

Butki, B. D., & Andersen, M. B. (1994). Mentoring in sport psychology: Students' perceptions of training in publications and presentation guidelines. *The Sport Psychologist, 8*, 143–148.

Carron, A. V. (1993). The Coleman Roberts Griffith address: Toward the integration of theory, research, and practice in sport psychology. *Journal of Applied Sport Psychology, 5*, 207–221.

Clarke, K. S. (1984). The USOC Sports Psychology Registry: A clarification. *Journal of Sport Psychology, 6*, 365–366.

Danish, S. J., & Hale, B. D. (1981). Toward an understanding of the practice of sport psychology. *Journal of Sport Psychology, 3*, 90–99.

Danish, S. J., & Hale, B. D. (1982). Let the discussions continue: Further considerations on the practice of sport psychology. *Journal of Sport Psychology, 4*, 10–12.

Danish, S. J., Petitpas, A. J., & Hale, B. D. (1990). Sport as a context for developing competence. In T. Gullotta, G. Adams, & R. Monteymar (Eds.), *Developing social competency in adolescence* (vol. 3, pp. 169–194). Newbury Park, CA: Sage.

Danish, S. J., Petitpas, A. J., & Hale, B. D. (in press). Life development intervention for athletes: Life skills through sports. *The Counseling Psychologist* (in special issue on sport psychology—expected date: summer 1993).

Danish, S. J., Petitpas, A. J., & Hale, B. D. (1992). A developmental-educational intervention model of sport psychology. *The Sport Psychologist, 6*, 403–415.

DeFrancesco, C., & Cronin, J. J. (1988). Marketing the sport psychologist. *The Sport Psychologist, 2*, 28–38.

Dishman, R. K. (1983). Identity crises in North American sport psychology: Academics in professional issues. *Journal of Sport Psychology, 5*, 123–134.

Ellickson, K. A., & Brown, D. R. (1990). Ethical considerations in dual relationships: The sport psychologist-coach. *Journal of Applied Sport Psychology, 2*, 186–190.

Gardner, F. L. (1991). Professionalization of sport psychology: A reply to Silva. *The Sport Psychologist, 5*, 55–60.

Gill, D. L. (1994). A feminist perspective on sport psychology practice. *The Sport Psychologist, 8*, 411–426.

Gould, D. (1990). AAASP: A vision for the 1990's. *Journal of Applied Sport Psychology, 2*, 99–116.

Gould, D., Tammen, V., Murphy, S., & May, J. (1989). An examination of U. S. Olympic sport psychology consultants and the services they provide. *The Sport Psychologist, 3*, 300–312.

Granito, Jr., V. J., & Wenz, B. J. (1995). Reading list for professional issues in applied sport psychology. *The Sport Psychologist, 9*, 96–103.

Hale, B. D., & Danish, S. J. (1999). Putting the accreditation cart before the AAASP horse: A reply to Silva, Conroy and Zizzi. *Journal of Applied Sport Psychology, 11*, 321–328.

Halliwell, W. (1989). Applied sport psychology in Canada. *Journal of Applied Sport Psychology, 1*, 35–44.

Hardy, C. J. (1994). Nurturing our future through effective mentoring: Developing roots as well as wings. AAASP 1993 Presidential Address. *Journal of Applied Sport Psychology, 6*, 196–204.

Harrison, R. P., & Feltz, D. L. (1979). The professionalization of sport psychology: Legal considerations. *Journal of Sport Psychology, 1*, 182–190.

Hays, K. F. (1995). Putting sport psychology into (your) practice. *Professional Psychology: Research and Practice, 26*, 33–40.

Heyman, S. R. (1982). A reaction to Danish and Hale: A minority report. *Journal of Sport Psychology, 4*, 7–9.

Heyman, S. R. (1984). The development of models for sport psychology: Examining the USOC guidelines. *Journal of Sport Psychology, 6*, 125–132.

Heyman, S. R. (1987). Counseling and psychotherapy with athletes: Special considerations. In J. R. May & M. J. Asken (Eds.), *Sport psychology: The psychological health of the athlete* (pp. 135–156). New York: PMA Publishing Corp.

Heyman, S. R. (1990). Ethical issues in performance enhancement approaches with amateur boxers. *The Sport Psychologist, 4*, 48–54.

Kirschenbaum, D. S., Parham, W. D., & Murphy, S. M. (1993). Provision of sport psychology services at Olympic events: The 1991 U.S. Olympic Festival and beyond. *The Sport Psychologist, 7*, 419–440.

Krane, V. (1994). A feminist perspective on contemporary sport psychology research. *The Sport Psychologist, 8*, 393–410.

Krane, V., Andersen, M. B., & Strean, W. B. (1997). Issues of qualitative research methods and presentation. *Journal of Sport & Exercise Psychology, 19*, 213–218.

Landers, D. M. (1983). Whatever happened to theory testing in sport psychology? *Journal of Sport Psychology, 5*, 135–151.

Mahoney, M. J., & Suinn, R. M. (1986). History and overview of modern sport psychology. *The Clinical Psychologist, 10*, 64–68.

McCullagh, P. (1998). What is the applied in applied sport psychology? The role of integration. *Journal of Applied Sport Psychology, 10*, S1–S10.

Murphy, S. (Ed.). (1993). *Clinical sport psychology.* Champaign: Human Kinetics.

Nideffer, R. M. (1981). *The ethics and practice of applied sport psychology.* Ithaca, NY: Mouvement Publications.

Nideffer, R. M., Dufresne, P., Nesvig, D., & Selder, D. (1980). The future of applied sport psychology. *Journal of Sport Psychology, 2*, 170–174.

Nideffer, R. M., Feltz, D., & Salmela, J. (1982). A rebuttal to Danish and Hale: A committee report. *Journal of Sport Psychology, 4*, 3–6.

Ogilvie, B. C. (1979). The sport psychologist and his professional credibility. In P. Klavora & J. V. Daniel (Eds.), *Coach, athlete, and the sport psychologist* (pp. 44–55). Toronto, Ontario, Canada: University of Toronto.

Ogilvie, B. C. (1989). Applied sport psychology: Reflections on the future. *Journal of Applied Sport Psychology, 1*, 4–7.

Petitpas, A. J., Brewer, B. W., Rivera, P. M., & Van Raalte, J. L. (1994). Ethical beliefs and behaviors in applied sport psychology: The AAASP Ethics Survey. *Journal of Applied Sport Psychology, 6,* 135–151.

Petitpas, A. J., Giges, B., & Danish, S. J. (1999). The sport psychologist-athlete relationship: Implications for training. *The Sport Psychologist, 13,* 344–357.

Petrie, T. A., & Diehl, N. S. (1995). Sport psychology in the profession of psychology. *Professional Psychology: Research and Practice, 26,* 288–291.

Petrie, T. A., & Watkins, Jr., C. E. (1994a). A survey of counseling psychology programs and exercise/sport science departments: Sport psychology issues and training. *The Sport Psychologist, 8,* 28–36.

Petrie, T. A., & Watkins, Jr., C. E. (1994b). Sport psychology training in counseling psychology programs: Is there room at the inn? *The Counseling Psychologist, 22,* 335–341.

Ravizza, K. (1988). Gaining entry with athletic personnel for season-long consulting. *The Sport Psychologist, 2,* 243–254.

Rejeski, W. J., & Brawley, L. R. (1988). Defining the boundaries of sport psychology. *The Sport Psychologist, 2,* 231–242.

Sachs, M. L. (1991). Reading list in applied sport psychology: Psychological skills training. *The Sport Psychologist, 5,* 88–91.

Sachs, M. L. (1993). Professional ethics in sport psychology. In R. N. Singer, M. Murphey, & K. Tennant, (Eds.), *Handbook on research in sport psychology.* New York: Macmillan Publishing Company.

Sachs, M. L. (1999). Comment on Petitpas, Danish, and Giges, The sport psychologist-athlete relationship: Implications for training. *The Sport Psychologist, 13,* 358–361.

Schell, B., Hunt, J., & Lloyd, C. (1984). An investigation of future market opportunities for sport psychologists. *Journal of Sport Psychology, 6,* 335–350.

Silva, J. M., III (1989). The evolution of AAASP and JASP. *Journal of Applied Sport Psychology, 1,* 1–3.

Silva, J. M., III (1989). Toward the professionalization of sport psychology. *The Sport Psychologist, 3,* 265–273.

Silva, J. M., III (1992). On advancement: An editorial. *Journal of Applied Sport Psychology, 4,* 1–9.

Silva, J. M., III (1996). 1995 Coleman Roberts Griffith address: Profiles of excellence. *Journal of Applied Sport Psychology, 8,* 119–130.

Silva, J. M., III, Conroy, D. E., & Zizzi, S. J. (1999) Critical issues confronting the advancement of applied sport psychology. *Journal of Applied Sport Psychology, 11,* 298–320.

Simons, J. P., & Andersen, M. B. (1995). The development of consulting practice in applied sport psychology: Some personal perspectives. *The Sport Psychologist, 9,* 449–468.

Singer, R. N. (1989). Applied sport psychology in the United States. *Journal of Applied Sport Psychology, 1,* 61–80.

Singer, R. N. (1992). What in the world is happening in sport psychology. *Journal of Applied Sport Psychology*, *4*, 63–76.

Smith, D. (1992). The coach as sport psychologist: An alternate view. *Journal of Applied Sport Psychology*, *4*, 56–62.

Smith, R. E. (1989). Applied sport psychology in an age of accountability. *Journal of Applied Sport Psychology*, *1*, 166–180.

Smith, Y. R. (1991). Issues and strategies for working with multicultural athletes. *Journal of Physical Education, Recreation, and Dance*, *62*(3), 39–44.

Straub, W. F., & Hinman, D. A. (1992). Profiles and professional perspectives of 10 leading sport psychologists. *The Sport Psychologist*, *6*, 297–312.

Strean, W. B., & Roberts, G. C. (1992). Future directions in applied sport psychology research. *The Sport Psychologist*, *6*, 55–65.

Taylor, J. (1991). Career direction, development, and opportunities in applied sport psychology. *The Sport Psychologist*, *5*, 266–280.

Taylor, J. (1994). Examining the boundaries of sport science and psychology trained practitioners in applied sport psychology: Title usage and area of competence. *Journal of Applied Sport Psychology*, *6*, 185–195.

Taylor, J. (1995). A conceptual model for integrating athletes' needs and sport demands in the development of competitive mental preparation strategies. *The Sport Psychologist*, *9*, 339–357.

United States Olympic Committee. (1983). United States Olympic Committee establishes guidelines for sport psychology services. *Journal of Sport Psychology*, *5*, 4–7.

Van Raalte, J. L., Brewer, D. D., Brewer, B. W., & Linder, D. E. (1993). Sport psychologists' perceptions of sport and mental health practitioners. *Journal of Applied Sport Psychology*, *5*, 222–233.

Vealey, R. S. (1988). Future directions in psychological skills training. *The Sport Psychologist*, *2*, 318–336.

Waite, B. T., & Pettit, M. E. (1993). Work experiences of graduates from doctoral programs in sport psychology. *Journal of Applied Sport Psychology*, *5*, 234–250.

Weinberg, R. S. (1989). Applied sport psychology: Issues and challenges. *Journal of Applied Sport Psychology*, *1*, 181–195.

Weiss, M. R. (1998). "Passionate collaboration": Reflections on the directions of applied sport psychology in the coming millennium. *Journal of Applied Sport Psychology*, *10*, S11–S24.

Williams, J. M. (1995). Applied sport psychology: Goals, issues, and challenges. *Journal of Applied Sport Psychology*, *7*, 81–91.

Zaichkowsky, L. D., & Perna, F. M. (1992). Certification of consultants in sport psychology: A rebuttal to Anshel. *The Sport Psychologist*, *6*, 287–296.

Zeigler, E. F. (1987). Rationale and suggested dimensions for a code of ethics for sport psychologists. *The Sport Psychologist*, *1*, 138–150.

Appendix I

Reading List in Applied Sport Psychology: Psychological Skills Training

Michael L. Sachs, Temple University
Alan S. Kornspan, University of Akron

Note: This reading list originally appeared in *The Sport Psychologist* as Sachs, M. L. (1991). Reading list in applied sport psychology: Psychological skills training, *The Sport Psychologist, 5,* 88–91.

The reading list was updated in the third, fourth, and fifth editions of the directory and has been updated further in this sixth edition to include books and reviews published since the fifth edition.

Applied sport psychologists are frequently asked how to find information about psychological skills training (PST). In an effort to answer this question, the following reading list was developed; it identifies books in applied sport psychology that focus on PST. The information may carry a different label, such as mental training, but each book focuses on a set of psychological skills that will help athletes enhance their performance. These psychological skills include relaxation, concentration, visualization, goal setting, and so on.

The list was drawn from a review of library materials, from the appendix in Vealey's (1988) excellent article on future directions in PST, and from an examination of the following journals: *The Sport Psychologist* (*TSP*): the *Journal of Applied Sport Psychology* (*JASP*); the *Journal of Sport & Exercise Psychology* (*JSEP*, formerly the *Journal of Sport Psychology*); and the *Journal of Physical Education, Recreation, and Dance* (*JOPERD*).

In some cases the books listed have been reviewed in one or more of the journals examined. These book reviews are noted, if available, following each book listing. The primary goal of this listing is not to judge the quality of the books listed, although the book reviews may help in this regard. Indeed, the books range from scientifically oriented texts designed for those with more scholarly interests to popular press paperbacks designed for the layperson. Similarly, the quality of the books ranges from comparatively poor to excellent.

The reader looking for a good place to get started in applied sport psychology, even considering the diversity of orientation in the books available, would be most likely to benefit from the following books from the list, as they are among the best available: Martens (1987), Orlick (1990), and Williams (1997). Progressing from these general volumes to more specific ones, there are many books dealing with golf, tennis, and skiing, as well as books focusing on running, basketball, bodybuilding, and other sports.

Are these books effective? Some are designed to be used in academic settings as parts of courses or workshops. Others have been written to stand alone, to presumably give readers the basics in applied sport psychology and to let them proceed from there. The number of books available (and the variety of sports covered) is increasing exponentially, with many authors seeking to get *their* psychological skills training book to press as soon as possible.

Studies are not yet available in the sport psychology literature concerning the efficacy of psychological skills training books. One meta-analysis of self-administered treatment programs found them to be effective in comparison with no treatment, and not significantly different from therapist-administered programs of psychotherapy (Scogin, Bynum, Stephens, & Calhoon, 1990). However, limitations of the work precluded the authors from indicating that self-administered treatments were as effective as programs administered by therapists.

Readers looking for a broader array of sensory stimulation modes will find many videotapes and audiotapes available in applied sport psychology. Many of these are listed, and some are reviewed, in issues of *The Sport Psychologist*.

A noteworthy development since the previous publication and update of this list has been the considerable number of workbooks and related guides made available to athletes and coaches, guides that assist them in direct work through the various areas within psychological skills training. Martens (1987) has had an excellent workbook available for coaches for quite some time, but more recently, a number of authors, particularly Dalloway (1992, 1993a, 1993b, 1993c, 1994); Miner, Shelley, & Henschen (1995); and Taylor (1993, 1994a, 1994b, 1994c, 1994d) have developed additional publications of note.

Recent developments have included books addressing psychological skills training and children, as well. Orlick in particular (1992, 1993) has published a number of books that "translate these lessons [of elite performers and use of psychological skills] into practical guidelines for quality parenting and quality living" (1992, back cover).

Vealey (1988) indicated that the Hendricks and Carlson (1982) and Kappas (1984) books were out of print and not available at a number of libraries that she searched. Readers who have trouble obtaining such volumes should enlist the aid of the librarian in requesting materials through interlibrary loan. This is often the only way of obtaining some of the older and lesser known (not to mention out-of-print) titles. As a final note, there are many excellent articles on applied sport psychology in the journals listed previously, particularly *The Sport Psychologist* and the *Journal of Applied Sport Psychology*.

Albinson, J. G., & Bull, S. J. (1988). *The mental game plan*. London, Ontario: Spodym. Book review: *TSP*, 1990, *4*, 76–77.

Alder, H., & Morris, K. (1996). *Masterstroke: Use the power of your mind to improve your golf with NLP neurolinguistic programming*. London: Piatkus.

Alexander, D. (1994). *Think to win*. Cambridge, MA: R. Bentley. (auto racing).

Allen, G. (1983). *The mental game: The inner game of bowling*. Deerfield, IL: Tech Ed Publishing Co.

American Sport Education Program. (1994). *SportParent*. Champaign, IL: Human Kinetics.

Anderson, E. (1994). *Training games: Coaching runners creatively*. Mountain View, CA: TAFNEWS Press.

Andersonn, C., & Andersonn, B. (2000). *Will you still love me if I don't win?* Dallas, TX: Taylor Publishing Co.

Backley, S., & Stafford, I. (1996). *The winning mind: A guide to achieving success and overcoming failure*. London: Aurum Press.

Barden, R. C., Jackson, B., & Ford, M. E. (1992). *Optimal performance in tennis: Mental skills for maximum achievement in athletics and life*. Plymouth, MN: Optimal Performance Systems Research. Book review: *TSP*, 1995, *9*, 112–113.

Barzdukas, A. (1995). *Gold minds: Gold medal mental strategies for everyday life*. Indianapolis, IN: Masters Press.

Baum, K., & Trubo, R. (1999). *The mental edge: Maximize your sports potential with the mind-body connection.* New York: Berkley Publishing Company.

Bell, K. F. (1983). *Championship thinking: The athlete's guide to winning performance in all sports.* Englewood Cliffs, NJ: Prentice-Hall.

Bell, K. F. (1983). *Target on gold: Goal setting for swimmers and other kinds of people.* Austin, TX: Keel Publications.

Bennett, J. G., & Pravitz, J. E. (1982). *The miracle of sports psychology.* Englewood Cliffs, NJ: Prentice-Hall. Book review: *JOPERD,* 1984, *55*(5), 98–99.

Bennett, J. G., & Pravitz, J. E. (1987). *Profile of a winner: Advanced mental training for athletes.* Ithaca, NY: Sport Science International. Book review: *TSP,* 1987, 1, 361–363.

Benzel, D. (1989). *Psyching for slalom: An illustrated guide to the mind and muscle of the complete skier.* Winter Park, FL: World Publications.

Braden, V., & Wool, R. (1993). *Vic Braden's mental tennis: How to psych yourself to a winning game.* Boston: Little, Brown and Company.

Brennan, S. J. (1990). *Competitive excellence: The psychology and strategy of successful team building.* Omaha, NE: Peak Performance Publishing. Book review: *TSP,* 1991, *5,* 290–291.

Brennan, S. J. (1993). *The mental edge: Basketball's peak performance workbook* (2nd ed.). Omaha, NE: Peak Performance Publishing. Book review: *TSP,* 1994, *8,* 321–323.

Brown, R. A. (1994). *The golfing mind: The psychological principles of good golf.* New York: Lyons & Burford.

Bull, S. J. (1991). *Sport psychology: A self-help guide.* Swindon: Crowood.

Bull, S. J., Albinson, J. G., & Shambrook, C. J. (1996). *The mental game plan: Getting psyched for sport.* Eastbourne: Sports Dynamics.

Bump, L. (1989). *Sport psychology study guide* (and accompanying workbook). Champaign, IL: Human Kinetics. Book review: *TSP,* 1990, *4,* 72–73.

Burnett, D. J. (1993). *Youth sports & self-esteem: A guide for parents.* Indianapolis, IN: Masters Press.

Butler, R. J. (1996). *Sports psychology in action.* Boston, MA: Butterworth Heinemann.

Cahill, B. R., & Pearl, A. J. (1993). *Intensive participation in children's sports.* Champaign, IL: Human Kinetics.

Clarkson, M. (1999). *Competitive fire.* Champaign, IL: Human Kinetics.

Clayton, L., & Smith, B. S. (1992). *Coping with sport injuries.* New York: Rosen Publishing Group.

Cogan, K. D., & Vidmar, P. (2000) *Sport psychology library: Tennis.* Morgantown, WV: Fitness Information Technology.

Cohn, P. J. (1994). *The mental game of golf: A guide to peak performance.* South Bend, IN: Diamond Communications. Book review: *TSP,* 1996, *10,* 213–216.

Cohn, P. J. (2000). *Peak performance golf: How good golfers become great ones.* Chicago, IL: Contemporary Books.

Cohn, P. J., & Winters, K. (1995). *The mental art of putting: Using your mind to putt your best.* South Bend, IN: Diamond Communications, Inc.

Colby, M. (1996). *Motor learning applied to sports* (2nd ed.). Boston, MA: American Press.

Coles, J. (1999). *Three shot golf*. Springfield, NJ: Burford Books.

Coop, R. H., & Fields, Bill. (1993). *Mind over golf: Play your best by thinking smart*. New York: Macmillan Publishing Company.

Cooper, A. (1998). *Playing in the zone: Exploring the spiritual dimensions of sports*. Boston: Shambhala.

Cratty, B. J. (1984). *Psychological preparation and athletic excellence*. Ithaca, NY: Mouvement Publications. Book review: *JSP*, 1986, *8*, 252–254.

Cunningham, L. (1981). *Hypnosport: How you can improve your sporting performances*. Glendale, CA: Westwood.

Curtis, J. D. (1989). *The mindset for winning*. La Crosse, WI: Coulee Press. Book review: *JSEP*, 1990, *12*, 439–441.

Dalloway, M. (1992). *Visualization: The master skill in mental training*. Phoenix, AZ: Optimal Performance Institute Press. Book review: *TSP*, 1995, *9*, 109–111.

Dalloway, M. (1993a). *Concentration: Focus your mind, power your game*. Phoenix, AZ: Optimal Performance Institute Press. Book review: *TSP*, 1995, *9*, 109–111.

Dalloway, M. (1993b). *Drive and determination: Developing your inner motivation*. Phoenix, AZ: Optimal Performance Institute Press. Book review: *TSP*, 1995, *9*, 109–111.

Dalloway, M. (1993c). *Risk taking: Performing your best during critical times*. Phoenix, AZ: Optimal Performance Institute Press. Book review: *TSP*, 1995, *9*, 109–111.

Dalloway, M. (1994). *Reflections on the mental side of sports*. Phoenix, AZ: Optimal Performance Institute Press. Book review: *TSP*, 1996, *10*, 300–301.

Decoursey, D., & Linder, D. E. (1990). *Visual skiing: Essential mental and physical skills for the modern skier*. New York: Doubleday.

Devenzio, D. (1997). *Think like a champion: A guide to championship performance in all sports*. Charlotte, NC: Fool Court Press.

Domey, R. L. (1989). *Mental training for shooting success* (2nd ed.). Pullman, WA: College Hill Communications.

Dorfman, H. A., & Kuehl, K. (1995). *The mental game of baseball: A guide to peak performance*. (2nd ed.) South Bend, IN: Diamond Communications, Inc. Book review: *TSP*, 1991, *5*, 92–93.

Douillard, J. (1994). *Body, mind and sport: The mind-body guide to lifelong fitness and your personal best*. London: Bantam Inc.

Edgette, J. S. (1996). *Heads up! Practical sports psychology for riders, their trainers, and their families*. New York: Doubleday.

Elliot, R. (1991). *The competitive edge: Mental preparation for distance running*. Mountain View, CA: TAFNEWS Press.

Engh, F. (2000). *Why Johnny hates sports*. Garden City Park, NY: Avery Publishing Group.

Evans, E. (1990). *Mental toughness training for cross-country skiing*. New York: The Stephen Greene Press/Pelham Books.

Farley, K. L., & Curry, S. M. (1994). *Get motivated: Daily psych-ups*. New York: Fireside/Simon & Schuster.

Figone, A. (1991). *Teaching the mental aspects of baseball: A coach's handbook*. Madison, WI: Brown & Benchmark.

Fine, A. H., & Sachs, M. L. (1997). *The total sports experience for kids: A parent's guide to success in youth sports*. South Bend, IN: Diamond Communications, Inc.

Fortanasce, V. M. (1995). *Life lessons from Little League: A guide for parents and coaches*. New York: Image/Doubleday.

Foster, S., & Prussack, T. (1999). *Skate your personal best: A guide to mastering intermediate and advanced technique, achieving optimal performance skills and skating excellence*. San Francisco, CA: Rudi Publishing.

Fox, A. (1993). *Think to win: The strategic dimension of tennis*. New York: Harper.

Gallwey, W. T. (1998). *The inner game of golf* (rev. ed.). New York: Random House.

Garfield, C. A., & Bennett, H. Z. (1984). *Peak performance: Mental training techniques of the world's greatest athletes*. Los Angeles: Jeremy P. Tarcher, Inc. Book review: *JOPERD*, 1985, *56*(9), 77–78.

Gauron, E. F. (1984). *Mental training for peak performance*. Lansing, NY: Sport Science Associates. Book review: *JSP*, 1987, *9*, 83–84.

Gibson, M. (1994). *Going for it! A gym bag companion for living our dreams*. Perkasie, PA: Wind Dancer Publications.

Glad, W., & Beck, C. (1999). *Focused for golf*. Champaign, IL: Human Kinetics.

Goldberg, A. S. (1998). *Sports slump busting*. Champaign, IL: Human Kinetics.

Goldberg, A. (1988). *The sports mind: A workbook of mental skills for athletes*. Northampton, MA: Competitive Advantage.

Graham, D., & Yocum, G. (1990). *Mental toughness training for golf*. New York: Stephen Greene Press/Pelham Books.

Grant, R. W. (1988). *The psychology of sport: Facing one's true opponent*. Jefferson, NC: McFarland.

Hackfort, D. (1994). *Psycho-social issues and interventions in elite sport*. New York: P. Lang.

Hardy, L., Jones, J. G., & Gould, D. (1996). *Understanding psychological preparation for sport: Theory and practice of elite performers*. New York: J. Wiley.

Harley, N. R. (1994). *Let's go skiing with a psychiatrist: The mental game of sensational skiing*. Vail, CO: Vail Press.

Harris, D. V., & Harris, B. L. (1984). *The athlete's guide to sports psychology: Mental skills for physical people*. New York: Leisure Press.

Hassler, J. K., & Jahiel, J. (1993). *In search of your image: A practical guide to the mental and spiritual aspects of horsemanship*. Colora, MD: Goals Unlimited Press.

Henderson, J. (1991). *Think fast: Mental toughness training for runners*. New York: Pengiun Books.

Henderson, J. (Ed.) (1972). *Practical running psychology*. Mountain View, CA: *Runner's World* Magazine.

Hendricks, G., & Carlson, J. (1982). *The centered athlete: A conditioning program for your mind.* Englewood Cliffs, NJ: Prentice-Hall.

Hogg, J. M. (1995a). *Mental skills for competitive swimmers.* Edmonton, Alberta, Canada: Sport Excel Publishing.

Hogg, J. M. (1995b). *Mental skills for competitive swimmers: A workbook to improve mental performance.* Edmonton, Alberta, Canada: Sport Excel Publishing.

Hogg, J. M. (1995c). *Mental skills for swim coaches: A coaching text on the psychological aspects of competitive swimming.* Edmonton, Alberta, Canada: Sport Excel Publishing.

Hogg, J. M. (1997). *Mental skills for young athletes: A mental skills workbook for athletes 12 and under.* Edmonton, Alberta, Canada: Sport Excel Publishing. Book review: *TSP*, 1998, *12*, 358–360.

Holzel, P., & Holzel, W. (1996). *Learn to ride using sports psychology: A training aid for riders and instructors.* North Pomfret, VT: Trafalgar Square.

Huang, C. A., & Lynch, J. (1992). *Thinking body, dancing mind: Taosports for extraordinary performance in athletics, business, and life.* New York: Bantam Books.

Jackson, A. (1995). *Eye on the ball, mind on the game.* New York: Barnes & Noble.

Jackson, S. A., & Csikszentmihalyi, M. (1999). *Flow in sports.* Champaign, IL: Human Kinetics.

Jaeger, A. J. (1994). *Getting focused, staying focused: A Far Eastern approach to sports and life.* Glendale, CA: Griffith Printing.

Janssen, J. J., & Candrea, M. (1994). *Mental toughness training for softball: A guide and workbook for athletes and coaches.* Casa Grande, AZ: Southwest Camps Publications.

Jones, C. (1999). *What makes winners win: Thoughts and reflections from successful athletes.* New York: Broadway Books.

Jordan, J. H. (1995). *Total mindbody training: A guide to peak athletic performance.* Hartford: Turtle Press.

Jordan, T. J., & De Michele, P. E. (1997). *Overcoming the fear in riding.* Sharon Hill, PA: Breakthrough Publications.

Kappas, J. G. (1984). *Self-hypnosis: The key to athletic success.* Englewood Cliffs, NJ: Prentice-Hall.

Kauss, D. R. (1980). *Peak performance: Mental game plans for maximizing your athletic potential.* Englewood Cliffs, NJ: Prentice-Hall. Book review: *JSP*, 1982, *4*, 410–413.

Keogh, B. K., & Smith, C. E. (1985). *Personal par: A psychological system of golf for women.* Champaign, IL: Human Kinetics. Book review: *JOPERD*, 1986, *57*(8), 83.

Keyes, M. J. (1996). *Mental training for shotgun sports.* Auburn, CA: Shotgun Sports, Inc.

Kirschenbaum, D. S. (1997). *Mind matters: Seven sportpsych steps to maximize performance.* Carmel, IN: Cooper Publishing Group.

Kogler, A. (1993). *Preparing the mind: Improving fencing performance through psychological preparation.* Lansdowne, PA: ConterParry Press.

Kubistant, T. (1986). *Performing your best: A guide to psychological skills for high achievers.* Champaign, IL: Human Kinetics.

Kubistant, T. (1988). *Mind pump: The psychology of bodybuilding*. Champaign, IL: Leisure Press.

Kubistant, T. (1994). *Mind links: The psychology of golf*. Reno, NV: Performance and Productivity Specialists.

Liggett, D. (2000). *Sport hypnosis*. Champaign, IL: Human Kinetics.

Lilliefors, J. (1978). *The running mind*. Mountain View, CA: World Publications, Inc.

Loehr, J. E. (1982). *Mental toughness training for sports: Achieving athletic excellence training*. Lexington, MA: Stephen Greene.

Loehr, J. E. (1990). *The mental game*. New York: The Stephen Greene Press/Pelham Books.

Loehr, J. E. (1994). *The new toughness training for sports: Achieving athletic excellence*. New York: Dutton.

Loudis, L. A., Lobitz, W. C., & Singer, K. M. (1986). *Skiing out of your mind*. Champaign, IL: Leisure Press.

Lucas, G. (1987). *Images for golf: Visualizing your way to a better game*. Calgary: Arizona Academic Sport Resources.

Lynberg, M. (1993). *Winning: Great coaches and athletes share their secrets of success*. New York: Doubleday.

Lynch, J., & Scott, W. (1999). *Running within: A guide to mastering the body-mind-spirit connection for ultimate training and racing*. Champaign, IL: Human Kinetics.

Lynch, J. (1987). *The total runner: A complete mind-body guide to optimal performance*. Englewood Cliffs, NJ: Prentice-Hall. Book review: *TSP*, 1987, *1*, 265–266.

Mackenzie, M. M., & Denlinger, Ken. (1990). *Golf: The mind game*. New York: Dell. Book review: *TSP*, 1992, *6*, 314.

Mackenzie, M. M., & Denlinger, K. (1991). *Skiing: The mind game*. New York: Dell.

Mackenzie, M. M., & Denlinger, K. (1991). *Tennis: The mind game*. New York: Dell.

Margenau, E. (1990). *Sports without pressure: A guide for parents & coaches of young athletes*. New York: Gardner Press.

Martens, R. (1987). *Coaches' guide to sport psychology*. Champaign, IL: Human Kinetics. Book review: *TSP*, 1990, *4*, 78.

Martin, G. L. (1997). *Sport psychology consulting: Guidelines from behavioral analysis*. Winnipeg, Manitoba, Canada: Sport Sciences Press. Book review: *TSP*, 1998, *12*, 104–105.

Martin, G. L., & Ingraham, D. (1993). *New mental skills for better golf: Test your self-talk*. Winnipeg, Manitoba, Canada: Sport Sciences Press.

Martin, G. L., Toogood, A., & Tkachuk, G. (1997). *Behavioral assessment forms for sport psychology consulting*. Winnipeg, Manitoba, Canada: Sport Sciences Press. Book review: *TSP*, 1998, *12*, 104–105.

May, J. R., & Asken, M. J. (Eds.). (1987). *Sport psychology: The psychological health of the athlete*. New York: PMA Publishing Corp. Book review: *TSP*, 1989, *3*, 274–277.

Meyer, J. E., & Plodzien, C. A. (1988). *Excelling in sports through thinking straight*. Springfield, IL: Charles C. Thomas. Book review: *JSEP*, 1990, *12*, 437–438.

Micheli, L. J. (1990). *Sportswise: An essential guide for young athletes, parents, and coaches.* Boston: Houghton Mifflin Company.

Mikes, J. (1987). *Basketball fundamentals: A complete mental training guide.* Champaign, IL: Leisure Press. Book review: *JOPERD,* 1987, *58*(9), 141–142.

Miller, L. (1996). *Golfing in the zone: Merging mind, body, and spirit through golf.* New York: MJF Books.

Miller, S., & Hill, P. M. (1999). *Sport psychology for cyclists.* Boulder, CO: Velo Press.

Millman, D. (1999). *Body mind mastery: Creating success in sport and life.* Novato, CA: New World Library.

Mills, B. D. (1994). *Mental training and performance enhancement: A guide for volleyball coaches and players.* Dubuque, IA: Eddie Bowers Publishing, Inc. Book review: *TSP,* 1996, *10,* 415–416.

Miner, M. J., Shelley, G. A., & Henschen, K. P. (1995). *Moving toward your potential: The athlete's guide to peak performance.* Farmington, UT: Performance Publications.

Missoum, G. (1991). *Guide du training mental.* Paris: RETZ. Book review: *TSP,* 1992, *6,* 315–316.

Moran, A. P. (Ed.). (1996). *The psychology of concentration in sport performers: A cognitive analysis.* Hove: Psychology Press.

Murphy, S. (1996). *The achievement zone: Eight skills for winning all the time from the playing field to the boardroom.* New York: G. P. Putnam's Sons.

Murphy, S. (1999). *The cheers and the tears: A healthy alternative to the dark side of youth sports today.* San Francisco: Jossey-Bass Publishers.

Nakamura, R. M. (1996). *The power of positive coaching.* Sudbury, MA: Jones and Bartlett Publishers, Inc.

Nideffer, R. M. (1981). *The ethics and practice of applied sport psychology.* Ithaca, NY: Mouvement Publications. Book review: *JOPERD,* 1982, *53*(4), 100.

Nideffer, R. M. (1985). *Athletes' guide to mental training.* Champaign, IL: Human Kinetics.

Nideffer, R. M. (1992). *Psyched to win.* Champaign, IL: Leisure Press: Book reviews: *JSEP,* 1993, *15,* 355–356. *TSP,* 1993, *7,* 204–206.

Nowicki, D. (1993). *Gold medal mental workout: A step-by-step program of mental exercises to make you a winner every time.* Island Pond, VT: Stadion Publishing Co., Inc.

Orlick, T. (1986). *Coaches training manual to psyching for sport.* Champaign, IL: Leisure Press. Book review: *TSP,* 1987, *1,* 82.

Orlick, T. (1986). *Psyching for sport: Mental training for athletes.* Champaign, IL: Leisure Press. Book review: *TSP,* 1987, *1,* 82.

Orlick, T. (1990). *In pursuit of excellence: How to win in sport and life through mental training.* (2nd ed.). Champaign, IL: Human Kinetics. Book review: *TSP,* 1992, *6,* 99–100.

Orlick, T. (1992). *Nice on my feelings.* Sacramento, CA: ITA Publications.

Orlick, T. (1993). *Free to feel great: Teaching children to excel at living.* Carp, Ontario, Canada: Creative Bound, Inc.

Orlick, T. (1995). *Nice on my feelings: Nurturing the best in children and parents.* Carp, Ontario, Canada: Creative Bound, Inc.

Orlick, T. (1998). *Embracing your potential.* Champaign, IL: Human Kinetics.

Orlick, T., & Partington, J. (1986). *Psyched: Inner views of winning.* Ottawa, Canada: The Coaching Association of Canada. Book review: *TSP,* 1987, *1,* 166–167.

Owens, D., & Kirschenbaum, D. (1997). *Smart golf: How to simplify and score your mental game.* San Francisco: Jossey-Bass Publishers.

Pargman, D. (1986). *Stress and motor performance: Understanding and coping.* Ithaca, NY: Mouvement Publications. Book review: *TSP,* 1988, *2,* 266–267.

Phillips, L., & Stahl, B. (2000). *Parenting, sportsmom style: Real-life solutions for surviving the youth sports scene.* Maumee, OH: 307 Books.

Pirozzolo, F. J., & Pate, R. (1996). *The mental game pocket companion for golf.* New York: Harper Collins Publishers.

Pitcher, B. L. (1996). *The Mental Proficiency System: A proven, step-by-step guide to thinking and planning your way to lower golf scores.* Safety Harbor, FL: Pitcher Golf Group.

Porter, C. W. (1993). *Top golf: Peak performance through brain body integration.* Sparks, NV: Life Enhancement Services.

Porter, K., & Foster, J. (1986). *The mental athlete.* Dubuque, IA: Wm. C. Brown Co. Book review: *TSP,* 1988, *2,* 173–174.

Porter, K., & Foster, J. (1990). *Visual athletics.* Dubuque, IA: Wm. C. Brown Co.

Railo, W. (1986). *Willing to win.* West Yorkshire, England: Springfield Books Limited. Book review: *JSP,* 1987, *9,* 186–189.

Ravizza, K., & Hanson, T. (1995). *Heads-up baseball: Playing the game one pitch at a time.* Indianapolis: Masters Press.

Richard, J. (1991). *Not too high, not too low: Stress management strategies for professional baseball players and their fans.* Dubuque, IA: Kendall/Hunt.

Rodionow, A. W. (Ed.). (1982). *Psychology for training and competition.* L. Pickenhain, Trans. Berlin: Sportverlag Berlin. Book review: *TSP,* 1989, *3,* 278–280.

Roland, D. (1997). *The confident performer.* Paddington, NSW. Australia: Currency Press Ltd. Book review: *TSP,* 1998, *12,* 228–229.

Rotella, R. J., & Bunker, L. K. (1981). *Mind mastery for winning golf.* Englewood Cliffs, NJ: Prentice-Hall.

Rotella, R. J., & Bunker, L. K. (1982). *Mind, set and match.* Charlottesville, VA: LINKS, Inc.

Rotella, R. J., & Bunker, L. K. (1987). *Parenting your superstar.* Champaign, IL: Human Kinetics. Book review: *TSP,* 1989, *3,* 281–282.

Rotella, R., & Cullen, B. (1995). *Golf is not a game of perfect.* New York: Simon & Schuster.

Rotella, R., & Cullen, B. (1996). *Golf is a game of confidence.* New York: Simon & Schuster.

Rotella, R., & Cullen, B. (1997). *The golf of your dreams.* New York: Simon & Schuster.

Rushall, B. S. (1979). *Psyching in sports.* London: Pelham Books.

Rushall, B. S. (1986). *The psychology of successful cross-country ski racing.* Ottawa, Ontario, Canada: Cross Country Canada.

Rushall, B. S. (1991). *Imagery training in sports: A handbook for athletes, coaches, and sport psychologists*. Spring Valley, CA: Sport Science Associates.

Rushall, B. S. (1992). *Mental skills training for sports: A manual for athletes, coaches, and sport psychologists*. Spring Valley, CA: Sport Science Associates.

Rushall, B. S. (1995). *Think and act like a champion*. Spring Valley, CA: Sport Science Associates.

Rushall, B. S., & Potgieter, J. (1987). *The psychology of successful competing in endurance events*. Pretoria: South African Association for Sport Science, Physical Education, and Recreation.

Sailes, G. A. (1995). *Mental training for tennis*. Dubuque, IA: Kendall/Hunt Publishers.

Savoie, J. (1992). *That winning feeling: A new approach to riding using psychocybernetics*. London: Allen.

Schultheis, R. (1996). *Bone games: Extreme sports, shamanism, zen and the search for transcendence*. New York: Breakaway Sports.

Scott, M. D., & Pellicioni, L., Jr. (1982). *Don't choke: How athletes can become winners*. Englewood Cliffs, NJ: Prentice-Hall. Book review: *JOPERD*, 1984, *55*(2), 73.

Selleck, G. A. (1995). *How to play the game of your life: A guide to success in sports and life*. South Bend, IN: Diamond Communications, Inc.

Shapiro, A. (1996). *Golf's mental hazards: Overcome them and put an end to the self-destructive round*. New York: Fireside/Simon and Schuster.

Sheikh, A. A., & Korn, E. R. (Eds.). (1994). *Imagery in sports and physical performance*. Amityville, NY: Baywood.

Simek, T. C., & O'Brien, R. M. (1981). *Total golf: A behavioral approach to lowering your score and getting more out of your game*. New York: Doubleday & Company. Book review: *JOPERD*, 1982, *53*(4), 102, 104.

Singer, R. N. (1986). *Peak performance . . . and more*. Ithaca, NY: Mouvement Publications. Book review: *JOPERD*, 1987, *58*(9), 141.

Slaikeu, K., & Trogolo, R. (1999). *Focused for tennis*. Champaign, IL: Human Kinetics.

Smith, A. M. (1991). *Power play: Mental toughness for hockey and beyond*. Rochester, MN: Power Play.

Smith, E. W. L. (1989). *Not just pumping iron: On the psychology of lifting weights*. Springfield, IL: Charles C. Thomas.

Smith, N. J., Smith, R. E., & Smoll, F. L. (1983). *Kidsports: A survival guide for parents*. Reading, MA: Addison-Wesley Publishing Company.

Smith, R. E., & Smoll, F. L. (1996). *Way to go, coach: A scientifically proven approach to coaching effectiveness*. Portola Valley, CA: Warde.

Smoll, F. L., & Smith, R. E. (1987). *Sport psychology for youth coaches: Personal growth to athlete excellence*. Washington, DC: National Federation for Catholic Youth Ministry. Book review: *TSP*, 1988, *2*, 175–177.

Smoll, F. L., & Smith, R. E. (1995). *Children and youth in sport: A biopsychosocial perspective*. Dubuque, IA: Brown and Benchmark.

Stein, M., & Hollowitz, J. (1994). *Psyche and sports: Baseball, hockey, martial arts, running, tennis, and others.* Wilmette, IL: Chiron.

Straub, W. F., & Williams, J. M. (Eds.). (1984). *Cognitive sport psychology.* Lansing, NH: Sport Science Associates.

Strossen, R. J. (1994). *IronMind: Stronger minds, stronger bodies.* Nevada City, CA: IronMind Enterprises, Inc.

Sugarman, K. (1999). *Winning the mental way: A practical guide to team building and mental training.* Burlingame, CA: Step Up Publishing.

Suinn, R. M. (1986). *Seven steps to peak performance: The mental training manual for athletes.* Lewiston, NY: Hans Huber Publishers. Book reviews: *TSP*, 1987, *1*, 359–360. *JSEP*, 1989, *11*, 343–345.

Swindley, D. (1996). *Decide to win: A total approach to winning in sport and life.* London: Ward Lock.

Syer, J., & Connolly, C. (1984). *Sporting mind, sporting body: An athlete's guide to mental training.* New York: Cambridge University Press.

Taylor, D. (1989). *Challenge yourself: Goal-setting workbook for athletes.* Coquitlam, British Columbia, Canada: Challenge Yourself Press.

Taylor, J. (1993). *The mental edge for competitive sports* (3rd ed.). Aspen, CO: Alpine* Taylor Consulting. Book review: *TSP*, 1996, *10*, 298–299.

Taylor, J. (1994a). *The mental edge for alpine ski racing.* Aspen, CO: Alpine*Taylor Consulting.

Taylor, J. (1994b). *The mental edge for golf.* Aspen, CO: Alpine*Taylor Consulting.

Taylor, J. (1994c). *The mental edge for tennis.* Aspen, CO: Alpine*Taylor Consulting.

Taylor, J. (1994d). *The mental edge for skiing.* Aspen, CO: Alpine*Taylor Consulting.

Terry, P. (1989). *The winning mind.* Wellingborough, Northamptonshire, England: Thorsons Publishing Group. Book reviews: *JSEP*, 1990, *12*, 434–436; *TSP*, 1990, *4*, 437–439.

Thomas, J. R. (Ed.) (1977). *Youth sports guide for coaches and parents.* Washington, DC: AAHPERD Publications.

Underwood, T. (1998). *Christian golf psychology.* Grand Island, NE: Cross Training Publishing.

Ungerleider, S. (1996). *Mental training for peak performance: Top athletes reveal the mind exercises they use to excel.* Emmaus, PA: Rodale Press, Inc.

Van Raalte, J. L., & Silver-Bernstein, C. (1999). *Sport psychology library: Tennis.* Morgantown, WV: Fitness Information Technology, Inc.

Vardy, D. (1996). *The mental game of golf.* Thrumpton: Castle.

Vernacchia, R. A., McGuire, R. T., & Cook, D. L. (1992). *Coaching mental excellence: "It does matter whether you win or lose . . . "* Dubuque, IA: Brown & Benchmark. Book review: *TSP*, 1993, *7*, 210–212.

Vicory, J. (1996). *Mind golf: It's brain over ball.* Aurora, IL: Kelmscott Press.

Waitley, D. (1994). *The new dynamics of winning: Gain the mind-set of a champion.* London: Brealey. (Originally published 1993 by Nightingale-Conant.)

Wallach, J. (1995). *Beyond the fairway: Zen lessons, insights, and inner attitudes of golf.* New York: Bantam Books.

Wanless, M. (1991). *Ride with your mind: An illustrated masterclass in right brain riding.* North Pomfrey, VT: Trafalgar Square Publishing.

Weinberg, R. S. (1988). *The mental advantage: Developing your psychological skills in tennis.* Champaign, IL: Leisure Press. Book reviews: *TSP*, 1988, *2*, 357–358.*JSEP*, 1990, *12*, 98–99.

Whittam, P. (1995). *Tennis talk, psych yourself in to win!!! Affirmations for mental fitness in tennis.* Bahamas: Sapphire Publishing Corporation.

Williams, J. M. (Ed.). (1997). *Applied sport psychology: Personal growth to peak performance* (3rd ed.). Palo Alto, CA: Mayfield.

Wilt, F., & Bosen, K. (1971). *Motivation and coaching psychology.* Los Altos, CA: TAFNEWS Press.

Winter, B. (1981). *Relax and win: Championship performance in whatever you do.* La Jolla, CA: A. S. Barnes and Company. Book reviews: *JOPERD*, 1982, *53*(7), 86. *JSP*, 1983, *5*, 466–467.

Winter, G. (1992). *The psychology of cricket: How to play the inner game of cricket.* Melbourne, Australia: Sun.

Winter, G., & Martin, C. (1988). *A practical guide to sport psychology.* Underdale, Australia: SA Sports Institute.

Wiren, G., Coop, R., & Sheehan, L. (1985). *The new golf mind.* New York: Simon & Schuster.

Wolff, R. (1993). *Good sports.* New York: Dell.

Yandell, J. (1999). *Visual tennis.* Champaign, IL: Human Kinetics.

Young, B., & Bunker, L. K. (1995). *The courtside coach.* Charlottesville, VA: LINKS, Inc.

Zaichkowsky, L., D., & Sime, W. E. (Eds.). (1982). *Stress management for sport.* Reston, VA: American Association for Health, Physical Education, Recreation, and Dance.

Zinsser, N. (1991). *Dear Dr. Psych.* Little Brown: Boston.

Zulewski, R. (1994). *The parent's guide to coaching physically challenged children.* Cincinnati, OH: Betterway Books.

References

Scogin, F., Bynum, J., Stephens, G., & Calhoon, S. (1990). Efficacy of self-administered treatment programs: Meta-analytic review. *Professional Psychology: Research and Practice, 21*(1), 42–47.

Vealey, R. S. (1988). Future directions in psychological skills training. *The Sport Psychologist, 2*, 318–336.

Appendix J

Reference List of Mental Training/ Sport Psychology Videos

Alan S. Kornspan, University of Akron
Christopher Lantz, Truman State University
Bart S. Lerner, Arizona School of Professional Psychology
Scott R. Johnson, West Virginia University

Author Notes: Alan S. Kornspan, Department of Physical and Health Education; Christopher Lantz, Department of Health and Exercise Science; Scott R. Johnson, School of Physical Education. Correspondence concerning this article should be addressed to Alan S. Kornspan, 2774 Lochraven, Apt. G., Copley, OH 44321; telephone number: (330) 665-3396. Electronic mail may be sent via the Internet to au440@yfn.ysu.edu

Reprinted from A. S. Kornspan, C. Lantz, B. S. Lerner, and S. R. Johnson. (1998). "A Reference List of Mental Training/Sport Psychology Videos." In W. K. Simpson, A. LeUnes, & J. S. Picou (Eds.), *Applied Research in Coaching and Athletics Annual*. Boston: American Press.

Abstract

The continued growth of sport psychology has resulted in an influx of mental training techniques. These techniques are presented in a variety of books, journals, and audio/visual materials. While reference lists exist for sport psychology texts (Allen, 1994; Sachs & Kornspan, 1995) and journal articles (Granito & Wenz, 1995), there remained no such resource for locating and obtaining sport psychology videos. This article presents an extensive list of mental training and sport psychology videos that can be used by sport psychologists, coaches, and athletes. In addition, this list provides purchasing information such as addresses, telephone numbers, and price of the video.

Reference List of Mental Training/Sport

Psychology Videos

As the field of sport psychology experiences increasing popularity, members of the athletic community are recognizing the benefits of psychological skills training. As a result, coaches and athletes are obtaining sport psychology information from books and videos. As technology continues to advance in the classroom and on the field, many coaches and sport psychologists are beginning to use videos to introduce athletes to psychological skills training.

Often, the coach or sport psychologist will introduce athletes to mental skills training through the use of videotapes. Murphy (1991) explains how he has used the video "Visualization: What You See Is What You Get" to lead into group discussions. For example, Murphy explained, "I might have one group identify ways visualization can be used in practice and may tell another group to watch for ways visualization can be used at competition" (p. 95). Gould (1987) suggests that videos introducing mental training can be useful, but the teacher, coach, or sport psychologist should provide guidance to athletes on the use of the video. Further, Weinberg (1990) suggests that some videos may be limited in that they do not give specific demonstrations of how to use the psychological techniques. However, Weinberg suggests that videos can be useful in introducing basic information for those who are unfamiliar with applied sport psychology.

Although sport psychology videos may be useful (Gould, 1987; Murphy, 1988; Weinberg, 1990), a problem exists in that only a very limited number of videos have been reviewed in the literature. Also, the phone numbers and prices that are listed in the video review are often outdated. Thus coaches and sport psychology consultants may have great difficulty in locating and purchasing sport psychology videos. While reference lists exist for sport psychology texts (Allen, 1994; Sachs & Kornspan, 1995) and journal articles (Granito & Wenz, 1995), there remained no such resource for locating and obtaining sport psychology videos.

An effort to provide the coaching community with information on sport psychology videos began with a comprehensive list generated via various computerized searches. After completing the list, addresses and telephone numbers of the distributors were obtained. Current prices (as of 1997), telephone numbers, and addresses for 39 videos were located. It should be noted that these videos address a wide range of sport psychology and coaching topics. It is not the purpose of this article to review the videos presented but to provide the information necessary to help individuals in locating videos of interest.

References

Allen, M. B. (1994). Authorship in sport psychology: A reference list. *The Sport Psychologist, 8,* 94–99.

Gould, D. (1987). Mental training for peak athletic performance [Review of the video program *Mental training for peak athletic performance*]. *The Sport Psychologist, 1,* 364–365.

Granito, V., & Wenz, B. (1995). Reading list for professional issues in applied sport psychology. *The Sport Psychologist, 9,* 96–103.

Murphy, S. M. (1991). Visualization: What you see is what you get [Review of the video program *Visualization: What you see is what you get*]. *The Sport Psychologist, 5,* 94–95.

Sachs, M. L., & Kornspan, A. (1995). Reading list in applied sport psychology: Psychological skills training. In M. Sachs, K. Burke, & L. Butcher (Eds.), *Directory of graduate programs in applied sport psychology* (4th ed.) (pp. 216–227). Morgantown, WV: Fitness Information Technology.

Weinberg, R. (1990). Sports psychology: The winning edge in sports [Review of the video program *Sports psychology: What winning edge in sports*]. *The Sport Psychologist, 4,* 192–194.

Video List

Bassham, L. (1989). *Mental management seminar, part 1. The principles of mental management* [Videotape]. (Available from Mental Management Systems, P.O. Box 225, Seguin, TX, 78155).

Bassham, L. (1989). *Mental management seminar, part 2. Mental tools and techniques* [Videotape]. (Available from Mental Management Systems, P.O. Box 225, Seguin, TX, 78155).

Bassham, L. (1989). *Mental management seminar part 3. Mental tools and techniques* [Videotape]. (Available from Mental Management Systems, P.O. Box 225, Seguin, TX, 78155.

Blanchard, K. (1994). *The golf university swing school videos. Mastering the mental game of golf* [Videotape]. (Available from The Golf University, 17550 Bernardo Oaks Drive, San Diego, CA 92128, 1-800-426-0966, $24.95).

Botterill, C., & Orlick, T. (1988). *Visualization: What you see is what you get* [Videotape]. (Available from Coaching Association of Canada, 1600 James Naismith Drive,

Gloucester, ON K1B 5N4 Canada, 613-748-5624, $19.95 Canadian). Video Review: Murphy, S.M. (1991). Visualization: What you see is what you get [Review of the video program *Visualization: What you see is what you get*]. *The Sport Psychologist, 5,* 94–95.

Braden, V. (1994). *Mental tennis: Hidden secrets to why you win and lose!* [Videotape]. (Available from Vic Braden Tennis College, 23335 Avenida La Caza, Coto de Caza, CA 92769; 1-800-42COURT, $39.95).

Cairns, K. (1989). *Our inner selves, (Program 2)* [Videotape]. (Available from Human Kinetics Publishers, P.O. Box 5076, Champaign, IL 61825-5076; 1-800-747-4457, $15.95).

Cohn, P., & Waite, G. (1996). *Make your most confident stroke: A guide to a one putt mindset* [Videotape]. (Available from Peak Performance Sports, 7380 Sand Lake Rd., Suite 500, Orlando, FL 32819; 1-888-742-7225, $22.95).

Cox, B. (1982). *Sports psychology for youth coaches* [Videotape]. (Available from Distinctive Home Videos, 391 El Portal Road, San Mateo, CA 94402; 415-344-7756, $59.95).

Cox, B. (1982). *Tom Tutko's coaching clinic* [Videotape]. (Available from Distinctive Home Videos, 391 El Portal Road, San Mateo, CA 94402; 415-344-7756, $39.95).

Curtis, J. (1988). *The mindset for winning* [Videotape]. (Available from Cambridge Career Products, Cambridge Physical Education & Health, P.O. Box 2153, Department PE15, Charleston, WV 25328-2153; 1-800-468-4227, $39.95).

Duda, J., & Retton, M. L. (1994). *Mental readiness* [Videotape]. (Available from USA Gymnastics, 1036 N. Capital Ave., Suite E. 235, Indianapolis, IN, 46204; 1-800-4US-AGYM, $4.95).

Ellis, R. (1990). *Mental mechanics and hitting simplification* [Videotape]. (Available from Championship Books and Video Productions, 2730 Graham St., Ames, IA 50010; 1-800-873-2730, $29.95).

Goshen, B. (1987). *The mental game* (Videotape]. (Available from Professional Image, 9422 E. 55th Place, Tulsa, OK, 74145-8154, 918-622-8899, $39.95). Video Review: Sime, W.E. (1992). The mental game [Review of the video program *The mental game*]. *The Sport Psychologist, 6,* 204–205.

Gould, D. (1987). *Sport psychology* [Videotape]. Champaign, IL: Human Kinetics Publishers. (Available from Human Kinetics Publishers, P.O. Box 5076, Champaign, IL 61825-5076; 1-800-747-4457, $70.00).

Hamshire, R., Iveson, I., & Catell, R. (1994). *Winning with sports psychology* [Videotape]. Available from I.C.C. Entertainment P/L, The Marina 13/1 Bradley Ave., Kirribill, NSW, 2061, Australia, 6129955-2297; US $29.95). Video Review: Sargent, G. (1995). Winning with sports psychology [Review of the video program *Winning With Sports Psychology*]. *The Sport Psychologist, 4,* 433–434.

Hogan, C. (1988). *Nice shot* [Videotape]. (Available from Cambridge Career Products, Cambridge Physical Education & Health, P.O. Box 2153, Department PE15, Charleston, WV 25328-2153; 1-800-468-4227, $29.95). Video Review: Armstrong, H.E. (1990) *Nice Shot* [Review of the video program *Nice Shot*]. *The Sport Psychologist, 4,* 433–434.

Jacobs, A., Hill, C., & Allen, L. (1987). *Sports psychology: The winning edge in sports.* (Available from Cambridge Career Products, Cambridge Physical Education & Health P.O. Box 2153, Department PE15, Charleston, WV 25328-2153; 1-800-468-4227, $89.95). Video Review: Weinberg, R. (1990). Sports psychology: The winning edge in sports [Review of the video program *Sports psychology: The winning edge in sports*]. *The Sport Psychologist, 4,* 192–194.

LaTreill, D., & Theilen, A. (1994). *Mental golf* [Videotape]. (Availability, Vestron Video, 15400 Sherman Way, P.O. Box 10124, Van Nuys, CA 91410-0124; $19.95).

Loehr, J. (1989). *Mental toughness training for tennis: "The 16 Second Cure"* [Videotape]. (Available from LGE/Sport Science, 9757 Lake Nona, Orlando, FL 32827-7017; 1-800-543-7764, $30.00).

Loehr, J. (1989). *Tips to mental toughness* [Videotape]. (Available from LGE/Sport Science, 9757 Lake Nona, Orlando, FL 32827-7017; 1-800-543-7764, $40.00).

Martin, C., & Winter, G. (1990). *What is sport psychology?* [Videotape]. (Available from South Australian Sports Institute, P.O. Box 219, Brooklyn Park, SA 5032).

Martin, G. (1989). *Sport psychology for figure skaters*. [Videotape]. (Available from Canadian Figure Skating Association, 200 Main St., Winnipeg, Manitoba R3C 4MZ; 204-985-4064, $28.00 Canadian). Video Review: Jackson, S. (1991). Sport psyching for figure skaters. [Review of the video program *Sport psyching for figure skaters*]. *The Sport Psychologist, 5*, 194–195.

Mudra, D. (1986). *The creative edge in sports psychology*. [Videotape]. (Availabe from Championship Books and Video Productions, 2730 Graham St., Ames, IA 50010; 1-800-873-2730, $29.95).

Murphy, S., & McCann, S. (1994). *Sports mental training*. [Videotape]. (Available from USOC, Judine Anseimo, Sports Science & Technology Division, USOC, One Olympic Plaza, Colorado Springs, CO 80909; $4.99).

National Collegiate Athletic Association. (1988). *Athletes at risk*. [Videotape]. (Available from Karol Media, 350 N. Pennsylvania Ave., Wilkesbarre, PA 18773, 1-800-526-4773, $17.95).

National Collegiate Athletic Association. (1988). *Drugs and the collegiate athlete*. [Videotape]. (Available from Karol Media, 350 N. Pennsylvania Ave., Wilkesbarre, PA 18773, 1-800-526-4773, $17.95).

National Collegiate Athletic Association. (1989). *Afraid to eat: Eating disorders and student-athletes*. [Videotape]. (Available from Karol Media, 350 N. Pennsylvania Ave., Wilkesbarre, PA 18773, 1-800-526-4773, $17.95).

National Collegiate Athletic Association. (1989). *Eating disorders: What can you do?* [Videotape]. (Available from Karol Media, 350 N. Pennsylvania Ave., Wilkesbarre, PA 18773, 1-800-526-4773, $14.95).

Nideffer, R., & Coffey, R. (1989). *Psychological preparation of the elite athlete*. [Videotape]. (Availabe from Australian Coaching Council, P.O. Box 176, Belconnen, ACT 2616).

Orlick, T. (1995). *Coaching the spirit of sport: Building self-esteem*. [Videotape]. Ontario, Canada: Canadian Sport Association. (Available from The Spirit of Sport Foundation, 1600 J. Naismith Drive, Gloucester, Ontario, K1B 5N4; 1-800-672-7775, $17.95).

Porter, K., & Foster, J. (1985). *Mental training for peak athletic performance*. Eugene, OR: Westcom Productions, Inc. (Available from Cambridge Career Products, Cambridge Physical Education & Health, P.O. Box 2153, Department PE15, Charleston, WV 25328-2153, 1-800-468-4227, $59.95). Video Review: Gould, D. (1987). Mental training for peak athletic performance [Review of the video program *Mental training for peak athletic performance*]. *The Sport Psychologist, 1*, 364–365.

Ravizza, K. (1989). *Stress management for baseball: 3–2 count bases loaded, "no sweat."* [Videotape]. (Available from Australian Baseball Federation, P.O. Box 58, Malvern, Victoria, Australia, 3144).

Scolinos, J. (1983). *Mental approach to baseball.* [Videotape]. (Available from Australian Baseball Federation, P.O. Box 58, Malvern, Victoria, Australia, 3144).

Stewart, A., & Heading, R. (1990). *Psychology and motivation in Australian football.* [Videotape]. (Available from National Football Council, 120 Jolimont Road, Jolimont, Victoria, Australia).

Stockton, B.A. (1985). *Coaching psychology.* [Videotape]. (Available from Championship Books and Video Productions, 2730 Graham St., Ames, IA 50010; 1-800-873-2730, $39.95).

Sutphen, R. (1989). *Golf: Mindprogramming to increase your skill.* [Videotape]. (Available from Valley of the Sun Publishing, P.O. Box 683, Ashland, OR 97520-0023; 1-800-225-4717, $19.95).

Voderman, C. (1988). *Mind over matter.* [Videotape]. (Available from National Coaching Foundation, 4 College Close, Beckett Park, Leeds, England LS6 3QHUK).

Whitaker, J. (1991). *Brainwaves golf.* [Videotape]. (Available from Televisual Communications, 300 S. Duncan Ave., Suite 112, Clearwater, FL 34615; 813-442-6480, $19.95).

Appendix K

Geographical List of Graduate Programs

There are six countries represented in this directory. The total number of programs represented is 103, as follows:

Australia: . . . . 7 programs

Canada: . . . . 12 programs

Great Britain: . . . . 7 programs

Singapore: . . . . 1 program

South Africa: . . . . 1 program

United States: . . . . 75 programs (in 35 states)

Total: . . . . 103 programs

Australia

University of Canberra

Deakin University, Rusden Campus

University of Queensland

University of Southern Queensland

Victoria University

University of Western Australia

University of Western Sydney

Canada

University of Alberta

Lakehead University

University of Manitoba

McGill University

Université de Montréal

University of Ottawa

Université du Québec à Trois-Rivières

Queen's University

Université de Sherbrooke

University of Waterloo

University of Western Ontario

York University

Great Britain

Chichester Institute of Higher Education

DeMontfort University Bedford

University of Edinburgh

University of Exeter

Leeds Metropolitan University

Manchester Metropolitan University

Staffordshire University

Singapore

Nanyang Technological University

South Africa

University of Stellenbosch

281

United States

Arizona
Arizona School of Professional Psychology
Arizona State University
University of Arizona

California
California State University, Fresno
California State University, Fullerton
California State University, Long Beach
California State University, Sacramento
University of California, Los Angeles
Humboldt State University
John F. Kennedy University
San Diego State University
San Diego University for Integrative Studies
San Jose State University
University of Southern California

Colorado
University of Northern Colorado

Connecticut
Southern Connecticut State University

Florida
Florida State University
University of Florida

Georgia
Georgia Southern University
University of Georgia

Idaho
Boise State University
University of Idaho

Illinois
Illinois State University
University of Illinois
Northern Illinois University
Southern Illinois University, Carbondale
Southern Illinois University Edwardsville
Western Illinois University

Indiana
Ball State University
Indiana University
Purdue University

Iowa
Iowa State University
University of Iowa

Kansas
Kansas State University
University of Kansas

Kentucky
Spalding University

Louisiana
Southeastern Louisiana University

Maryland
University of Maryland, College Park

Massachusetts
Boston University
Springfield College (Graduate Studies)
Springfield College (Psychology Department)

Michigan
Michigan State University
Wayne State University

Minnesota
Mankato State University
University of Minnesota

Missouri
University of Missouri, Columbia
University of Missouri, Kansas City

Montana
University of Montana

New Hampshire
University of New Hampshire

New Mexico
The University of New Mexico

New York
Ithaca College

282

North Carolina

University of North Carolina, Greensboro

North Dakota

University of North Dakota

Ohio

Bowling Green State University

Cleveland State University

Miami University

Oregon

Oregon State University

Pennsylvania

The Pennsylvania State University

Temple University

South Carolina

Furman University

Tennessee

University of Memphis (Human Movement Sciences and Education)

University of Memphis (Psychology)

University of Tennessee, Knoxville

Texas

University of Houston

University of North Texas

University of Texas, Austin

Texas Christian University (Kinesiology)

Texas Tech University

Utah

Utah State University

University of Utah

Virginia

University of Virginia

Virginia Commonwealth University

Washington

Western Washington University

West Virginia

West Virginia University

Wisconsin

University of Wisconsin, Milwaukee

Appendix L
Contact Persons

University of Alberta . . . . Anne Jordan
John Hogg

Arizona School of Professional Psychology . . . . Frank Gardner

Arizona State University . . . . Darren C. Treasure

University of Arizona . . . . Jean M. Williams
Peggy Collins

Ball State University . . . . S. Jae Park

Boise State University . . . . Linda M. Petlichkoff

Boston University . . . . Leonard Zaichkowsky

Bowling Green State University . . . . Vikki Krane
Bonnie Berger

California State University, Fresno . . . . Rebecca Crampton

California State University, Fullerton . . . . Bill Beam

California State University, Long Beach . . . . Michael Lacourse

California State University, Sacramento . . . . Karen L. Scarborough

UCLA . . . . Graduate Program
Director

University of Canberra . . . . John B. Gross

Chichester Institute of Higher Education . . . . Jan Graydon

Cleveland State University . . . . Susan Ziegler

Deakin University, Rusden Campus . . . . Rob Sands
Sue South

DeMontfort University Bedford . . . . Howard K. Hall

University of Edinburgh . . . . Dave Collins

University of Exeter . . . . Ken Fox

Florida State University . . . . David Pargman
Gershon Tenenbaum

University of Florida . . . . Christopher M. Janelle

Furman University . . . . Frank M. Powell

Georgia Southern University . . . . Kevin L. Burke

University of Georgia . . . . Rod K. Dishman
Patrick J. O'Connor

University of Houston . . . . Dale G. Pease

Humboldt State University . . . . Al Figone

University of Idaho . . . . Damon Burton

Illinois State University . . . . Anthony J. Amorose
Bill Vogler

University of Illinois . . . . Edward McAuley

Indiana University . . . . John S. Raglin

Iowa State University . . . . Rick Sharp

University of Iowa . . . . Dawn E. Stephens

Ithaca College . . . . Greg A. Shelley

Kansas State University . . . . David Dzewaltowski

University of Kansas . . . . David Templin

John F. Kennedy University . . . . Gail Solt

Lakehead University . . . . Jane Crossman

Leeds Metropolitan University . . . . Mark Nesti

Manchester Metropolitan University . . . . Nick Smith

University of Manitoba (Physical Education) . . . . Dennis Hrycaiko

University of Manitoba (Psychology) . . . . Garry Martin

Mankato State University . . . . Wayne C. Harris

University of Maryland, College Park . . . . Brad D. Hatfield

McGill University . . . . Graham Neil

University of Memphis . . . . Mary Fry
(Hum. Mvmt. Sciences & Educ.)

University of Memphis (Psychology) . . . . Andrew Meyers

Miami University . . . . Robert Weinberg

Michigan State University . . . . Martha Ewing

University of Minnesota . . . . Diane Wiese-Bjornstal

University of Missouri, Columbia . . . . Richard H. Cox

University of Missouri, Kansas City . . . . Joan Gallos

University of Montana . . . . Lewis A. Curry

Université de Montréal . . . . Wayne R. Halliwell

Nanyang Technological University . . . . Daniel Smith
Harry Tan
Nick Aplin

University of New Hampshire . . . . Heather Barber

The University of New Mexico . . . . Joy Griffin

University of North Carolina, Greensboro	Diane L. Gill
	Daniel Gould
	Jeffrey A. Katula
University of North Dakota	Sandra (Moritz) Short
University of North Texas (Kinesiology)	Peggy Richardson
	Scott Martin
University of North Texas (Psychology)	Trent Petrie
	Karen Cogan
University of Northern Colorado	Robert Brustad
Northern Illinois University	Laurice Zittel
Oregon State University	Vicki Ebbeck
University of Ottawa	Lise O'Reilly
The Pennsylvania State University	David Conroy
	Sam Slobunov
	David Yukelson
Université du Québec à Trois Rivières	Pierre Lacoste
Queen's University	John Albinson
University of Queensland	Stephanie Hanrahan
San Diego State University	Dennis J. Selder
San Diego University for Integrative Studies	Cristina Bortoni Versari
San Jose State University	David M. Furst
Université de Sherbrooke	Paul Deshaies
Southeastern Louisiana University	Dan Hollander
University of Southern California	John Callaghan
Southern Connecticut State University	David S. Kemler
Southern Illinois University, Carbondale	Elaine Blinde
Southern Illinois University, Edwardsville	Curt L. Lox
	Brian Butki
University of Southern Queensland	Steven Christensen
	Gerry Fogarty
	Andrea Lamont-Mills
Spalding University	Thomas Titus
Springfield College (Graduate Studies)	Betty L. Mann
Springfield College (Psychology Dept.)	Al Petitpas
Staffordshire University	Geoffrey Paull
University of Stellenbosch	Justus R. Potgieter
Temple University	Carole A. Oglesby
	Michael L. Sachs

286

University of Tennessee, Knoxville . . . . Craig A. Wrisberg

University of Texas, Austin . . . . John B. Bartholomew

Texas Christian University (Kinesiology) . . . . Gloria B. Solomon

Texas Tech University . . . . Lanie Dornier

Utah State University . . . . Richard Gordin

University of Utah . . . . Keith Henschen

Victoria University . . . . Mark Andersen
Daryl Marchant

University of Virginia . . . . Maureen Weiss

Virginia Commonwealth University . . . . Steven J. Danish

University of Waterloo . . . . L.R. Brawley

Wayne State University . . . . Jeff Martin

West Virginia University . . . . Andrew Ostrow

University of Western Australia . . . . J. Robert Grove
Sandy Gordon

Western Illinois University . . . . Laura Finch

University of Western Ontario . . . . Craig R. Hall

University of Western Sydney . . . . Patsy Tremayne

Western Washington University . . . . Ralph A. Vernacchia

University of Wisconsin, Milwaukee . . . . Barbara B. Meyer

York University . . . . Programme Assistant

Appendix M
Telephone Number List of Contact Persons

The following list provides telephone numbers for the contact persons in this directory (in some cases, only one person, generally the primary sport psychology contact person, is listed per program). The list is provided by area code and telephone number. Occasionally, students wish to find institutions in particular geographical areas and, within those areas, in particular area codes. The following list will help locate institutions by area code more efficiently. Telephone numbers are provided first for the United States, then for Australia, Canada, Great Britain, Singapore, and South Africa.

United States

203.392.6040	Southern Connecticut St. Univ.	David S. Kemler
208.426.1231	Boise State University	Linda Petlichkoff
208.885.2186	University of Idaho	Damon Burton
213.740.2971	Univ. of Southern California	John Callaghan
215.204.1948	Temple University	Carole A. Oglesby
215.204.8718	Temple University	Michael L. Sachs
216.687.4876	Cleveland State University	Susan Ziegler
217.333.6487	University of Illinois	Edward McAuley
301.405.2489	Univ. of Maryland, College Park	Brad Hatfield
303.351.1737	Univ. of Northern Colorado	Robert Brustad
304.293.3295	West Virginia University	Andrew Ostrow
309.298.2350	Western Illinois University	Laura Finch
309.438.8590	Illinois State University	Anthony J. Amorose
310.825.2617	UCLA	Grad Prog Director
313.577.1381	Wayne State University	Jeff Martin
317.285.1458	Ball State University	S. Jae Park
319.335.9348	University of Iowa	Dawn E. Stephens
336.334.3037	U. North Carolina, Greensboro	Daniel Gould
336.334.4683	U. North Carolina, Greensboro	Diane L. Gill
336.334.3271	U. North Carolina, Greensboro	Jeffrey A. Katula
352.392.0584	University of Florida	Christopher Janelle
360.650.3514	Western Washington University	Ralph Vernacchia
406.243.5242	University of Montana	Lewis A. Curry
408.924.3039	San Jose State University	David M. Furst

413.748.3125	Springfield Coll. (Grad School)	Betty L. Mann
413.748.3325	Springfield Coll. (Psych. Dept)	Al Petitpas
414.229.4591	Univ. of Wisconsin, Milwaukee	Barbara B. Meyer
419.372.2334	Bowling Green State University	Bonnie Berger
419.372.7233	Bowling Green State University	Vikki Krane
435.797.1506	Utah State University	Richard Gordin
480.965.8489	Arizona State University	Darren Treasure
502.585.9911	Spalding University	Thomas Titus
504.549.3870	Southeastern Louisiana Univ.	Dan Hollander
505.277.3534	The University of New Mexico	Joy Griffin
507.389.1818	Mankato State University	Wayne C. Harris
510.254.0110	John F. Kennedy University	Gail Solt
512.471.4407	University of Texas, Austin	John B. Bartholomew
513.529.2700	Miami University	Robert Weinberg
515.294.8650	Iowa State University	Rick Sharp
517.353.4652	Michigan State University	Martha Ewing
520.621.6984	University of Arizona	Jean M. Williams
520.621.7456	University of Arizona	Peggy Collins
541.737.6800	Oregon State University	Vicki Ebbeck
559.278.7094	California State University, Fresno	Rebecca Crampton
562.985.4558	Cal. State Univ., Long Beach	Michael Lacourse
573.882.7602	Univ. of Missouri, Columbia	Richard H. Cox
602.216.2600	Arizona School of Prof. Psych.	Frank Gardenr
602.965.7664	Arizona State University	Daniel M. Landers
603.862.2058	University of New Hampshire	Heather Barber
607.274.1275	Ithaca College	Greg A. Shelley
612.625.6580	University of Minnesota	D. Wiese-Bjornstal
617.353.3378	Boston University	L. Zaichkowsky
618.453.3119	Southern Illinois U. Carbondale	Elaine Blinde
618.650.2306	Southern Illinois U. Edwardsville	Brian Butki
618.650.5961	Southern Illinois U. Edwardsville	Curt L. Lox
619.594.1920	San Diego State University	Dennis J. Selder
701.777.4325	University of North Dakota	Sandra (Moritz) Short
706.542.4382	University of Georgia	Patrick O'Connor
706.542.9840	University of Georgia	Rod K. Dishman

707.826.3557	Humboldt State University	Al Figone
713.743.9838	University of Houston	Dale G. Pease
714.278.3432	Cal. State Univ., Fullerton	Bill Beam
801.581.7558	University of Utah	Keith Henschen
803.294.3418	Furman University	Frank M. Powell
804.924.7860	University of Virginia	Maureen Weiss
804.828.4384	Virginia Commonwealth Univ.	Steven J. Danish
806.742.3371	Texas Tech University	Lanie Dornier
812.855.1844	Indiana University	John S. Raglin
814.865.3451	Pennsylvania State University	David E. Conroy
814.865.3146	Pennsylvania State University	Sam Slobounov
814.865.0407	Pennsylvania State University	David Yukelson
815.753.1425	Northern Illinois University	Laurice Zittel
816.235.2236	Univ. of Missouri, Kansas City	Joan Gallos
817.565.3427	University of North Texas	Scott Martin
817.565.3427	University of North Texas	Peggy Richardson
817.257.6866	Texas Christian U. (Kinesiology)	Gloria B. Solomon
850.644.8793	Florida State University	David Pargman
850.644.8780	Florida State University	Gershon Tenenbaum
858.638.1999	San Diego Univ. for Integ. Studies	Cristina Bortoni Versari
865.974.1283	U. of Tennessee, Knoxville	Craig A. Wrisberg
901.678.4986	Univ. of Memphis (Human Mvmt.)	Mary Fry
901.678.2146	Univ. of Memphis (Psych.)	Andrew Meyers
912.681.5267	Georgia Southern University	Kevin L. Burke
913.532.0708	Kansas State University	D. Dzewaltowski
913.864.0778	University of Kansas	David Templin
916.278.7309	Cal. State Univ., Sacramento	Karen Scarborough
940.565.2671	University of North Texas	Karen Cogan
940.565.4718	University of North Texas	Trent Petrie

Australia

(03) 9244 7244	Deakin Univ., Rusden Campus	Rob Sands
(06) 2012009	University of Canberra	John B. Gross
61-3-9248-1132	Victoria University	Mark Andersen
61-3-9248-1135	Victoria University	Daryl Marchant
61-7-3365-6453	University of Queensland	Stephanie Hanrahan

61-8-9380-2361	Univ. of Western Australia	Sandy Gordon
61-8-9380-2361	Univ. of Western Australia	J. Robert Grove
61-7-46-31-1703	Univ. of Southern Queensland	Andrea Lamont-Mills
61-7-46-31-2379	Univ. of Southern Queensland	Gerry Fogarty
61-7-46-31-2707	Univ. of Southern Queensland	Steven Christensen
62-2-9772-6568	Univ. of Western Sydney	Patsy Tremayne

Canada

204.474.8589	University of Manitoba (Psych)	Garry Martin
204.474.8764	University of Manitoba (Phys Ed)	Dennis Hrycaiko
416.736.5728	York University	Programme Assistant
514.343.7008	Université de Montréal	Wayne Halliwell
514.398.4188	McGill University	Graham Neil
519.679.2111	University of Western Ontario	Craig R. Hall
519.885.1211	University of Waterloo	L.R. Brawley
613.562.5800	University of Ottawa	Lise O'Reilly
613.545.2666	Queen's University	John Albinson
780.492.3198	University of Alberta	Anne Jordan
780.492.2830	University of Alberta	John Hogg
807.343.8642	Lakehead University	Jane Crossman
819.376.5128	U. du Québec a Trois-Rivières	Pierre Lacoste
819.821.8000	Université de Sherbrooke	Paul Deshaies

Great Britain

0113-2837566	Leeds Metropolitan University	Mark Nesti
01234-793316	DeMontfort Univ., Bedford	Howard K. Hall
01243-816320	Chichester Inst. of Higher Ed.	Jan Graydon
44-131-312-6001	Unversity of Edinburgh	Dave Collins
+44-(0)-392-264792	University of Exeter	Ken Fox
Fax 44-161-2475455	Manchester Metropolitan Univ.	Nick Smith
44-1782-412515	Staffordshire University	Geoffrey Paull

Singapore

65-460-5358	Nanyang Technological Univ.	Harry Tan
65-460-5364	Nanyang Technological Univ.	Nick Aplin
65-460-5368	Nanyang Technological Univ.	Daniel Smith

South Africa

| 27-21-8084915 | University of Stellenbosch | Justus Potgieter |

Appendix N
Email Addresses for Contact Persons

The following lists email addresses for the contact persons in this directory alphabetically, first by program, then by individual. Please note that email addresses change frequently, and some of the addresses in this directory may be outdated by the time you read this. For those addresses that are no longer valid, or to locate those individuals who don't have addresses listed, surfing the Internet, particularly accessing a program's website, may enable you to locate a college/university address directory and find the correct address or to locate an address when one is not listed.

Alphabetically, by Program

University of Alberta

John Hogg . . . . jhogg@PER.UALBERTA.CA

Anne Jordan . . . . Ajordan@PER.UALBERTA.CA

Arizona School of Professional Psychology

Frank Gardner . . . . fgardner@azspp.edu

Arizona State University

Darren Treasure . . . . Darren.Treasure@asu.edu

University of Arizona

Jean M. Williams . . . . williams@u.arizona.edu

Peggy Collins . . . . lcollins@u.arizona.edu

Boise State University

Linda Petlichkoff . . . . lpetlic@boisestate.edu

Boston University

Leonard Zaichkowsky . . . . sport@acs.bu.edu

Bowling Green State University

Vikki Krane . . . . VKRANE@BGNET.BGSU.EDU

Bonnie Berger . . . . BBERGER@BGNET.BGSU.EDU

California State University, Fresno

Rebecca Crampton . . . . rebeccac@csufresno.edu

California State University, Long Beach

Michael Lacourse . . . . mlacours@csulb.edu

California State University, Sacramento

Karen Scarborough . . . . scarboro@csus.edu

University of California, Los Angeles (UCLA)

Graduate program director . . . . gradadm@psych.ucla.edu

University of Canberra
John Gross . . . . gross@science.canberra.edu.au

Chichester Institute of Higher Education
Jan Graydon . . . . 100443.2067@compuserve.com

Deakin University, Rusden Campus
Rob Sands . . . . rsands@deakin.edu.au

DeMontfort University Bedford
Howard K. Hall . . . . HKHall@DMU.AC.UK

University of Edinburgh
Dave Collins . . . . d.collins@ed.ac.uk

Florida State University
David Pargman . . . . dpargman@edres.fsu.edu

University of Florida
Christopher M. Janelle . . . . CJANELLE@HHP.UFL.EDU

Furman University
Frank M. Powell . . . . frank.powell@furman.edu

Georgia Southern University
Kevin L. Burke . . . . KevBurke@gsaix2.cc.GASOU.edu

University of Georgia
Rod K. Dishman . . . . rdishman@coe.uga.edu
Patrick J. O'Connor . . . . poconnor@arches.uga.edu

University of Houston
Dale G. Pease . . . . DPEASE@UH.EDU

University of Idaho
Damon Burton . . . . dburton@uidaho.edu

Illinois State University
Anthony J. Amorose . . . . ajamoro@ilstu.edu

University of Illinois
Edward McAuley . . . . a-mc3@uiuc.edu

Indiana University
John S. Raglin . . . . raglinj@indiana.edu

Iowa State University
Rick Sharp . . . . rlsharp@iastate.edu

University of Iowa
Dawn Stephens . . . . dawn-e-stephens@uiowa.edu

Ithaca College
Greg A. Shelley . . . . GSHELLEY@Ithaca.Edu

Kansas State University

David Dzewaltowski . . . . DADX@KSU.KSU.EDU

Lakehead University

Jane Crossman . . . . Jane.Crossman@lakeheadu.ca

Leeds Metropolitan University

Mark Nesti . . . . M.Nesti@lmu.ac.uk

Manchester Metropolitan University

Nick Smith . . . . N.C.SMITH@MMU.ac.uk

University of Maryland, College Park

Brad D. Hatfield . . . . bh5@umail.UMD.edu

McGill University

Graham Neil . . . . Neil@EDUCATION.MCGILL.CA

University of Memphis (Hum. Mvmt. Sciences and Educ.)

Mary Fry . . . . fry.mary@coe.memphis.edu

University of Memphis (Psychology)

Andrew Meyers . . . . AMEYERS@MEMPHIS.EDU

Miami University

Robert Weinberg . . . . WEINBER@MUOHIO.EDU

University of Minnesota

Diane Wiese-Bjornstal . . . . dwiese@tc.umn.edu

University of Missouri, Columbia

Richard H. Cox . . . . coxrh@missouri.edu

University of Missouri, Kansas City

Joan Gallos . . . . Gallos@umkc.edu

University of Montana

Lewis A. Curry . . . . curry58@selway.umt.edu

Nanyang Technological University

Daniel Smith . . . . desmith@nie.edu.sg

Harry Tan . . . . ekhtan@nie.edu.sg

Nick Aplin . . . . ngaplin@nie.edu.sg

University of New Hampshire

Heather Barber . . . . HB@CISUNIX.UNH.EDU

The University of New Mexico

Joy Griffin . . . . jgriffin@unm.edu

University of North Carolina, Greensboro

Diane Gill . . . . diane_gill@uncg.edu

Dan Gould . . . . drgould@uncg.edu

Jeffrey A. Katula . . . . jakatula@uncg.edu

University of North Dakota
Sandra (Moritz) Short . . . .   sandra_moritz@und.nodak.edu

University of North Texas (Kinesiology)
Scott Martin . . . .   SMARTIN@COEFS.COE.UNT.EDU

Peggy Richardson . . . .   RCHRDSN@COEFS.COE.UNT.EDU

University of North Texas (Psychology)
Karen Cogan . . . .   COGAN@DSA.UNT.EDU

Trent Petrie . . . .   PETRIET@UNT.EDU

University of Northern Colorado
Robert Brustad . . . .   bbrustad@hhs.UnivNorthCo.edu

Oregon State University
Vicki Ebbeck . . . .   vicki.ebbeck@orst.edu

University of Ottawa
Lise O'Reilly . . . .   lcosa@uottawa.ca

The Pennsylvania State University
David E. Conroy . . . .   DAVID-CONROY@PSU.EDU

Sam Slobounov . . . .   sms13@PSU.EDU

David Yukelson . . . .   Y39@PSU.EDU

Queens University
John Albinson . . . .   albinson@qucdn.queensu.ca

University of Queensland
Stephanie Hanrahan . . . .   steph@hms.uq.edu.au

San Diego State University
Dennis J. Selder . . . .   DSELDER@MAIL.SDSU.EDU

San Diego University for Integrative Studies
Cristina Bortoni Versari . . . .   cversari@sduis.edu

San Jose State University
David M. Furst . . . .   furstd@email.sjsu.edu

Université de Sherbrooke
Paul Deshaies . . . .   PDESHAIES@FEPS.USHERB.CA

Southeastern Louisiana University
Dan Hollander . . . .   dhollander@selu.edu

University of Southern California
John Callaghan . . . .   callagha@mizar.usc.edu

Southern Connecticut State University
David S. Kemler . . . .   Kemler@scsu.ctstateu.edu

Southern Illinois University, Carbondale
Elaine Blinde . . . .   Blinde@siu.edu

Southern Illinois University, Edwardsville

Curt L. Lox . . . . clox@siue.edu

Brian Butki . . . . bbutki@siue.edu

University of Southern Queensland

Steven Christensen . . . . christen@usq.edu.au

Gerry Fogarty . . . . fogarty@usq.edu.au

Andrea Lamont-Mills . . . . lamontm@usq.edu.au

University of Stellenbosch

Justus R. Potgieter . . . . JRP@MATIES.SUN.AC.ZA

Temple University

Carole A. Oglesby . . . . reds@astro.temple.edu

Michael L. Sachs . . . . msachs@nimbus.temple.edu

University of Tennessee, Knoxville

Craig A. Wrisberg . . . . caw@utk.edu

University of Texas, Austin

John B. Bartholomew . . . . john.bart@mail.utexas.edu

Texas Christian University (Kinesiology)

Gloria B. Solomon . . . . G.SOLOMON@TCU.EDU

Texas Tech University

Lanie Dornier . . . . lanie@ttu.edu

Utah State University

Richard Gordin . . . . gordin@cc.usu.edu

Victoria University

Mark Andersen . . . . mark.andersen@vu.edu.au

Daryl Marchant . . . . daryl.marchant@vu.edu.au

University of Virginia

Maureen Weiss . . . . mrw5d@virginia.edu

Virginia Commonwealth University

Steven J. Danish . . . . sdanish@saturn.vcu.edu

University of Waterloo

L.R. Brawley . . . . lrbrawle@healthy.uwaterloo.ca

Wayne State University

Jeff Martin . . . . 993975@wayne.edu

West Virginia University

Andrew Ostrow . . . . aostrow2@wvu.edu

University of Western Australia

Sandy Gordon . . . . sgordon@cyllene.uwa.edu.au

J. Robert Grove . . . . Bob.Grove@uwa.edu.au

Western Illinois University

Laura Finch . . . . LM-Finch@wiu.edu

University of Western Ontario

Craig R. Hall . . . . chall@julian.uwo.ca

University of Western Sydney

Patsy Tremayne . . . . p.tremayne@uws.edu.au

Western Washington University

Ralph A. Vernacchia . . . . anthony@cc.wwu.edu

University of Wisconsin, Milwaukee

Barbara B. Meyer . . . . bbmeyer@uwm.edu

York University

Barry Fowler . . . . EAHS@YORKU.CA

Alphabetically, by Contact Person

John Albinson . . . . albinson@qucdn.queensu.ca
    Queens University

Anthony J. Amorose . . . . ajamoro@ilstu.edu
    Illinois State University

Mark Andersen . . . . mark.andersen@vu.edu.au
    Victoria University

Nick Aplin . . . . ngaplin@nie.edu.sg
    Nanyang Technological University

Heather Barber . . . . HB@CISUNIX.UNH.EDU
    University of New Hampshire

John B. Bartholomew . . . . john.bart@mail.utexas.edu
    University of Texas, Austin

Bonnie Berger . . . . bberger@bgnet.bgsu.edu
    Bowling Green State University

Elaine Blinde . . . . Blinde@SIU.EDU
    Southern Illinois University, Carbondale

L.R. Brawley . . . . lrbrawle@healthy.uwaterloo.ca
    University of Waterloo

Robert Brustad . . . . bbrustad@hhs.UnivNorthCo.edu
    University of Northern Colorado

Kevin L. Burke . . . . KevBurke@gsaix2.cc.GASOU.edu
    Georgia Southern University

Damon Burton . . . . dburton@uidaho.edu
    University of Idaho

Brian Butki . . . . bbutki@sieu.edu
    Southern Illinois University, Edwardsville

John Callaghan . . . . callagha@mizar.usc.edu
    University of Southern California

Steven Christensen . . . . christen@usq.edu.au
    University of Southern Queensland

Karen Cogan .... COGAN@DSA.UNT.EDU
    University of North Texas (Psychology)

Dave Collins .... d.collins@ed.ac.uk
    University of Edinburgh

Peggy Collins .... lcollins@u.arizona.edu
    University of Arizona

David E. Conroy .... DAVID-CONROY@PSU.EDU
    The Pennsylvania State University

Richard H. Cox .... coxrh@missouri.edu
    University of Missouri, Columbia

Rebecca Crampton .... rebeccac@csufresno.edu
    California State University, Fresno

Jane Crossman .... Jane.Crossman@lakeheadu.ca
    Lakehead University

Lewis A. Curry .... curry58@selway.umt.edu
    University of Montana

Steven J. Danish .... sdanish@saturn.vcu.edu
    Virginia Commonwealth University

Paul Deshaies .... PDESHAIES@FEPS.USHERB.CA
    Université de Sherbrooke

Rod K. Dishman .... rdishman@coe.uga.edu
    University of Georgia

Lanie Dornier .... lanie@ttu.edu
    Texas Tech University

David Dzewaltowski .... DADX@KSU.KSU.EDU
    Kansas State University

Vicki Ebbeck .... vicki.ebbeck@orst.edu
    Oregon State University

Laura Finch .... LM-Finch@wiu.edu
    Western Illinois University

Gerry Fogarty .... fogarty@usg.edu.au
    University of Southern Queensland

Barry Fowler .... EAHS@YORKU.CA
    York University

Mary Fry .... fry.mary@coe.memphis.edu
    University of Memphis (Hum. Mvmt. Sciences)

David M. Furst .... furstd@email.sjsu.edu
    San Jose State University

Joan Gallos .... gallos@umkc.edu
    University of Missouri, Kansas City

Frank Gardner .... fgardner@azspp.edu
    Arizona School of Professional Psychology

Diane Gill .... diane_gill@uncg.edu
    University of North Carolina, Greensboro

Richard Gordin .... gordin@cc.usu.edu
    Utah State University

Sandy Gordon . . . . sgordon@cyllene.uwa.edu.au
    University of Western Australia

Dan Gould . . . . drgould@uncg.edu
    University of North Carolina, Greensboro

Jan Graydon . . . . 100443.2067@compuserve.com
    Chichester Institute of Higher Education

Joy Griffin . . . . jgriffin@unm.edu
    The University of New Mexico

John Gross . . . . gross@science.canberra.edu.au
    University of Canberra

J. Robert Grove . . . . Bob.Grove@uwa.edu.au
    University of Western Australia

Craig R. Hall . . . . CHALL@JULIAN.UWO.CA
    University of Western Ontario

Howard K. Hall . . . . HKHall@DMU.AC.UK
    DeMontfort University Bedford

Stephanie Hanrahan . . . . steph@hms01.hms.uq.edu.au
    University of Queensland

Brad D. Hatfield . . . . bh5@umail.umd.edu
    University of Maryland, College Park

John Hogg . . . . jhogg@PER.UALBERTA.CA
    University of Alberta

Dan Hollander . . . . dhollander@selu.edu
    Southeastern Louisiana University

Anne Jordan . . . . Ajordan@PER.UALBERTA.CA
    University of Alberta

Jeffrey A. Katula . . . . jakatula@uncg.edu
    University of North Carolina, Greensboro

David S. Kemler . . . . Kemler@scsu.ctstateu.edu
    Southern Connecticut State University

Vikki Krane . . . . VKRANE@BGNET.BGSU.EDU
    Bowling Green State University

Michael Lacourse . . . . mlacours@csulb.edu
    California State University, Long Beach

Andrea Lamont-Mills . . . . lamontm@usq.edu.au
    University of Southern Queensland

Curt L. Lox . . . . clox@siue.edu
    Southern Illinois University Edwardsville

Daryl Marchant . . . . daryl.marchant@vu.edu.au
    Victoria University

Jeff Martin . . . . 993975@wayne.edu
    Wayne State University

Scott Martin . . . . smartin@coefs.coe.unt.edu
    University of North Texas (Kinesiology)

Edward McAuley . . . . a-mc3@uiuc.edu
    University of Illinois

Barbara Meyer . . . . bbmeyer@umw.edu
    University of Wisconsin, Milwaukee

Andrew Meyers . . . . AMEYERS@MEMPHIS.EDU
    University of Memphis (Psychology)

Graham Neil . . . . Neil@EDUCATION.MCGILL.CA
    McGill University

Mark Nesti . . . . M.Nesti@lmu.ac.uk
    Leeds Metropolitan University

Patrick J. O'Connor . . . . poconnor@arches.uga.edu
    University of Georgia

Carole A. Oglesby . . . . reds@astro.temple.edu
    Temple University

Lise O'Reilly . . . . lcosa@uottawa.ca
    University of Ottawa

Andrew Ostrow . . . . aostrow2@wvu.edu
    West Virginia University

David Pargman . . . . dpargman@edres.fsu.edu
    Florida State University

Dale G. Pease . . . . DPEASE@UH.EDU
    University of Houston

Linda Petlichkoff . . . . lpetlic@boisestate.edu
    Boise State University

Trent Petrie . . . . PETRIET@UNT.EDU
    University of North Texas (Psychology)

Justus R. Potgieter . . . . JRP@MATIES.SUN.AC.ZA
    University of Stellenbosch

Frank M. Powell . . . . frank.powell@furman.edu
    Furman University

John S. Raglin . . . . raglinj@indiana.edu
    Indiana University

Peggy Richardson . . . . rchrdsn@coefs.coe.unt.edu
    University of North Texas (Kinesiology)

Michael L. Sachs . . . . msachs@nimbus.temple.edu
    Temple University

Rob Sands . . . . rsands@deakin.edu.au
    Deakin University, Rusden Campus

Karen Scarborough . . . . scarboro@csus.edu
    California State University, Sacramento

Dennis J. Selder . . . . DSELDER@MAIL.SDSU.EDU
    San Diego State University

Rick Sharp . . . . rlsharp@iastate.edu
    Iowa State University

Greg A. Shelley . . . . Gshelley@Ithaca.Edu
    Ithaca College

Sandra (Moritz) Short . . . . sandra_moritz@und.nodak.edu
    University of North Dakota

Sam Slobounov . . . . sms18@PSU.EDU
    The Pennsylvania State University

Daniel Smith . . . . desmith@nie.edu.sg
    Nanyang Technological University

Nick Smith . . . . N.C.SMITH@MMU.ac.uk
    Manchester Metropolitan University

Gloria B. Solomon . . . . G.SOLOMON@TCU.EDU
    Texas Christian University (Kinesiology)

Dawn Stephens . . . . dawn-e-stephens@uiowa.edu
    University of Iowa

Harry Tan . . . . ekhtan@nie.edu.sg
    Nanyang Technological University

Darren Treasure . . . . Darren.Treasure@asu.edu
    Arizona State University

Patsy Tremayne . . . . p.tremayne@uws.edu.au
    University of Western Sydney

Ralph A. Vernacchia . . . . anthony@cc.wwu.edu
    Western Washington University

Cristina Bortoni Versari . . . . cversari@sduis.edu
    San Diego University for Integrative Studies

Robert Weinberg . . . . WEINBER@MUOHIO.EDU
    Miami University

Maureen Weiss . . . . mrw5d@virginia.edu
    University of Virginia

Diane Wiese-Bjornstal . . . . dwiese@umn.edu
    University of Minnesota

Jean M. Williams . . . . williams@u.arizona.edu
    University of Arizona

Craig A. Wrisberg . . . . caw@utk.edu
    University of Tennessee, Knoxville

David Yukelson . . . . Y39@PSU.EDU
    The Pennsylvania State University

Leonard Zaichkowsky . . . . sport@acs.bu.edu
    Boston University

Appendix O
Surfing the Net: Using the Internet for Success

Lindsey Blom, Georgia Southern University
Kevin L. Burke, Georgia Southern University
David Dillard, Temple University
Vince J. Granito, John Carroll University
Michael L. Sachs, Temple University

This appendix includes three sections. The first section is written by David Dillard and provides a background primer for effective use of computer and Internet-information skills in sport psychology. The second section, written by Lindsey Blom, Kevin Burke, Vince Granito, and Michael Sachs, offers some detailed information on surfing the web within exercise and sport psychology, along with an extensive list of websites for that area. The third section, written by Lindsey Blom and Kevin Burke, presents information about online sport psychology courses and programs, a growing option in the field.

Computer and Internet-Information Skills for Sport Psychology
David Dillard
Reference Librarian and Subject Specialist
Temple University
215.204.4584
jwne@astro.temple.edu

Since around 1970, computers have had a tremendous impact, as information resources, on the conduct of all types of information seeking, ranging from casual searches to serious research in almost any subject field. The Internet is merely the latest development in this chain of innovations. For scholarly research, the bibliographic databases that began to appear in the early 1970s are arguably more useful than the Internet because they provide a gateway to collections of subject-specific academic research articles from the significant journals, as well as to other information resources in the given field. Some of the literature is taken from peer-reviewed journals, while other articles are culled from the trade journals and other sources of literature in the particular discipline of the database.

While many databases are very scholarly, a large group of them focus on popular magazines and newspapers; these are very good resources for finding discussions of current news and controversies. Among these databases are *Readers Guide to Periodical Literature*, *Magazine Index*, *Newspaper Index*, *Newsbank*, *Periodical Abstracts*, *Ethnic Newswatch*, and *Lexis-Nexis Universe*. Such databases are becoming more readily available at academic and public libraries.

One key to searching a database is vocabulary. Databases usually provide thesauri that indicate which subject headings are used in their files. Plain English-language thesauri, especially the *Synonym Finder* (Rodale Press), are very good places to find

302

groups of synonyms to make search results more complete. For further information about the effective use of computers and the Internet, browse the Educational CyberPlayGround at www.edu-cyberpg.com.

For specific information about the database-searching process, see my articles at the Educational Cyberplayground. The second article includes a detailed example of a complete search. To find the articles, follow this path: Click on "Welcome," then "Ringleaders," then go to my page near the bottom, under "Reference."

Databases tend to be eclectic, drawing literature from subject disciplines that are neighbors to the field of coverage. For example, *ERIC*, a United States government-sponsored database that indexes and abstracts education periodicals and unpublished documents, culls relevant articles from fields as diverse as communications, psychology, recreation, sociology, and human resources, along with its core coverage of the education journals and sources. On the other hand, some databases, like *Social Work Abstracts*, stay much more strictly within the confines of their subject field's publications.

Databases do tend to be predictable in their coverage. They index a specific group of periodicals, either selectively or from cover to cover. They catalogue a specific time range. Generally, they do not cover even superb and highly relevant articles from journals not on their coverage list of periodicals. This is one reason for searching interdisciplinary topics in several relevant databases; this way, you can obtain a wider range of relevant citations from a variety of viewpoints on the search topic.

Sport psychology, an interdisciplinary field, finds its knowledge and information scattered in a number of disciplines and databases. *SportDiscus*, from the Sports Information Resource Center; *PsychINFO*, from the American Psychological Association; and *ERIC*, from the Educational Resources Information Center, are possibly the three most important databases for the sport psychology researcher. There are, however, other databases that can be very useful for some of the research in the field. Two of these are *Sociological Abstracts* and *ABI-Inform*. *ABI-Inform* covers business trade and journal literature and is now found as part of *ProQuest Direct*, where ABI is supplemented by coverage of popular and social science periodicals. Additional databases relevant to sport psychology research include the *Commonwealth Agricultural Bureau* database, with its strong subfile in recreation; *Mental Health Abstracts*; and *Medline*. For discussion of kinesiology, ergonomics, and sports-injury issues, *Medline* is supplemented in coverage by databases such as *BIOSIS (Biological Abstracts)*, *EMBASE (Excerpta Medica)*, and *CINAHL (Combined Index to Nursing and Allied Health)*. *Dissertation Abstracts* is an important database for discovering completed dissertations relevant to research in sport psychology. Additionally, the International Institute for Sport and Human Performance at the University of Oregon (Eugene, OR 97403-1243) publishes a bulletin of microform publications of theses and dissertations in the exercise and sport sciences, including exercise and sport psychology. Their Internet URL is <darkwing.uorego.edu/~micropub/>.

Some may think that business literature is not relevant to sport psychology. However, it becomes much more applicable when one looks at modern athletics at the college and professional levels. Sport at these levels is run as a business. Much has been written in the business literature on issues such as wage negotiations, high salaries, legal issues of contracts, and side ventures like product promotion. Such articles provide insight regarding the impact these distractions have on athletic performance. Similarly, education databases like *ERIC* and *Education Abstracts* provide a large body of material on children as related to sports, physical education, physical development, and much more. The selection of databases used in sport psychology research depends, of course, on the mix of databases that have potential relevance to the topic of study.

The Internet is a totally different mixture of resources than one finds in the prim and neat world of databases. The tremendous range of resources range from high quality to poor, creating the immediate problem of determining credibility. Some well-written web pages are written in the most erudite prose merely to sell a product. There are no rules on the Internet about peer review. Hucksters and criminals have as much freedom to create web pages as do professors and scientists. Never before has a medium enabled such a wide range of people to publish so much material and to do so instantaneously. You must therefore be far more critical in your acceptance of these materials than those of academic publications. Critical analysis of sources is always important; however, the importance of critical analysis is greatly increased when you use the Internet. For example, in scholarly literature, hoaxes like the Piltdown man are the exception. On the web, however, entire web pages from a variety of governmental, organizational, and corporate sources are devoted to making people aware of the various "news" stories available on the Internet that are, in fact, complete hoaxes.

Finding relevant information is another complex issue. Databases usually operate on software that permits complex and frequently multistep search statements designed to exhaust the multifaceted topic under study. Search engines theoretically help users search for information quickly and efficiently on the web; however, search tools on the web permit only very rudimentary search statements, and each search engine works somewhat differently than the others. Some search engines do an excellent job of finding information; some are moderately successful; and some are just plain awful. The best search engine to use is the one that finds a satisfactory answer to the question you are working on at the time. One question can get better results from a particular search engine than can another question; therefore, there is no one search engine that is always, or perhaps even usually, the best place to visit. Furthermore, results for the same search in the same search engine can differ even when the searches are done minutes apart. One reason for this is a difference in how heavily the search engine is being used at the time of each search.

Different search engines have different strengths, depending on how they are structured. Some work better in broad-concept searches, while others are good at finding nitty-gritty pieces of information. Importantly, a search engine is not limited to searching the content of web pages. There are metatags. These metatags are unseen by the website reader but are provided by the web page owner to describe the contents of the website to the search engine. Aggressive marketers may use words that will attract search engine user 'hits' but that are not honestly descriptive of the site. Metatag abuse can get a website thrown off a search engine. Due to the large number of sites coming into being every day, these discrepancies are very hard for search engines to detect. Just as there is an email-based discussion group for sport psychologists (SPORTPSY), there is a discussion group, I-Search, which includes web businessmen and website owners along with search engine experts. Discussion on I-Search includes issues such as (a) techniques to get web pages listed on search engines, and (b) ways to attain higher position rankings in search results from word searches using search engines in which the websites are described by key words. Information and sources on the web are indexed in more ways than by academic, objective analyses of the subject content of websites.

With all of these problems, why bother using the Internet as an information tool? Like most coins, this issue has two sides. Search engines (the better ones, at least), despite any weaknesses and flaws, are very powerful tools for finding information. Several very good ones bear mentioning. In preparing my discussion of hoaxes, to make sure the information about Piltdown was correct, I went to Google, a product of Netscape, and searched this phrase: "pilt and hoax". In less than 30 seconds the first record showed me that indeed the Piltdown man was the hoax I was thinking about, and the first three records of the nine returned were sources that discussed the concept I was checking. The first item I found was an extensive article on the topic with a 49-item bibliography of publications about Piltdown man. This resource, regardless of the fact that it came from the web, would be a credible place to commence research on the topic. The third item on the list was quite another story; it was a term paper that defended creationism and used Piltdown man as an example of substantial evidence to refute Darwin's theories. More importantly, it came from a web service for students, called School Sucks, which serves these students as a resource for obtaining prewritten term papers that will save them the trouble of writing their own.

Most people who use the Internet a great deal have their own favorite list of preferred search engines, and for many people, this is subject to change as they learn of new and better ones. Different tasks will tend to point to different search tools. Yahoo and the Open Directory Project, for example, are excellent resources for a basic concept search or when you want to look at a web directory of specific kinds of websites, such as sites for medical employment. Google is a tremendous resource and a recent development that came from work at Stanford University, where it was created. It is now owned by Netscape (America Online) and is where I usually begin a web search. AltaVista is a quality search tool as well and is good at finding discussion group contributions from archived, web-accessible discussion group postings. Excite and Northern Light also have very good search tools. Dogpile and Metafind are examples of multiple search engine search resources; these tools will take your search query and run it sequentially through a number of different search engines, giving results from each. Dogpile, for example, searches 14 different search engines. This is a good resource for doing troublesome searches in which it is difficult to find reliable answers to meet the informational need. These are some of the general all-subject search engines I currently recommend.

Another resource for searching and exploring the web is the excellent site made available to the public for free by the *Encyclopedia Britannica* (www.britannica.com/). This not only contains the full text of the encyclopedia, but also provides search results that lead to websites from their Internet website search engine. These searches generally lead to reliable and high-quality websites.

Quite a few specialized search engines focus on specific fields, and here are two examples. The first is Omni, which focuses on medical web resources: <omni.ac.uk/search/>. The second is Sponet (www.sponet.de/), a resource that focuses on sport science, biomechanics, and exercise physiology.

There is more to the pathways of the Internet than search engines. To gain skill in using the Internet, it is important that you explore and that you create a working file of sites that are of potential value for research or personal interests. It is helpful to record websites deemed of future value either in subject folders in your email, in a subject-arranged, loose-leaf binder, or as bookmarks on your web browser. You can use a web-based email account (such as Hotmail or YahooMail) as a storage device for favorite websites; you can also use email services such as Netscape Communicator or Internet Explorer Outlook. In these cases it is possible to click on web addresses found in the stored email messages and go to those websites directly from the email message. I tracked down Omni and Sponet from my personal record-keeping system for web information.

You can utilize the Internet in infinite ways to gain knowledge. I have covered three major techniques thus far: searching, guided exploration, and record keeping for future learning activities. The fourth and last method I will address is interpersonal communication, something that is lacking in databases completely unless you know the helpdesk phone number of the database or the search software provider. On the Internet there are newsgroups and discussion groups on almost any subject, topic, or field that you can name. Finding informative, quality discussion groups on topics that interest you affords you the opportunity to read commentary on issues that come up on those lists. You can find out what others think about those issues and respond if you want to make comments or differ with the ideas presented. A normal function of such discussion lists is to obtain specific information by asking for answers, ideas, or assistance. Some email discussion lists are one-way electronic newsletters or magazines and do not permit reader postings. Search engines are available that specialize in discussion groups and list the discussion groups they index topically; you can use these search engines to find discussion groups that focus on your interests.

Indeed, there is a multitude of resources and tools on the web that can be helpful or educational. This brief introduction to computerized information tools serves only to open the door and to alert you to the benefits and dangers to be found in this new eZnvironment. If you believe my use of the word *danger* to be too strong, consider the computer virus problem and the havoc it is wreaking on expensive computers and networks. There are many reasons for educated, wise, and careful use of the Internet, such as learning to identify and to avoid scams and hoaxes. Discussion groups focused on web issues are therefore helpful to include in your list of subscriptions. They will enhance your ability to use the Internet more effectively and more safely. They are especially beneficial for users who are just beginning to explore this constantly changing environment.

Surfing the Net

Lindsey Blom, Georgia Southern University
Kevin L. Burke, Georgia Southern University
Vince J. Granito, John Carroll University
Michael L. Sachs, Temple University

Attaining information about the field of sport psychology in general, or about graduate programs specifically, is in many cases as easy as typing on a computer keyboard. Thanks to the convenience of the Internet, a wealth of sport psychology information lies at your fingertips. Many colleges and universities make available through their World Wide Web sites much of the same graduate program information published in graduate catalogues. (For the graduate programs in this directory in Appendix P check the listing of available websites as of July 1, 2000.) You may be able to find graduate program applications, assistantship information and applications, graduate course offerings and requirements, and information about (perhaps even photos of) the graduate faculty involved in the programs that interest you.

The Internet, specifically email, can allow you to contact faculty at programs of interest (see Appendix N for email addresses of contact persons for the graduate programs in this directory). Other sources (e.g., *AAASP Membership Directory*) provide email addresses for colleagues in the field with whom you can discuss the hot sport-psychology topics of the day and/or where to eat at the site of the next sport psychology conference. Email is certainly a viable (and in some ways preferable) option for communication, as compared to letters, faxes, or telephone calls.

Numerous sites on the Internet address exercise- and sport-related issues. The most established site in sport psychology is SPORTPSY, originally established in 1987 at the University of Maryland at Baltimore and still coordinated by Michael Sachs at Temple University. SPORTPSY deals with a wide variety of areas in exercise and sport psychology, from discussions on issues such as certification and confidentiality to conference information, job announcements, and requests for information on topics within the field. You can join by sending the following command at your command line: TELL LISTSERV AT LISTSERV.TEMPLE.EDU SUB SPORTPSY your name

or by sending the following message to LISTSERV@LISTSERV.TEMPLE.EDU

SUB SPORTPSY your name

SPORTPSY is at LISTSERV.TEMPLE.EDU and if the above commands don't work, just write to Michael Sachs directly at msachs@nimbus.temple.edu and he can add you himself (given his "vast" powers as list coordinator).

The World Wide Web has grown exponentially, and a dizzying number of sites have been developed from a diverse population ranging from individual faculty members to international organizations. Search engines are available to help users search for information on various topics (see David Dillard's article in this directory or your local Internet/World Wide Web guru for suggestions on the latest/best resources). The list that follows was compiled by the four authors (with some helpful additions from Dr. Jack Lesyk of the Ohio Center for Sport Psychology. Check out his website under Sport Psychology Related Sites), and addresses are hopefully still correct. No attempt has been made to screen these sites for the quality of their information. Most of the information should be of good quality and derived from reputable sources; however, especially for "personal" websites, there is no screening regarding information posted on a website. Therefore, the cardinal rule is always "User Beware."

Enjoy your surfing (always physical activity involved!) through the Internet.

Websites for Sport and Exercise Psychology

Associations and Organizations

American College of Sports Medicine
www.acsm.org/

American Medical Society for Sports Medicine
www.sportsmed.upmc.edu/~amssm/

American Psychological Association
www.apa.org/

American Sport Education Program
www.asep.com/

Association for the Advancement of Applied Sport Psychology
www.aaasponline.org/

The Center for Sport Psychology & Performance Excellence
www.sportpsych.unt.edu/index.html

Coaching Association of Canada
www.coach.ca/

Division 47 (Exercise and Sport Psychology) of the American Psychological Association
www.psyc.unt.edu/apadiv47

Fitness Information Technology
www.fitinfotech.com

German Association of Sport Psychology
www.uni-leipzig.de/~asp/english/index.html

Human Kinetics Publishers
www.humankinetics.com/

International Institute for Sport & Human Performance
darkwing.uoregon.edu/~iishp/index.html

Los Angeles Sport Psychology Network
www-scf.usc.edu/~clcooper/laspn.htm

Michigan State University's Youth Sports Institute
www.edc.msu.edu/units/Dept/PEES/ysi/ysihome.html

National Alliance for Health, Physical Education, Recreation, and Dance
www.aahperd.org/

National Alliance for Youth Sports
www.nays.org/

National Strength and Conditioning Association
www.nsca-lift.org

North American Society for Psychology of Sport and Physical Activity
grove.ufl.edu/~naspspa/naspspa.org/

Women's Sports Foundation
www.womenssportsfoundation.org

Sport Psychology-Related Sites

Art, Writing, and Sport Services
www.awss.com/index.htm

Australian College of Applied Psychology
www.acap.edu.au/index.html

Center for Sport Psychology Web Conferences
webct.courses.unt.edu/public/sportpsych/

Enhanced Performance Systems
www.enhanced-performance.com/

Focused Training
focusedtraining.com/

Golf Psych: The Leading Golf Psychology System
www.golfpsych.com/

John Murray (articles on the mental side of tennis)
tennisserver.com/

Journal of Psychology and the Behavioral Sciences
alpha.fdu.edu/psychweb/JPBS.htm

Los Angeles Sport Psychology Network
www-scf.usc.edu/~clcooper/laspn.htm

The Mental Edge Article
www.ultranet.com/~dupck/mntledge.html

Mind Tools column on Sport Psychology
www.mindtools.com/

Ohio Center for Sport Psychology (Jack Lesyk)
www.sportpsych.unt.edu/index.html

Peak Performance Online
www.pponline.co.uk/

Peak Performance Sports
www.peaksports.com/

The Performance Advisor
members.home.net/performance.advisor/index.htm

The Physician & Sports Medicine (using the mind power for healing)
www.physsportsmed.com/

Positive Coaching Alliance
www.positivecoach.org

Potentium: The Coaching Network
www.potentium.ca/

Psyched 4 Sports
www.psyched4sports.com/

Psychology in Extreme Conditions
www.geocities.com/CapeCanaveral/Launchpad/1033/index.htm

Psychology in Spain
www.cop.es/

Sport Psychology
hometown.aol.com/gardconsul/fitness/index.htm

Sport Psychology
sport-psychology.com

Sport Psychology and Golf
golfweb.com/instruction/cohn/

Sport Psychology Information
spot.colorado.edu/~collinsj/

Sport Psychology with Karlene Sugarman
www.psychwww.com/sports/index.htm

Sport Psychology in Spain
www.ucm.es/OTROS/Psyap/hispania/cruz.htm

Sport Science
www.sportsci.org/

Sporting Excellence
ds.dial.pipex.com/town/avenue/xhi48/target-resources/index.htm

Sports Coach
www.brianmac.demon.co.uk/

Sports Psychology
www.sportspsychology.com/

Cristina Versari (self-help and psychology magazine)
www.cybertowers.com/self-help/

Women's Mental Game Plan
www.inc.com/users/mentalgame.html

Sport Psychology Products

American Psychological Association Books
www.apa.org/books/homepage.html

Brent Rushall (sport psychology workshops offered for coaches)
www-rohan.sdsu.edu/dept/coachsci/index.htm

Optimal Performance Institute
www.bookzone.com/optimal/

Sport Psychology for Athletes
www.drrelax.com/baseball.htm

Sport Psychology Oversite
www.personalumich.edu/~bing/oversite/sportpsych.html

Sport Psychology Questions and Answers
www.sportdoc.com/

Sport Psychology Services (Apex)
www.ux1.eiu.edu/~cfglc/Apexmain.htm

University of Washington's Husky Sport Psychology Services
depts.washington.edu/hsps/

Winners Unlimited Inc.
www.winnersunlimited.com/

Resource List

FitnessLink
www.fitnesslink.com

Just SPORTS for Women (issues related to women and sport)
justwomen.com/

Mental Health Net (Web resource for health and sport psychology)
www.cmhc.com/guide/pro07.htm

Psychwatch-Sport Psychology
www.psychwatch.com/sport_psychology.htm

Sport Psychology Links
www-rohan.sdsu.edu/~psyched/Links.html

Sport Psychology-research sources
server.bmod.athabascau.ca/html/aupr/sport.htm

Strength Online
www.deepsquatter.com/strength/subscribe.htm

Supertraining (book about training)
www.geocities.com/Colosseum/8682/siff.htm

Specific Sport Information Sites

Amateur Softball Association
www.softball.org/

American Youth Soccer Association
www.soccer.org/

CNN Sports
cnnsi.com/index.html

Coaching Youth Sports
www.youth-sports.com

Complete Soccer Academy
www.socceracademy.com/

Cool Running
www.coolrunning.com

The Cooper Institute for Aerobic Research
www.cooperinst.org/

The Cyclotherapist (cycling and sport psychology)
thecyclotherapist.com/

ESPN's Sport Zone
espn.go.com/

Go, girl! Magazine (sports and fitness for women)
www.gogirlmag.com/

Golf
www.igolf.com/

The Golf Psychology Training Center
www.drsport.com/

Golf Web
www.golfweb.com/

Major League Baseball
www.majorleaguebaseball.com/

Mind Games: Sport Psychology for Every Sport
drrelax.com/run.html
drrelax.com/pwrlift.htm
drrelax.com/soccer.htm
drrelax.com/baseball.htm
drrelax.com/volley.htm
drrelax.com/bskball.htm

Multi-sport (running)
www.multispoort.com/

National Basketball Association
www.nba.com/

NCAA
www.ncaa.org

NCAA Championships
www.ncaachampionships.com/index.html

National Hockey League
www.nhl.com/

The National Strength and Conditioning Association
www.nsca-lift.org/menu.htm

Peak Running Performance
www.peakrun.com/index.html

SearchUp
www.searchup.com/sports/

Sport Information
www.sportquest.com/

Sport Information Resource Center (SIRC)
sirc.ca/

Stadiums and Arenas
www.wwcd.com/stadiums.html

Swimming Science Journal
www-rohan.sdsu.edu/dept/coachsci/swimming/index.htm

Sydney 2000 Olympic Games
www.sydney.olympic.org/

Title IX Information
bailiwick.lib.uiowa.edu/ge/

U.S. Olympic Committee
www.usoc.org/

U.S. Youth Soccer Association
www.usysa.org/

USA Hockey
www.usahockey.com/

USA Today Sports Section
www.usatoday.com/sports/sfront.htm

USA Wrestling
www.usawrestling.org/

United States Golf Association
www.usga.org/

United States Swimming
www.usswim.org/

United States Tennis Association
www.usta.com/

The Virtual Resource Centre for Sports Information
www.sportquest.com/search.html
www.sportdiscus.com/

Online Sport Psychology Courses

Lindsey Blom and Kevin L. Burke
Georgia Southern University

A fast-growing and exciting dimension of the field of exercise and sport psychology is the availability of courses (and even complete degree programs) online. The following list is most likely incomplete due to the exponential development of such offerings. However, it provides a starting point for possibilities; networking with colleagues, belonging to SPORTPSY, and using available search engines may help you to uncover other possibilities. Please note that the following information was provided by the programs indicated and should be checked with the programs for accuracy. No endorsement of any particular program(s) is implied.

Capella University

All courses in the School of Psychology are offered in an online-course format. Courses are accessed through the Capella University website and start at the beginning of a quarter. Each course is divided into 10 learning units, and learners complete 1 unit each week. Approximately 2 weeks will be left at the end of the course before the quarter is officially over, allowing learners plenty of time to complete the final course paper before the next quarter begins. Each course is assigned 5 quarter credits, enrolls 15 20 learners, and has an instructor. The instructor for each course posts assignments and discussion questions each week. At the beginning of each week, learners log into their courses to get the assignments and read the questions; later, they log in and post their indepth responses to the discussion questions as well as read and respond to their fellow learners' responses. It is advised that learners will spend a minimum of 10 hours per course, each week. About half of this time will actually be spent online.

PSY8840: Principles of Sport Psychology

This course is an overview of the field of sport psychology. It covers a broad range of topics that will be investigated in greater detail in additional courses. Topics include personality, attention, anxiety and arousal, arousal adjustment strategies, cognitive-behavioral intervention, causal attribution, motivation, selfconfidence, psychobiology, and social issues of sport. The learner will leave this course with an eclectic understanding of sport psychology.

PSY8841: Performance Enhancement in Sports

Performance enhancement is the most common issue dealt with by sport psychologists. Knowing how to improve performance through mental strategies in the arena of sport is a critical factor in an athletic success. This course examines the mechanisms by which athletes can exceed their perceived physical limitations and explores strategies such as visualization, meditation, hypnosis, autogenic training, biofeedback, and progressive relaxation.

PSY8842: Applied Sport Psychology

This course focuses on how the sport psychologist interacts with individuals within a sport context. Methods of providing effective professional guidance in the areas of learning, motivation, and social interaction are examined, as is mental training for performance enhancement. The course also explores such issues as referrals, drug abuse, burnout, injury, and termination from athletics.

PSY8843: Exercise Psychology

This class covers all the psychological aspects of exercise, including the theoretical foundations of motives for exercise, exercise adherence, personality factors in exercise, and psychological effects of exercise. The course also addresses applied issues such as motivation, cognitive- and behavioral-change strategies, leadership, and counseling in exercise.

PSY8844: Psychology of Injury

This course examines the effects of the injured athlete. It investigates the psychological factors of injury from the points of view of the athlete, the coach, the physician, and the sport psychologist. The behavioral risk factors, injury prevention, and overstraining will be studied as a means of prevention. Injury assessment and the management of injury treatment from assessment to recovery is a central focus and will also include the biomedical issues of injury. Additionally, the course covers the interaction of the sport psychologist and the sports medicine team.

PSY8845: Current Issues in Sport Psychology

This class involves indepth reading and critical analysis of current issues in sport psychology. The content of this course examines, in depth, current research and theoretical directions in the field.

Contact Information: . . . . PO Box 64658
St. Paul, MN 55164-0658
Phone: 612.339.8650
Toll-free: 800.987.2282

Desert Southwest Fitness, Inc.

Provides continuing education for health and fitness professionals. Offers a number of courses relevant to exercise and sport psychology. The Summer/Fall 1999 catalogue of correspondence courses includes courses on psychology for health fitness professionals, fitness motivation, and other related areas.

Contact Information: . . . . Desert Southwest Fitness Inc.
602 East Roger Road, Tucson, AZ 85705
1.800.873.6759
1.520.292.0011
1.520.292.0066 (fax)
www.dswfitness.com

Fairleigh Dickinson University

PSYC 6901: Interventions in Sport Psychology

Graduate Credits: 3.0

Instructor: Mitch Abrams, PsyD

This course examines the application and effectiveness of psychological interventions for enhancing performance in sports. Major topics include historical and contemporary foundations of sport psychology, psychological factors and peak performance, establishing commitment and selfcontrol, mental imagery and performance, improving confidence and performance, building concentration, development and implementation of a psychological training program, effective communication, dealing with staleness and burnout, and the use of nonpsychological ergogenic aids.

Contact Information: . . . .   University College: Arts, Sciences,
and Professional Studies,
TeaneckHackensack Campus
School of Psychology 201.692.2300
Graduate Division*
Spring 2000 (January 24 to May 13)

Website: . . . .   www.fdu/academic/uc/psych/sportpsych/

Mitch Abrams: . . . .   MAbrams589@aol.com

* Please note that admission to the Graduate Division of Fairleigh Dickinson University as a nonmatriculating student requires proof of an undergraduate degree from a 4year, baccalaureate-granting institution. Advanced undergraduate students may also enroll in this course, as long as they have permission from their home institutions. Students must also have access to a personal computer and the Internet in order to enroll in this course.

Parkland Community College

The online course is a 3-credit-hour college course that is fully transferable. It may be taken for Psychology credit through Mesa Community College or for Physical Education credit through Parkland Community College.

Sport Psychology Online

Instructor: Brooke Estabrook

This course gives the students the opportunity to learn about sport psychology theories and about ways to apply them to practical, real-life situations. Class activities involve reading the text and lecture materials, participating in discussions on our bulletin board, learning about applied sport psychology projects, and exploring options available in the field. The student must complete the class within 8 weeks of the receipt of his or her passwords, but it is possible to complete the class in far less time (the course is self-paced).

Contact Information: . . . .   Parkland College
2400 West Bradley Avenue
Champaign, Illinois 61821
217.351.2200
1.800.346.8089

Website: . . . .   online.parkland.cc.il.us/index.htm

Brooke Estabrook: . . . .   estabrook@mail.mc.maricopa.edu

San Diego University for Integrative Studies

Established April 3, 2000 (This University also has an entry in the main body of the directory)

Online students can earn master's and doctoral degrees in sport psychology, sport counseling, and transpersonal psychology. Each class presents essential information for counselors and professional therapists. The courses chosen reflect our commitment to offering our students access to the very best in current information and to giving them the unique opportunity to experience education through modern technology.

Assessment and Evaluation in Sport Psychology and Sport Counseling Utilizing the TAIS

Instructor: Robert Nideffer, PhD

The course addresses the theory underlying TAIS (Test of Attentional and Interpersonal Style) and its practical applications in sport psychology, business, and education. Dr. Nideffer will also discuss his cuttingedge, online system, ACE (Athlete's Competitive Edge), a new, short version of TAIS with an interactive report designed specifically for athletes and coaches. The course will address ways in which Dr. Nideffer's assessment methodology can be implemented for selection, screening, team building and performance enhancement in sports and other settings. Whether counseling athletes, business executives, or any other clients regarding their behavior under stress, the student will receive invaluable information regarding future therapeutic direction, commitment, and ultimate success.

Business Principles for the Professional: How to Start and Run a Business or Consulting Practice

Instructor: Jim Sinclair

Knowing how to start and run a business is essential for anyone who plans on going into private practice or consulting. All good businesses start with a business plan that is well thought out and is organized in such a fashion that it becomes a recipe for success. In this course, students will learn how to start, run, and build your business or private practice.

Career Transition and Athletic Retirement

Instructor: Cristina B. Versari, PhD

This course focuses on the career cycle of professional and elite athletes, with special emphasis on the career-transition process. Students will learn to assess, evaluate, and make proper recommendations to athletes in the areas of academic and career development and planning. Topics covered in this course include reasons for career transition among athletes, career-transition needs, and elements and models for successful career transition. Additionally, the course addresses the career transition problem areas in various aspects—psychological, physical, social, and economic.

Adult Fitness and Performance Enhancement

Instructor: Sherry Newsham, PhD

This course focuses on the study of various theories and techniques utilized to enhance performance in sports and other areas of physical and mental development. Students will have the opportunity to experience techniques and to develop their individual approaches to performance enhancement. Additional topics include the identification of primary factors in health risks, optimum training methods, and psychological issues confronted in personal physical challenges. By the end of the course, the student will have learned when and how to apply various sport psychology techniques such as anxiety reduction, physical relaxation, mental imagery, attention control, goal setting, positive thought control, and precompetition preparation.

Introduction to Sport Counseling

Instructor: Cristina B. Versari, PhD

This course focuses on the history of sport counseling/psychology, the controversies currently confronting practitioners, and the future opportunities. Students will become familiar with the different issues and crises experienced by athletes, as well as with the different intervention approaches currently practiced in sport counseling. Special emphasis is placed on a practical approach to working with athletes and sport professionals.

Psychology of Coaching

Instructor: Doug Gardner, EdD

Coaching at the school, amateur, or professional level has become complex, comprehensive, and in need of specialized and well-trained personnel. It is critical that anyone working within the sphere of an athlete or a team understands the coaching profession. The coach's goals and beliefs are often integrated into the performance outcome. As a sport counselor or a sport psychologist, understanding the psychology of the coaching process is essential; this course provides students with theoretical and practical knowledge of this process. Students will learn coaching strategies and techniques that will help them to work with this unique population.

Additional course descriptions are available at www.sduis.edu

For more information and to register contact SDUIS at admissions@sduis.edu

San Diego University for Integrative Studies
5703 Oberlin Drive, Suite 208
San Diego, CA 92121

Phone: 619.638.1999
Fax: 619.638.1990
Website: . . . . www.sduis.edu
Email: . . . . admissions@sduis.edu

United States Sports Academy

The United States Sports Academy offers distance-learning options in a number of its graduate programs. Course offerings include sport psychology and related topics.

Contact information:	The United States Sports Academy
	One Academy Drive
	Daphne, AL 36526-7055
Phone:	334.626.3303
Website:	www.ussa.edu

Walden University

Walden University's Psychology Division offers doctoral and master's degrees in psychology as well as a postdoctoral certificate. Study includes reading, observation, and research, and affords students a comprehensive exploration into the emotional and behavioral characteristics of individuals, groups, and activities.

PSYC 8560: Sport Psychology

(5 cr.)

This course explores the history and the emergence of sports psychology as a field within the psychology discipline. Early developments, major figures, and practical applications in work with individual athletes, teams, coaches, and observers are discussed.

Contact Information:	Walden University
	155 Fifth Avenue South
	Minneapolis, MN 55401
Phone:	800.WALDENU
	612.338.7224
Fax:	612.338.5092.

Widener University

Dr. Daniel Rodriguez, a faculty member in the Department of Psychology at Widener University (Chester, PA), offers a number of courses online, including one in sports psychology and one in health psychology. For further information, contact Dr. Rodriguez at daniel.rodriguez@widener.edu

Appendix P
Websites for Programs

The following listing provides website addresses for the programs listed in this directory. The listing is provided alphabetically by program. Only those programs that submitted website addresses by July 2000 are included in this list. Because web addresses frequently change and some programs have no website listed, you are encouraged to surf the web to locate or verify the current address of a program.

Arizona School of Professional Psychology
www.aspp.edu

Arizona State University
www.asu.edu/clas/espe/

University of Arizona
www.arizona.edu/~psych/

Ball State University
www.bsu.edu/physicaleducation/
www.bsu.edu/CAST/pe/index4.htm

Boise State University
kinesiology.boisestate.edu

Boston University
www.bu.edu/education

Bowling Green State University
bgsu.edu/departments/hmsls/gp.html

California State University, Fresno
www.csufresno.edu/pehp/programs/

California State University, Fullerton
www.fullerton.edu

California State University, Long Beach
www.csulb.edu/~kpe/

California State University, Sacramento
www.hhs.csus.edu/

University of Canberra
science.canberra.edu.au/sportstud/

Cleveland State University
www.csuohio.edu

DeMontfort University Bedford
www.dmu.ac.uk/dept/schools/pesl/spob/research_psych.html

University of Exeter
www.exeter.ac.uk/education/

Florida State University
www.fsu.edu/~edres/psychology/welcome.html

University of Florida
www.hhp.ufl.edu/ess/
www.hhp.ufl.edu/ess/mblab/
www.hhp.ufl.edu/ess/sppsylab/index.htm

Furman University
www.furman.edu/

Georgia Southern University
www.gasou.edu (Georgia Southern University Web Site)
www2.gasou.edu/KIN/index.htm (Department of Health & Kinesiology)
www2.gasou.edu/gradcoll/ (College of Graduate Studies)
www2.gasou.edu/KIN/index.htm (Charles J. Hardy's University Web Page)
www2.gasou.edu/KINMasters_Sport_Psych.htm (Sport Psychology Program
    Information)
www2.gasou.edu:80/facstaff/kevburke/ (Kevin L. Burke's University Web Page)

University of Georgia
www.coe.uga.edu/exs/

University of Houston
www.coe.uh.edu

Illinois State University
www.ilstu.edu

University of Illinois
www.kines.uiuc.edu
www.grad.uiuc.edu

Indiana University
www.indiana.edu/~kines/

Iowa State University
www.iastate.edu

University of Iowa
www.uiowa.edu/~shlps/grad.htm

Ithaca College
www.ithaca.edu/grad/grad1/

John F. Kennedy University
www.jfku.edu/

University of Kansas
www.soe.ukans.edu/courses/hper892/

Lakehead University
www.lakeheadu.ca/ (Click Admissions, then click Arts and Sciences.)

Manchester Metropolitan University
www.mmu.ac.uk

University of Manitoba (Physical Education)
www.Umanitoba.ca/Faculties/Physed/

McGill University
www.education.Mcgill.ca/phys_ed

University of Memphis (Human Movement Sciences)
www.hmse.memphis.edu/gopher.hmse.memphis.edu

University of Memphis (Psychology)
www.memphis.edu/psych.htm

Miami University
www.muohio.edu/~phscwis/phs_program.html

Michigan State University
www.educ.msu.edu/units/dept/kin/

University of Minnesota
www.kls.coled.umn.edu/

University of Missouri, Columbia
tiger.coe.missouri.edu/~ecp/

University of Missouri, Kansas City
www.CCTR.UMKC.EDU/DEPT/PHYSED/

Nanyang Technological University
www.spe.ntu.edu.sg:8080/

University of New Hampshire
WWW.UNH.EDU

The University of New Mexico
www.unm.edu/~sportad/

University of North Carolina, Greensboro
www.uncg.edu/

University of North Dakota
www.und.edu

University of North Texas
www.coe.unt.edu/

University of Northern Colorado
www.hhs.univnorthco.edu/

Northern Illinois University
www.niu.edu/acad/phed/

Oregon State University
www.osu.orst.edu/hhp/exss

University of Ottawa
www.health.uottawa.ca/hkgrad

The Pennsylvania State University

www.personal.psu.edu/dept/kinesiology	(Dept. of Kinesiology)
www.psu.edu/	(PSU)
www.hhdev.psu.edu/	(College of Human Development)
www.psu.edu/ur/prospective.html	(info for prospective students)
www.gradsch.psu.edu/	(Graduate School)
www.personal.psu.edu/dec9/	(David Conroy's webpage)
www.personal.psu.edu/sms18/	(Sam Slobounov's webpage)

Purdue University
www.purdue.edu/academic/hkls

University of Queensland
www.uq.edu.au/hms/
psych.psy.uq.edu.au/

San Diego State University
www.rohan.sdsu.edu/~psyched

San Diego University for Integrative Studies
www.sduis.edu

San Jose State University
www.sjsu.edu/depts/casa/dept/hup.html

Université de Sherbrooke
www.usherb.ca/programmes/maitrise/kinant.html

University of Southern California
www.usc.edu/dept/LAS/exsci/

Southern Connecticut State University
scsu.ctstateu.edu/

Southern Illinois University, Carbondale
www.siu.edu/departments/coe/physed/

Southern Illinois University Edwardsville
www.sieu.edu/HRPE/

University of Southern Queensland
www.usq.edu.au/faculty/science/depts/psych/psych.htm

Spalding University
www.spalding.edu/

Springfield College (Graduate Studies)
www.springfieldcollege.edu/

Springfield College (Psychology)
www.spfldcol.edu/

Staffordshire University
www.staffs.ac.uk/sands/scis/sport/

Temple University
www.temple.edu/education/pe

University of Tennessee, Knoxville
www.coe.utk.edu/units/cultural.html

Texas Christian University (Kinesiology)
www.tcu.edu/

Texas Tech University
www.ttu.edu/~hper/

Utah State University
www.usu.edu/

University of Utah
www.utah.edu

Victoria University
www.vu.edu.au/

Virginia Commonwealth University
www.has.vcu.edu/psy/cans97.html

University of Virginia
www.curry.edschool.virginia.edu/curry/dept/edbs/hlthpel/sprtpsy/

University of Waterloo
www.ahs.uwaterloo.ca/kin/kinhome.html

Wayne State University
www.hpr.wayne.edu

West Virginia University
www.wvu.edu/~physed/sportbeh/htm

University of Western Australia
www.general.uwa.edu.au/~hmweb/

Western Illinois University
www.wiu.edu/users/mipe/

University of Western Ontario
www.uwo.ca/kinesiology/

University of Western Sydney
www.macarthur.uws.edu.au/

Western Washington University
www.ac.wwu.edu/~pehr/gradbroc.html

University of Wisconsin, Milwaukee
www.uwm.edu/SAHP/gp/hk/ghkmenu.htm

York University
www.yorku.ca/academics/bfowler

Appendix Q
Location of Graduate Programs:
Physical Education and Psychology,
Master's and Doctoral Level

*Physical Education Programs**

Master's Programs (88 programs)

University of Alberta

Arizona State University

Ball State University

Boise State University

Bowling Green State University

California State University, Fresno

California State University, Fullerton

California State University, Long Beach

California State University, Sacramento

University of Canberra

Chichester Institute of Higher Education

Cleveland State University

Deakin University, Rusden Campus

DeMontfort University Bedford

University of Edinburgh

University of Exeter

University of Florida

Furman University

Georgia Southern University

University of Georgia

University of Houston

Humboldt State University

University of Idaho

Illinois State University

University of Illinois

Indiana University

Iowa State University

University of Iowa

Ithaca College

Kansas State University

Lakehead University

Leeds Metropolitan University

Manchester Metropolitan University

University of Manitoba

University of Maryland, College Park

McGill University

University of Memphis

Miami University

Michigan State University

University of Minnesota

University of Missouri, Kansas City

University of Montana

Université de Montréal

Nanyang Technological University

University of New Hampshire

University of New Mexico

___

* Primarily found in Departments of Physical Education, but also found under many other names, including Kinesiology, Exercise and Sport Sciences, etc.

University of North Carolina,
  Greensboro

University of North Dakota

University of North Texas

University of Northern Colorado

Northern Illinois University

Oregon State University

University of Ottawa

The Pennsylvania State University

Purdue University

Université du Québec à Trois-Rivières

Queen's University

University of Queensland

San Diego State University

San Jose State University

Université de Sherbrooke

Southeastern Louisiana University

University of Southern California

Southern Connecticut State University

Southern Illinois University, Carbondale

Southern Illinois University,
  Edwardsville

Springfield College (Health, Physical
  Education, and Recreation)

Staffordshire University

University of Stellenbosch

Temple University

University of Tennessee, Knoxville

University of Texas, Austin

Texas Christian University

Texas Tech University

Utah State University

University of Utah

Victoria University

University of Virginia

University of Waterloo

Wayne State University

West Virginia University

Western Illinois University

Western Washington University

University of Western Australia

University of Western Ontario

University of Western Sydney

University of Wisconsin, Milwaukee

York University

Doctoral Programs (44 programs)

University of Alberta

Arizona State University

Chichester Institute of Higher Education

Deakin University, Rusden Campus

DeMontfort University Bedford

University of Edinburgh

University of Exeter

University of Florida

University of Georgia

University of Houston

University of Idaho

University of Illinois

University of Iowa

University of Kansas

Leeds Metropolitan University

Manchester Metropolitan University

University of Maryland, College Park

Michigan State University

University of Minnesota

University of Missouri, Kansas City

Université de Montréal

Nanyang Technological University

University of New Mexico

University of North Carolina,
  Greensboro

University of Northern Colorado

Oregon State University

University of Ottawa

The Pennsylvania State University

Purdue University

University of Queensland

University of Southern California

Springfield College (Health, Physical Education, and Recreation)

Staffordshire University

University of Stellenbosch

Temple University

University of Tennessee, Knoxville

Texas Tech University

University of Utah

Victoria University

University of Virginia

University of Waterloo

West Virginia University

University of Western Australia

University of Western Ontario

Psychology Programs

Master's Programs (13 programs)

Arizona School of Professional Psychology

Boston University**

Florida State University***

John F. Kennedy University

University of Manitoba

Mankato State University

University of Memphis

University of Missouri, Columbia

University of Queensland

San Diego University for Integrative Studies

University of Southern Queensland

Spalding University

Springfield College (Psychology)

Doctoral Programs (17 programs)

Arizona School of Professional Psychology

University of Arizona

Boston University**

University of California, Los Angeles

Florida State University***

John F. Kennedy University

University of Manitoba

University of Memphis

University of Missouri, Columbia

University of Montana****

University of North Texas

University of Queensland

San Diego University for Integrative Studies

University of Southern Queensland

Spalding University

Texas Christian University

Virginia Commonwealth University

** Department of Developmental Studies and Counseling
*** Department of Educational Research, Program in Educational Psychology
**** Department of Counselor Education

Appendix R

Quick Chart of Program Information: Degrees Offered, Program Emphasis Rating, and Internship Possibility

Institution	Master's	Doctoral	Rating*	Internship
Univ. of Alberta	MA/MS	PhD	—	N
Arizona Sch. Prof. Psychology	MA	PsyD	2	Y
Arizona State Univ.	MS	PhD	5	Y
University of Arizona	—	PhD	5	Y
Ball State University	MA/MS	PhD	4	Y
Boise State University	MS	—	4	Y
Boston University	MEd	EdD	4	Y
Bowling Green State Univ.	MEd	—	4	N
Cal. State U., Fresno	MA	—	5	Y
Cal. State U., Fullerton	MS	—	3	Y
Cal. State U., Long Beach	MS	—	4	Y
Cal. State U., Sacramento	MS	—	4	Y
Univ. of Cal., Los Angeles	—	PhD	6	N
University of Canberra	—	GradDip	2	Y
Chichester Inst. Higher Ed	MPhil/MS	PhD	—	Y
Cleveland State Univ.	MEd	—	3	N
Deakin Univ., Rusden	MAS	PhD	—	N
DeMontfort Univ. Bedford	MPhil/MS	PhD	6	N
University of Edinburgh	MSc/MPhil	PhD	—	Y
University of Exeter	MS/MPhil	PhD	4	Y
Florida State Univ.	MS	PhD	4	Y
Univ. of Florida	MS	PhD	6=	Y
Furman University	MA	—	4=	Y
Georgia Southern Univ.	MS	—	2	Y
Univ. of Georgia	MA	PhD	7	N
Univ. of Houston	MEd/MS	PhD	6=	Y
Humboldt State Univ.	MA	—	—	Y

Institution	Master's	Doctoral	Rating*	Internship
Univ. of Idaho	MS	PhD	4	Y
Illinois State Univ.	MS	—	6	Y
Univ. of Illinois	MS	PhD	7=	N
Indiana University	MS	—	7	N
Iowa State University	MS	—	4	Y
University of Iowa	MA	PhD	7	N
Ithaca College	MS	—	2=	Y
John F. Kennedy Univ.	MA	PsyD	2=	Y
Kansas State University	MS	—	—	Y
University of Kansas	MS	EdD/PhD	—	Y(PhD)
Lakehead University	MS	—	4	Y
Leeds Metropolitan University	MS/MPhil	PhD	4	N
Manchester Metropolitan U.	MS/MPhil	PhD	4	N
University of Manitoba	MA/MS	PhD	4	Y
Mankato State Univ.	MA	—	—	Y
Univ. of MD, College Park	MA	PhD	6	N
McGill University	MA	—	5	N
University of Memphis (HMS)	MS	—	6	Y
University of Memphis (Psych)	MA/MS	PhD	6	Y
Miami University	MS	—	4	Y
Michigan State Univ.	MS	PhD	5	Y
University of Minnesota	MA/MEd	PhD	5	Y
U. of Missouri, Columbia	MA	PhD	5	Y
U. of Missouri, Kansas City	MA	PhD	7	Y
University of Montana	MS	EdD/PhD	4=	Y
Université de Montréal	MSc	PhD	—	N
Nanyang Technological U.	MA	PhD	—	Y
Univ. of New Hampshire	MS	—	4	Y
The Univ. of New Mexico	MS	PhD	4	Y
U. of NC, Greensboro	MS	PhD	4=	Y
Univ. of North Dakota	MS	—	4	Y
Univ. of North Texas	MS	PhD	=	Y
Univ. of Northern Colorado	MA	EdD	6=	Y
Northern Illinois Univ.	MSEd	—	4	N

Institution	Master's	Doctoral	Rating*	Internship
Oregon State University	MS	PhD	6	N
University of Ottawa	MA	PhD	1,6	Y
The Pennsylvania State Univ.	MS	PhD	5=	Y
Purdue University	MS	PhD	—	Y
U. Québec, Trois-Rivières	MS	—	—	Y
Queen's University	MA	—	—	Y
University of Queensland	MA/MS/MSEP	PhD	4=	Y(MSEP)
San Diego State Univ.	MA	—	4	Y
San Diego University for Integrative Studies	MA	PhD	2	Y(PhD)
San Jose State University	MA	—	6=	Y
Université de Sherbrooke	MS	—	5	N
Southeastern Louisiana Univ.	MA	—	6	Y
Univ. of Southern California	MA	PhD	6	N
S. Connecticut St. Univ.	MS	—	4=	Y
Southern Illinois Univ., Carbondale	MS	—	4=	Y
Southern Illinois Univ., Edwardsville	MSEd	—	5	Y
Univ. of Southern Queensland	MPsy/MPhil	Psy/PhD	—	Y
Spalding University	MA	PsyD	4=	Y
Springfield College (Grad. Studies)	MS	DPE	4	Y
Springfield College (Psy.)	MEd/MS	CAS	4=	Y
Staffordshire University	MPhil/MS	PhD	6=	Y
University of Stellenbosch	MHMvt	PhD	6	N
Temple University	MS	PhD	5	Y
Univ. of Tennessee, Knoxville	MS	PhD	4	Y
Univ. of Texas, Austin	MA/MEd	PhD	6	Y
Texas Christian Univ. (Kines.)	MS	—	4	Y
Texas Tech University	MS/MEd	EdD	6	Y
Utah State University	MS	—	3	Y
University of Utah	MS	PhD	—	Y
Victoria University	MAP/MAS	PhD	=	Y
Virginia Commonwealth U.	—	PhD	5	Y

Institution	Master's	Doctoral	Rating*	Internship
University of Virginia	MEd	PhD	6	Y
University of Waterloo	MS	PhD	—	Y(PhD)
Wayne State University	MEd	—	7	Y
West Virginia University	MS	EdD	5	Y
Western Illinois Univ.	MS	—	—	Y
Univ. of Western Australia	MS	PhD	4	Y
University of Western Sydney	MPsych	—	—	Y
Western Washington Univ.	MS	—	4	Y
Univ. of Western Ontario	MA	PhD	6	Y
U. of Wisconsin, Milwaukee	MS	—	5=	Y
York University	MS/MA	—	7	Y

Keys
Master's Degrees
CC—Coaching Certificate

GradDip—Graduate Diploma in Applied Psychology

MA—Master of Arts

MAP—Master of Applied Psychology

MAS—Master of Applied Science

MEd—Master of Education

MHK—Master of Human Kinetics

MHMvt—Master of Human Movement

MPE—Master of Physical Education

MPhil—Master of Philosophy

MPsy—Master of Psychology

MS—Master of Science

MSEd—Master of Science in Education

Doctoral degrees

DPE—Doctorate in Physical Education

EdD—Doctor of Education

PhD—Doctor of Philosophy

PsyD—Doctor of Psychology

CAS—Certificate of Advanced Study (not a doctoral degree but represents advanced study beyond the master's)

Program Emphasis Rating

Program respondents were asked to rate, on a 7-point Likert Scale, the number that best reflects the emphasis/orientation of their program.

An equals sign (=) indicates that the program offers opportunities to pursue an applied orientation OR a research orientation (as opposed to an equal emphasis on both).

Internship Possibility

Y—yes (possible or required)

N—no

About the Editors

Michael L. Sachs is a professor in the Department of Kinesiology in the College of Education at Temple University, specializing in exercise and sport psychology. He has been at Temple University since 1989. He received his PhD in sport psychology from Florida State University in 1980 and was an assistant professor at the University of Québec at Trois-Rivières from 1980–1983. From 1983–1989 he served as a research project coordinator at the Applied Research and Evaluation Unit in the Department of Pediatrics, University of Maryland School of Medicine. He has an extensive list of publications and presentations, including an associate editorship of *Psychology of Running* (Michael Sacks & Michael Sachs, Human Kinetics Publishers, 1981) and a coeditorship of *Running as Therapy: An Integrated Approach* (Michael Sachs & Gary Buffone, University of Nebraska Press, 1984; republished in 1997 by Jason Aronson Publishers as part of their Master Works Series). *The Total Sports Experience for Kids: A Parent's Guide to Success in Youth Sports* (1996, Diamond Communications, Inc.) is another recent publication coauthored by Aubrey Fine and Dr. Sachs. Dr. Sachs serves as an editorial board member and reviewer for numerous professional journals. He is a licensed psychologist in Maryland, as well as a certified consultant for the Association for the Advancement of Applied Sport Psychology. Dr. Sachs served as president of the Association for the Advancement of Applied Sport Psychology from 1991 to 1992. He is married and has two daughters. Dr. Sachs is interested in all sports and enjoys running as his primary means of exercise.

Kevin L. Burke is an associate professor and serves as graduate program director of the Department of Health & Kinesiology at Georgia Southern University. He also serves as program coordinator for the graduate program in sport psychology and director of the Sport Psychology Laboratory. He received a BA in psychology and recreational studies (double major) with a minor in sociology from Belmont Abbey College in 1982. Dr. Burke was a member of the Pi Gamma Mu National Social Science Honor Society. He also played on the men's tennis team and was a National Association of Intercollegiate Athletics Academic All-American Tennis Team nominee, making the NAIA All-District 26 Tennis Team in both singles and doubles play. Dr. Burke received his MA in social/organizational psychology from East Carolina University in 1984, where he was a member of Psi Chi, the National Honor Society in Psychology. He earned his PhD in sport psychology from Florida State University in 1988.

A fellow, charter member, and former secretary-treasurer of the Association for the Advancement of Applied Sport Psychology (AAASP), Dr. Burke also served on AAASP's original executive board as the first student representative. He has presented and published through local, state, regional, national, and international channels. In 1996, he coauthored the book, *Tennis*. He also coedited six editions of the *Directory of Graduate Programs in Applied Sport Psychology*. Dr. Burke currently serves on the editorial board for the *Journal of Applied Sport Psychology*, is an associate editor for the *Journal of Sport Behavior,* and is past associate editor for the *Journal of Interdisciplinary Research in Physical Education*. He also sits on the editorial board for *Strategies*. He has been a guest reviewer for *The Sport Psychologist*, the *Journal of Sport & Exercise Psychology*, and the *Research Quarterly for Exercise and Sport*. He has also served as a *Sport Psychologist Digest* compiler for the *Journal of Sport & Exercise Psychology* and as associate editor for the AAASP newsletter. Dr. Burke has served as a Research Dissemination Committee member of the Research Consortium of the American Alliance for Health, Physical Education, Recreation, and Dance, and as a Research Works contributing editor for the *Journal of Physical Education, Recreation, and Dance*.

Dr. Burke has assisted professional, college, high school, and recreational athletes from various sports in his roles as a sport psychology consultant and is a Certified Consultant, AAASP. His current research interests include optimism/pessimism, momentum, humor, concentration, sport officials, and the effectiveness of intervention techniques in sport and exercise. In 2000 Dr. Burke was nominated for the Georgia Southern University award for teaching. In 1999, he received the GSU College of Health and Professional Studies award for teaching. Dr. Burke received the GSU College of Health and Professional Studies award for scholarship in 1998, and he has also been nominated for the prestigious Dorothy V. Harris Young Scholar/Practitioner award and selected for leadership training. While in graduate school, he won an award for teaching. Dr. Burke has served as an intercollegiate basketball official. In 2000 he completed his 20th season as an interscholastic basketball official; he is certified at the state's highest level and serves as a state evaluator. He has officiated at the Georgia High School Association state tournament, boys' all-star game, and has been selected by the Georgia Athletic Coaches' Association as an all-star official. Dr. Burke has also served as the head coach of three NCAA Division I tennis teams. Dr. Burke has driven a stock car at Lowe's (Charlotte) Motor Speedway and Atlanta Motor Speedway and is a United States Tennis Association competitor. He enjoys running, recreational basketball, and softball.

Diana C. Schrader is completing her PhD in exercise and sport psychology at Temple University. She received a BA with honors in art history and a minor in dance from Ohio State University in 1977, specializing in Asian art. She received her master of creative arts in therapy from Hahnemann University of the Health Sciences in 1983, specializing in dance/movement therapy. After completing her master's, Ms. Schrader worked for 14 years as a psychotherapist and as an activity therapist for severely mentally ill patients in partial-hospital and inpatient settings. Her experience includes work with a wide range of people—adults, adolescents, and children—and a variety of psychiatric and substance-abuse populations. Her interests in exercise and sport psychology are diverse, and include elite athletes, collegiate student-athletes, eating disorders among athletes, anger management by athletes, and women and minorities in sport. Her internship experiences reflect these interests and include the Temple University Counseling Service and the U.S. Luge Association in Lake Placid, NY. She recently coauthored, with Dr. Carole Oglesby, a chapter in the second edition of *Racism in College Athletics: The African American Experience* (Brooks & Althouse, Fitness Information Technology, Inc., 2000). She has been a member of the Association for the Advancement of Applied Sport Psychology since 1996 and currently serves as a student regional representative. Ms. Schrader is married, and enjoys swimming, hiking, reading, traveling, and *Star Trek*.